Yale Historical Publications

# New York Jews and the Great Depression

## Uncertain Promise

**Beth S. Wenger**

Yale University Press

New Haven and London

Published with assistance from a gift from Mr. and Mrs. Edward L. Snitzer to the Myer and Rosaline Feinstein Center for American Jewish History, Temple University, for the best doctoral dissertation in American Jewish history, 1991–1993. Published under the direction of the Department of History of Yale University with assistance from the income of the Frederick John Kingsbury Memorial Fund.

Designed by Nancy Ovedovitz
Set in New Caledonia type by Northeastern Graphic Services, Inc.
Printed in the United States of America by Edwards Brothers, Inc., Ann Arbor, Michigan.

**Library of Congress Cataloging-in-Publication Data**
Wenger, Beth S., 1963–
New York Jews and the Great Depression : uncertain promise / Beth S. Wenger.
p. cm.
Includes bibliographical references and index.
ISBN 0-300-06265-6
1. Jews—New York (State)—New York—Economic conditions.
2. Depressions—1929—New York (State)—New York. 3. New York (N.Y.)—Ethnic relations. I. Title.
F128.9.J5W46 1996
305.892'407471—dc20 96–17786
CIP

A catalogue record for this book is available from the British Library.

The paper in this book meets the guidelines for permanence and durability of the Committee on Production Guidelines for Book Longevity of the Council on Library Resources.

10 9 8 7 6 5 4 3 2 1

*To my parents,*
*Nanette and Julius Wenger*

# Contents

# Figures and Tables

FIGURES

TABLES

# Acknowledgments

In researching and writing this book, I have had the good fortune to receive assistance and support from many sources. It is a pleasure to have the opportunity to acknowledge publicly the individuals and institutions who helped to make this book a reality.

This study began as a dissertation in the Yale University history department. As a graduate student, I received several fellowships that enabled me to devote full-time attention to research and writing. I am grateful for grants provided by the Andrew Mellon Foundation, the National Foundation for Jewish Culture, the Memorial Foundation for Jewish Culture, and the Josephine De Kármán Fellowship Trust. A faculty award from the Research Foundation of the University of Pennsylvania facilitated my ability to transform the dissertation into a book. I am especially grateful to have received a dissertation prize from the Center for American Jewish History, which provided a subvention for the book's publication.

My research would not have been possible without the resources of many libraries and archives and the assistance of their staffs. Michelle Feller-Kopman of the American Jewish Historical Society patiently fulfilled my often complicated requests. Barbara Dunlap, archivist for the City College of New York, helped me obtain some useful photographic material from the City College collection. Linda Lerman, the Judaica bibliographer at Yale University during my years as a graduate student, saved me countless hours through timely acquisitions of Yiddish newspaper collections. I am grateful to Stephen Solender for granting me access to the records of the Federation of Jewish Philanthropies and to Colonel S. J. Pomerenze for directing me to the collections housed in the Federation's Brooklyn warehouse. I owe a particular debt to Steven Siegel for revealing the extensive material about Depression-era Jewish employment agencies available at the Ninety-second Street Young Men's Hebrew Association. The valuable collections housed at the Joseph and Miriam Ratner Center for Conservative Judaism greatly enriched my investigation of New York synagogues. Professor Jack Wertheimer allowed me access to the Ratner Center's holdings at a time when many collections had just been acquired, and archivist Julie Miller offered important assistance in guiding me through the synagogue records. Shulamith Berger of Yeshiva University's archives also directed me to useful synagogue material, as did Robert Leifert, who generously opened Congregation Kehilath Jeshurun's collection to me. I am particularly indebted to Chancellor Ismar Schorsch for granting me permission to use the Rabbi Mordecai M. Kaplan diaries housed at the Jewish Theological Seminary. Suki Sandler formerly of the American Jewish Committee and Nicki Tanner of the Federation of Jewish Philanthropies provided access to the extensive oral history collections of their respective institutions. I owe a special thanks to the men and women who shared their memories of Depression-era New York with me.

I owe a different kind of debt to my teachers. My dissertation committee at Yale, Paula Hyman, Nancy Cott, and James Fisher, helped to shape the parameters of the project, and their comments on the dissertation guided me through the revision process. As a reader of the dissertation, Deborah Dash Moore offered her mastery of New York Jewish history and provided detailed suggestions for transforming the dissertation into a book. I thank her for being so generous with her time and advice and for helping me to sharpen the focus on the book's broader themes. My greatest debt is to Paula Hyman, my mentor and dissertation advisor, who continually encouraged me to confront complex historical problems and to work for precision in language and analysis. Her high standards of scholarship and her unfailing commitment to me have decisively shaped my intellectual development and helped me at every turn. I continue to depend upon her support and guidance.

I am grateful to the dissertation prize committee of the Center for American Jewish History—Murray Friedman, Jeffrey Gurock, Pamela Nadell, and Jonathan Sarna—for their critical comments on the manuscript. As a reader for

Yale University Press, Jonathan Sarna raised many provocative questions and offered valuable suggestions. Although I did not heed all of his advice, I hope he will recognize how his insights have improved the book and how much I appreciate his support of my scholarship. I also want to extend my thanks to Aryeh Goren who generously shared with me his mother's rich memoirs of Depression-era New York.

I thank Chuck Grench, my editor at Yale University Press, for believing in this project at a very early stage, patiently answering my questions, and supporting this work through the publication process. Jane Hedges carefully and skillfully edited the manuscript. Her close reading of the text and thoughtful suggestions for revision have made this a better book.

I have been able to complete this book while working in supportive institutional environments. My colleagues in the history department and in the Jewish Studies program at the University of Pennsylvania provided a hospitable atmosphere for teaching and research. A fellowship at Princeton University's Center for the Study of American Religion during the 1995–96 academic year enabled me to devote full-time attention to writing and revision. Without the peace and quiet of the office on Ivy Lane, I would not have been able to finish this book in such a timely fashion. I also wish to thank Chris Jones, a computer specialist at Princeton University, who rescued me from the brink of a technological disaster.

My thanks also go to Jeffrey S. Gurock and Marc Lee Raphael, editors of *An Inventory of Promises: Essays on American Jewish History in Honor of Moses Rischin*, where portions of chapter 6 were published as "Government Welfare and Jewish Communal Responsibility: The Evolution of Jewish Philanthropy in the Great Depression."

My friends and colleagues have been especially generous with their time and support. As a graduate student, I was fortunate to take part in a dissertation reading group. I wish to thank Martha Boonin-Vail, David Godshalk, Xiao Hong Shen, and Anne Standley, who were participants in our group in its first year, and in particular, Mia Bay, Jonathan Cedarbaum, Debbie Elkin, and Carol Sheriff, who read my dissertation in its entirety, providing critical comments as well as moral support. Many colleagues have been a part of the writing of this book. Karla Goldman reminded me of the worthiness of the project and offered reassurance at a moment when I needed it most. Jeffrey Shandler proved willing to be a sounding board for ideas. Over a cup of coffee at a Princeton diner, Cynthia Eller helped me to clarify the broader themes of the book and to devise an appropriate title. Marie Griffith occupied the office next door at Princeton and listened patiently to the trials and tribulations that accompanied the completion of this book.

Some of my greatest support came from those who offered no substantive comments on the book's content. Carolyn Braun's friendship and encouragement have been invaluable in the writing of this book and on so many other occasions. Terri Jacobson, Marcy Leach, and Karen Smith have delivered a combination of support and humor that only old friends can provide. Eric Miller has believed in me for years and offers more inspiration than he will ever know.

Finally, I wish to thank my family for their part in the creation of this book. Unfortunately, my grandparents, Edith and Aaron Kass and Fanny and Abraham Wenger, did not live to see this book completed, but some of their stories lie within its pages. My sisters, Debbie Wiatrak and Judy Wenger, along with my brother-in-law Brian Wiatrak and nephews Kevin and Jesse, listened for years, in one way or another, to the saga of this project. My sister Judy housed me during my many New York research trips and provided relaxing dinners after long days in the archives. In a family of physicians, the historical enterprise was not well understood. But my parents, Nanette and Julius Wenger, to whom this book is dedicated, have always supported my decision to pursue a different path.

# New York Jews and
# the Great Depression

# Introduction

"The apprehensiveness of American Jews," *Fortune* magazine told its readers in 1936, "has become one of the important influences in the social life of our time." In a detailed article, *Fortune*'s editors outlined Jewish fears about rising anti-Semitism and analyzed the factors that had led Jews to question their security in America. With the best of intentions, the magazine set out to correct any Gentile misconceptions that Jews dominated the American economy, to explain why Jews appeared "clannish" to their neighbors, and to convince American Jews that the fascism and intolerance spreading through Europe would not overtake the United States. Denouncing anti-Semitism while also criticizing "provocative Jewish defensive measures," the editors celebrated America's liberal spirit and insisted that there was "no reason for anxiety."[1] But the qualified reassurances of *Fortune* magazine did little to mitigate the mood of uncertainty among Depression-era Jews who shared an apprehension far more complex than simply the fear of anti-Semitism. For a Jewish population composed largely of immigrants and their children, the Great Depression brought economic setbacks, stalled mobility, and frustrated expectations. After attaining a level of stability and success in the first decades of the twentieth century, immigrant Jews expected that America would continue to offer their families opportunities for advancement and security. Instead, Jews in the Great Depression faced unprecedented financial hardships, barriers to their children's economic and educational progress, and a sudden increase in anti-Semitism. Young Depression-era Jews, raised to believe in the promise of America, encountered a shrinking pool of jobs and opportunities and a sharp rise in employment discrimination and university quotas. The Depression not only frustrated the personal ambitions of American Jews but also destabilized the foundations of Jewish communal life, as Jewish institutions faltered on the verge of bankruptcy and collapse. In a political climate full of challenges to the American social and economic system, Jews had good cause to reevaluate the promise of America for themselves and their community. A generation of American Jews, still actively engaged in constructing Jewish identity and community in America, furthered that process at a time when the American future seemed most uncertain. In an era of turbulence and change, confronted by the combined challenges of economic depression and escalating anti-Semitism, American Jews endured a period of unsettling transition and formative transformation.

The story of Jewish life in America has generally been told as a tale of success and mobility. At the turn of the century, Jewish immigrants built businesses and communal institutions, sent their children to school, and gained a solid foothold within the American economy. By the post–World War II era, Jews had become a successful middle-class group with an advanced educational and professional profile and a complex network of ethnic organizations and institutions. Given the cumulative successes of American Jews in the twentieth century, the Depression appears in most histories as a brief interruption in the overall pattern of Jewish life. The Great Depression, many historians have argued, delayed but did not significantly alter long-term Jewish trends.[2] To be sure, the economic mobility and organizational sophistication that began in the immigrant period resumed in the post–World War II era. Yet the Depression years were more than a momentary pause in the twentieth-century saga of American Jews. In the 1930s, Jews worried about their financial stability and security as a minority group in America, questioned the usefulness of their educational endeavors, and doubted whether their communal institutions would survive. A focus on the Depression years complicates the standard linear narrative of American Jewish success, revealing a time when Jews were not so confident about their prospects in America. Ultimately, American Jews and their institutions survived the Depression and thrived in the decades that followed, but the historical moment of the Great Depression, when the Jewish future seemed more precarious than ever, left an indelible imprint on the canvass of Jewish life in America.

The Great Depression has already assumed a pivotal role in many narratives of American Jewish experience but has also been subordinated to other more prominent themes of Jewish history. In the wake of the Holocaust, the thirties have become seared in Jewish memory as the Hitler era, a time when the weakened economy nurtured the growth of anti-Semitism, strengthened the movement for restrictions on immigration, and contributed to the lack of an American response to Nazism. The Jewish encounter with the Great Depression has largely been subsumed by a historical preoccupation with assessing American Jewish responses to the rise of Nazism in Germany. Jewish historians have produced scores of monographs that condemn, defend, or attempt to explain the actions of America's Jews in the years preceding the Holocaust.[3] As the Nazi threat mounted in Europe, anti-Semitism reached its zenith in the United States. Never before in American history had organized hate groups been so numerous, gaining strength and popularity with each successive year of the Depression. Because anti-Semitism so decisively influenced Jewish life in the 1930s, in forms ranging from employment discrimination to Jewish university quotas to the anti-Jewish propaganda of Father Coughlin and the Silver Shirts, Jewish scholars have been particularly concerned with studying anti-Semitic movements.[4] The combination of anti-Semitism at home and abroad was a constant current of Jewish life in the Depression years, a current more carefully documented than any other aspect of American Jewish experience in the 1930s.

Politics have also claimed a central place in the retelling of Jewish life during the Great Depression. Jewish intellectuals and activists have painted the thirties as a decade of political awakening, a time spent debating and protesting governmental and economic systems or taking part in heated discussions in the alcoves of City College. The writings of Alfred Kazin, Michael Gold, and Irving Howe offer a literary chronicle of the ideological and intellectual ferment of the 1930s.[5] Professional historians have also presented a detailed portrait of the political fervor of the Depression decade. The enormous range of political activity, from unionism and radical movements to the birth of the Jewish-Democratic coalition, have assumed center stage in scholarly discussions of the Depression years.[6] In Jewish political history, the thirties emerge as a decisive turning point, a period of heightened radicalism as well as the beginning of an enduring Jewish commitment to the Democratic Party.

In popular folklore, the Great Depression has garnered its share of nostalgic presentations. "There is a retrospective glamour in grayness," reckoned one City College alumnus, "the Great Depression has its worshippers."[7] As the "Militant Thirties," the "Anxious Years," or the "Dismal Decade," the 1930s have been alternately portrayed by Jewish writers as a time of great misery and of great cultural and political creativity. By some accounts the Depression years brought desperation and disappointment, yet tales of hardship have also been transformed into stories of family solidarity, personal growth, and triumph over adversity. The various representations of Jewish life in the 1930s—the restless energy and heady activity described by the New York Intellectuals, the painful recollections of anti-Semitism at home, the slow rise of Nazism and fascism abroad, and the less dramatic struggles to obtain education, secure employment, and maintain financial stability—all compose the mosaic of Jewish memory and experience in Depression-era America.

In economic terms, the Depression represents an aberration from the overall pattern of twentieth-century Jewish mobility. In most historical accounts, the economic setbacks and communal retrenchment of the decade appear merely as slight detours on the road to Jewish advancement. One historian of Jewish economic trends claimed that "from 1880 to 1940 . . . almost ideal objective conditions prevailed in the United States" to sustain uninterrupted upward mobility for Jews. The first half of the twentieth century has been described as a period in which "the second generation experienced economic mobility with a vengeance."[8] Even the formidable challenges faced by Jewish charities and the precipitous decline in synagogue memberships emerge in most accounts as only brief impediments in otherwise thriving Jewish communal endeavors. Such assessments, however, rest on anachronistic assumptions about the inevitability of American Jewish success and prosperity after World War II. To view the Great Depression only from the perspective of hindsight is to ignore the formidable challenges of the era and their consequences for Jews negotiating their way through a decade of turmoil and change.

This book examines the Great Depression as a brief but revealing historical moment, not a period that completely overturned the process of Jewish acculturation, but an era that forever reshaped the basic institutions of American Jewish life. As a critical juncture in American Jewish history, the Great Depression provides a particularly useful lens for exploring the evolution of American Jewry. Like other newly arrived immigrant groups, Jews did not encounter the Depression as an isolated event but rather as part of the ongoing challenges of assimilation and adjustment in America. At the time, Jews and other Americans had no idea that they were living in an era that would later become a celebrated historical epoch. The Great Depression was part of a much larger period of social change that spanned the interwar years. Many immigrants had experienced hard times before the Depression; they had already begun to create Jewish institutions capable of serving a changing Jewish community, and their native-born children were already pursuing new personal, educational, and occupational paths. Many patterns established in the first decades of the twentieth century persisted even amid the dramatic changes in Jewish life during the Depression years.

The Depression's challenges were by no means unique to American Jews. The economic crisis took its toll on Americans of all ethnic backgrounds and heralded an era of enormous cultural change. The emergence of Roosevelt and sweeping New Deal reforms, the resurgence of radicalism and the labor movement, and the birth of the welfare state constitute just a few of the social and political upheavals of the decade. American Jews shared in the economic privation, far-reaching social changes, and political innovations that preoccupied the nation during the 1930s. At the same time, Jewish experience in the Depression years was refracted through the distinct prism of Jewish culture, influenced by a specific Jewish occupational profile, and shaped by the character of Jewish family and community organization. Jews also carried a double burden in the 1930s, battling both the economic crisis and a growing anti-Semitic threat. To study American Jews during the Great Depression is not to assume that other Americans did not face similar financial setbacks or participate in many of the same social and political movements. A focus on Jewish experience in the Depression years demonstrates the particular development of Jewish community and culture in an age of social transformation. Within a nation refashioning its political, economic, and social structure, American Jews reinvented the personal and communal dimensions of ethnic culture.

The Great Depression was not a watershed in American Jewish history, but a period of crisis that revealed, and in some cases accelerated, long-term patterns of acculturation. The Depression occurred at a transitional moment in American Jewish life. By the mid-1920s, Jewish immigration had slowed to a trickle, a generation of immigrants had established roots on American soil, and a new American-born generation was coming of age. During the 1930s, American Jewry became for the first time a predominantly native-born rather than an immigrant population.[9] The Great Depression punctuated the maturation of the first mass generation of Jews born in the United States. Occurring precisely at the time when immigrant patterns were giving way to new formulations of Jewish community and culture, the Depression years set in motion Jewish patterns that would last for generations. Decisions made in the 1930s about education, marriage, and childbearing permanently transformed Jewish family structure and occupational characteristics. The economic crisis also forced lasting alterations in the institutional systems of Jewish life. Jewish philanthropic organizations and synagogues that had expanded rapidly in the prosperity of the 1920s faced unprecedented fiscal distress in the Depression years and reassessed their fundamental structure and purpose. The economic crisis, though not always a causal factor in these crucial changes, provided the confluence of historical conditions that redefined the collective portrait of American Jewry.

The focus of this book is New York's Jewish community. More than 40 percent of American Jews lived in New York during the Depression years, making the city a logical and valuable center for study.[10] Although the experience of New York's Jews differed in many respects from that of Jews in other American cities, New York's unparalleled concentration of Jews and vibrant Jewish culture provide an important guidepost for evaluating the impact of the Depression on American Jewry. Almost two million Jews lived in New York in the 1930s, making them the largest ethnic group in the city.[11] In the Depression era, East European Jewish immigrants and their children constituted the overwhelming majority of the New York Jewish population. Yet Jews of German and Sephardic descent, who had arrived earlier and were generally more established, retained their leadership role within the Jewish community. Despite a continued disparity in status and power, the once bitter division between Uptown and Downtown Jews, (between Jews of German descent and those of East European origin) had narrowed considerably by the 1930s, as immigrants became increasingly acculturated and raised their American-born children to adulthood. This book addresses the experiences of various sectors of the New York Jewish world but focuses primarily on the East European immigrants and their children who made up the bulk of the Jewish population and whose adjustment to America was influenced most decisively by the Great Depression.

For the diverse Jewish constituency of New York City, the Great Depression was not a monolithic event. The New York community contained Jews of different origin, class, status, religious affiliation, and political orientation. Some Jews, like some Americans, encountered the Depression as a time of poverty, unemployment, and utter desperation; many others never went hungry but endured varying levels of economic insecurity and uncertainty; still others hardly felt the impact of the Depression in their personal lives. As a disproportionately white-collar group, New York Jews experienced less unemployment relative to other sectors of the population.[12] Yet, given the vast class and cultural differences across the spectrum of New York Jewry, the Depression painted an uneven stroke across the city's diverse Jewish constituencies.

The Great Depression falls within the period of American Jewish history generally labeled the "second generation." This slippery term can denote an actual generation, namely the children of immigrants, as well as a chronological period extending from the 1920s through the post–World War II era.[13] The generational paradigm is less than exact, given the more than thirty-year period of mass migration and the continuing existence of an immigrant culture. The second generation, however, has rightly been called "a cultural generation," born out of the process of "scurrying between [the] two worlds" of a confined immigrant environment and an increasingly familiar American society. As the leading historian of this period has explained, "At home both in American urban culture and immigrant Jewish culture, second generation Jews could synthesize the two."[14] The Great Depression struck in the midst of the second generation's "remarkable synthesis" and brought an abrupt halt to the unprecedented Jewish economic success, upward mobility, and organizational expansion that had defined the 1920s.[15] During the twenties, New York Jews attained a degree of prosperity, abandoned the immigrant quarters of the Lower East Side, and established new working- and middle-class Jewish neighborhoods that suited their economic status and class aspirations. They sent their American-born children to the public schools, embracing the promise of education and preparing a new generation to enter white-collar professions.[16] In a decade of prosperity, New York Jews built scores of elaborate, modern synagogues and transformed the Federation of Jewish Philanthropies into a sophisticated citywide representative of the Jewish community.[17] One Jewish social worker commented that during the 1920s it seemed "as if a golden age were to be inaugurated . . . for the Jewish communities in this country. Then came the depression."[18]

For Jews who had placed their hopes for personal advancement and Jewish communal survival in the promise of America, the Depression represented a severe blow. As a group, immigrant Jews and their children had experienced America as both a land of opportunity and relative security; but the 1930s brought a serious challenge to Jewish economic well-being along with a resurgence of anti-Semitism. When the Depression struck, well-educated Jewish youth were left with few employment options. Working-class Jewish families sometimes teetered on the brink of eviction and destitution, forced to rely on extended family and neighborhood supports as well as government assistance. Synagogues and philanthropic institutions that had thrived in the twenties suddenly found themselves struggling to stay afloat. The temporary disruption of Jewish economic mobility, the financial setbacks experienced by Jewish individuals and communal institutions, the

challenges posed to social and familial stability, and the psychological repercussions of the crisis constitute only a few of the formidable problems
encountered by Depression-era Jewry. Arriving on the heels of prosperity
and expansion, the Great Depression represented a financial shock to New
York Jews, but more important, it forced them to make difficult personal and
communal decisions that influenced the shape of American Jewish life for
decades to come.

This book does not attempt to provide a comprehensive analysis of all
elements of Jewish experience in the thirties. Several sweeping national and
international developments of the Depression decade permanently altered
the Jewish world. The rise of Nazism in Europe, the anti-Semitic movements
gaining strength in the United States, and the task of absorbing European
Jewish refugees presented enormous challenges to Depression-era Jews.
Likewise, the resurgence of radicalism and the labor movement decisively
contributed to the mood and actions of American Jews as they battled the
economic crisis. The emerging Zionist consensus, the expressions of a new
generation of Jewish intellectuals, and Jewish entrance into the New Deal
coalition, were all part of the complex landscape of American Jewish history
in the Depression decade. Each of these issues warrants careful examination
and most have already received detailed treatment in other scholarly works.
This book does not seek to retell the history of the many crucial national and
international movements of the 1930s but focuses specifically on the social
history of Jewish life, culture, and community during the Great Depression.

By examining Jewish families and neighborhoods, the experiences of
Jewish youth, changing gender roles, political activity, and the responses of
Jewish communal institutions, this work uses the economic crisis to uncover
patterns of Jewish adaptation and identity in America. As Jewish families and
neighborhoods confronted the Depression, they reformulated ethnic family
patterns and Jewish political culture. Likewise, the city's Jewish federation
and its synagogues not only struggled to remain fiscally solvent but also
revised their communal programs to suit the rapidly changing requirements
of American life. As a period of far-reaching social, economic, and political
change, the Depression years provide a unique vantage point for exploring
the ongoing development of Jewish ethnicity, acculturation, and adjustment
in America.

A focus on the Depression's communal consequences brings to light
previously neglected aspects of Jewish experience in the 1930s and complicates the standard presentation of American Jewish history. The 1930s have
been virtually ignored by American Jewish historians, in part because there
has been so much interest in chronicling Jewish responses to Nazism and

anti-Semitism. By exploring Jewish experience during the Great Depression, this work both fills a gap in American Jewish history and illuminates larger patterns of twentieth-century Jewish life. Jewish historical research has centered primarily on the period of mass Jewish immigration (1881–1924), an era of enormous familial and communal adjustment.[19] With the exception of a few studies of second-generation Jewry that examine the interwar years, scholarly works about American Jews generally shift from accounts of immigrant Jewish experience to descriptions of an acculturated and comfortable post–World War II Jewish community.[20] The Depression years literally bridged the immigrant world of the early twentieth century and the highly integrated community of the postwar era. Understanding the transformations that occurred during the Great Depression helps to explain the evolution of American Jews from an immigrant culture to a post–World War II ethnic group.

The Great Depression constituted a defining moment for American Jews, inaugurating alterations in Jewish families, occupational structures, political preferences, and communal organization that changed the face of Jewish life in the twentieth century. Second-generation Jews emerged from the Depression removed from the factories and businesses that had employed their parents and pursuing almost exclusively white-collar professions. By the time they reached adulthood, native-born Jews moved to new neighborhoods, married later, and limited the size of their families. As middle-class suburbanites, they embraced Democratic politics as a liberal creed and used their philanthropic and religious institutions to express and maintain a sense of ethnic identity. These patterns, which came to define American Jews in the post–World War II era, took shape within the confusion, ferment, and fervor of the Great Depression.

# I

# An Ethnic Economy

*One terrible day in the early thirties we heard that the Bank of the United States—Jewish-owned!—had failed, and I sat in our apartment listening to my aunt and grandmother wailing over the loss of the few hundred dollars they had scraped together . . .*

*Things had gone profoundly wrong . . .*
—Irving Howe, *A Margin of Hope*

When the Bank of the United States failed in December of 1930, the family drama that Irving Howe recounted occurred in Jewish homes throughout New York City. The Jewish-owned bank held the savings of approximately one-fifth of New York Jews, and its closure left thousands of Jewish families and businesses devastated. The 1929 Wall Street Crash, a prelude to the Great Depression, created a degree of panic within the more established German-Jewish community and among those East European Jews who had speculated in the stock market. But most New York Jews, particularly the masses of new immigrants, had no strong connection to Wall Street, and the

Crash had little immediate impact on them, "like something unfolding on another planet." For New York's Jewish community, the failure of the Bank of the United States signaled the beginning of the Great Depression, transforming the Wall Street Crash from an impersonal event into a tragedy that touched the lives of family, friends, and neighbors.[1]

Since its establishment in 1913, the Bank of the United States had stood as a celebrated symbol of Jewish economic success. Its founder, Joseph Marcus, was an East European immigrant who began his career in the garment industry. When Marcus and his partner, Saul Singer, opened the Bank of the United States, they fulfilled the collective aspirations of a generation of immigrant Jews. America's banking industry offered few opportunities for Jews; even German Jews rarely attained high-ranking positions in U.S. banking, making the success of an immigrant endeavor particularly striking. The Bank of the United States grew into a thriving financial institution, carrying a name that boldly asserted that Jews belonged in America. With branches throughout the city, from the Lower East Side to Brooklyn and from the Bronx to Fifth Avenue, the bank embodied immigrant faith in the promise of American life. New York Jews eagerly embraced the new bank, opening savings accounts and borrowing money for fledgling businesses. By the time it closed its doors in 1930, the Bank of the United States claimed sixty New York branches and 400,000, mostly Jewish, depositors.

The 1930 failure of the Bank of the United States sent shockwaves through New York's Jewish community. When it closed, the city's icon of Jewish success was the largest financial institution in the country ever to suspend payments.[2] The bank's failure and the investigation that followed kept the Bank of the United States on the front page of the *New York Times* for weeks. The *Jewish Daily Forward*, the most widely read Yiddish newspaper, described in vivid detail the tumultuous scenes throughout the city, as Jewish depositors gathered outside the local branches, frantically attempting to withdraw their savings.[3] Many members of New York's garment industry had conducted their business with the Bank of the United States and scrambled to recover their assets from the failed bank. A wide range of Jewish organizations, from large labor groups such as the Industrial Council of Cloak, Suit, and Skirt Manufacturers, to the Broome Street Boys and Wilkins Avenue Neighborhood Associations, to delegations of Lower East Side housewives, rallied together to protect their interests. Within days, frustrated depositors had organized to sue the bank's directors who had knowingly sold stock in the unstable institution in the weeks before its closure. The 400,000 depositors ultimately settled for a percentage of their

Interior
BANK OF UNITED STATES
FREEMAN STREET BRANCH, AT SOUTHERN BOULEVARD, BRONX

Vault
BANK OF UNITED STATES
FREEMAN STREET BRANCH, AT SOUTHERN BOULEVARD, BRONX

JOSEPH S. MARCUS
Founder and President of the Bank of United States
RESOURCES OF WHICH ARE $74,000,000.

THE BANK OF
UNITED STATES

1. In its heyday, the Bank of the United States was a proud financial institution with branches throughout the city. This advertisement for the modern and stylish Freeman Street Branch in the Bronx prominently displays a photograph of the bank's immigrant Jewish founder, Joseph S. Marcus. Courtesy of the Bronx County Historical Society, Bronx, New York.

# A very personal matter

Your relationship with your bank is really a very personal matter. It can and should go deeper than making deposits and drawing checks. There are many occasions when your bank should give you valuable advice—on such transactions as making investments, sending money abroad, building an estate, planning all kinds of financial programs.

By having completely equipped banks in 58 communities, The Bank of United States believes it is making a definite contribution towards establishing an intimate contact between the individual and the banker. You are invited to confer with an executive at the nearest office.

### 4% Interest Paid on Thrift Accounts of $1 Up from the First of Every Month

# The Bank of United States

*Member Federal Reserve System*

## Main Office: Fifth Avenue at 44th St.

*58 Offices in Greater New York*

The Young Judaean, 111 Fifth Avenue, N. Y. Issued monthly, except for the months of July and August, by the Young Judaean Press. Entered as Second Class Matter at the Post Office at New York, N. Y., under the Act of March 3, 1879. Copyright 1928, by the Young Judaean Press. Subscriptions, $2.00 per year (12 issues). Single copy 20c. (Canada, $2.50; Foreign, $3.00. Subscribers are requested to report change of address promptly, always giving the old address.

2. *Less than a year before its failure, the Bank of the United States was promoting its services to the Jewish community through advertisements in Jewish newspapers and magazines. Courtesy of the American Jewish Historical Society, Waltham, Massachusetts.*

holdings gleaned from bank assets as well as loan support available through the cooperation of other New York banks.[4]

While angry customers clamored to recover their savings, the Jewish community struggled with the symbolic meaning of the bank's failure. The closure of the Jewish-owned bank shook the confidence of immigrant Jews. Not only did thousands of Jews lose their savings, but rumors circulated that the institution might have been saved were it not for anti-Semitic sentiments within the U.S. banking community. Immediately after the closure, the *Times* ran editorials arguing that the bank had sufficient assets to be reorganized and reopened and urging federal officials to salvage the institution.[5] Although the allegations were never proven, the impression that the bank's demise was the result of purposeful maneuvering by anti-Semitic banking officials lingered within the Jewish community. Even more upsetting for New York Jews, the federal investigation implicated the bank's directors for poor management and ill-advised fiscal decisions. The communal pride that the Bank of the United States had once inspired quickly turned to disappointment and embarrassment. "When a non-Jewish bank falls through, it is said only that an individual person or an individual institution did not act as it should have," explained the Yiddish paper, *The Day*. "But when a Jewish banker and a Jewish bank go bankrupt—people right away create the impression that it is the downfall of all Jewish bankers and all Jewish people."[6] In its heyday, the Bank of the United States had represented the collective hopes of the Jewish community. As one of the first setbacks of the Great Depression, its failure provided a lens for the shared fears and concerns of a generation of New York Jews.

After the failure of the Bank of the United States, *The Day*'s editors urged New York Jews not to overreact to the incident, assuring them that "America, be sure, is not going under."[7] As a relatively new immigrant group, Jews had only just begun to establish themselves in the United States. Most Americans worried about their economic security during the Great Depression, but those sentiments were particularly acute for Jewish families whose roots in the United States had been so recently planted. Although Jews had been remarkably successful in advancing their economic status and propelling their children into the white-collar class, they continued to feel vulnerable to the vicissitudes of the American economy and the potential for anti-Semitic backlash that often accompanied periods of economic distress. Such anxiety reflected the inherent contradictions and ambiguities of Jewish experience. The relative economic success of New York Jews co-existed with and perhaps even contributed to the fear that the gains made by a generation of Jewish immigrants might easily be lost. "The Jews were an anomaly," ex-

plained one New York historian. "Despite their obvious economic achievements, they felt the least secure of the immigrants groups."[8]

By the time the Depression struck, Jews had attained an economic status
unparalleled by other immigrant groups. In less than a generation, they had
risen from the proletarian to the white-collar class. Jews arrived in America
with prior experience in skilled labor and trading and were able to enter the
U.S. workforce in those occupations, avoiding less desirable and lower-pay-
ing unskilled jobs.[9] At the turn of the century, immigrant Jews dominated
the garment industry and staked out a firm position as petty merchants. In
1900, 60 percent of American Jews worked in blue-collar trades, but thirty
years later that number had been cut in half. During the Depression years,
as many as two-thirds of Jews nationwide worked in white-collar jobs.[10] The
New York Jewish community had a somewhat greater proportion of blue-
collar workers, approximately 35 percent of the city's Jewish population, due
to the continuing presence of immigrant Jews in the needle trades.[11] But in
New York, as in the rest of the country, the economic profile of Depression-
era Jews was clearly becoming white-collar.

During the Great Depression, Jewish occupational patterns remained
distinct from those of other American groups. In 1935, New York's Welfare
Council sponsored a detailed survey of the economic and social patterns of
the city's youth, recording the occupational characteristics of both parents
and children in Depression-era households. That survey placed 47 percent
of New York's Jewish families in the white-collar category. More than one-
third of young Jews came from families in which their fathers were proprietors, managers, or officials. In an era when most Jewish parents were
immigrants, their concentration in white-collar positions was more than
double that of the comparable non-Jewish sample. Approximately one-third
of immigrant Jews remained in the garment industry and in other manual
trades, but the Jewish presence in labor had begun a steady decline. In 1920,
Jews comprised 80 percent of membership in the International Ladies Garment Workers Union (ILGWU), but by the mid-1930s, the union claimed only
half as many Jewish members. Even those Jews who continued to work in
the garment and fur industries rarely held unskilled jobs. The Welfare
Council reported only 3 percent of Jewish households where fathers worked
as unskilled laborers, a number far below the 18 percent figure reported for
non-Jewish families.[12]

The children of immigrants demonstrated an even more pronounced
tendency to pursue white-collar employment. Contemporary observers
noted that the children of the typical immigrant factory worker "were not

Table 1. *Occupations of Jewish and Non-Jewish Youth in New York City in 1935 (ages 16 to 25 inclusive)*

|  | Jews | | Non-Jews | |
|  | Male | Female | Male | Female |
| --- | --- | --- | --- | --- |
| Total employed youth | 521 | 560 | 1152 | 1044 |
| Total reporting occupation | 516 | 555 | 1146 | 1042 |
| Occupation | Percentage Distribution | | | |
| Clerical workers | 55.8 | 73.5 | 40.7 | 45.3 |
| Semiskilled workers | 21.9 | 20.2 | 31.7 | 33.7 |
| Proprietary and managerial workers | 8.5 | 1.6 | 3.3 | 0.4 |
| Skilled workers | 6.5 | 0.6 | 9.4 | 0.8 |
| Professionals | 4.3 | 3.4 | 3.0 | 3.5 |
| Service workers | 1.5 | 0.7 | 5.6 | 16.2 |
| Unskilled workers | 1.5 | — | 6.3 | 0.1 |

Source: Nettie Pauline McGill, "Some Characteristics of Jewish Youth in New York City," *Jewish Social Service Quarterly* 14, no. 2 (December 1937): 263. This table indicates only general employment categories. The author provides a breakdown and tabulation of the occupations that constitute each category.

following him into the factory or trade, but were going into business, office work, or the professions." Although young Jews (ages 16 to 25) comprised one-third of New York's employed youth population, they accounted for 56 percent of youth in proprietary and managerial work, 43 percent of those in clerical and sales occupations, and 37 percent of youth working in the professional class. Jewish parents encouraged their children to shun factory work. Explaining the declining numbers of Jews in the needle trades, the ILGWU's director of research pointed to "the deep-seated reluctance of Jewish workers to have their children follow them into manual occupations."[13] Even as they organized unions and led strikes to improve labor conditions, Jewish immigrants' most fervent desire was for their sons and daughters to avoid factory work entirely. As table 1 shows, Jewish youth fulfilled their parents' aspirations, seeking white-collar occupations and remaining decidedly underrepresented in both skilled and unskilled labor throughout the Great Depression.[14]

The employment patterns of New York Jews helped them survive the economic crisis in a comparatively fortunate position. Jewish concentration in white-collar and skilled occupations resulted in less severe economic dislocation relative to groups that predominated in manual and un-skilled positions. Underrepresented in heavy industry and unskilled labor, the hardest hit sectors of the economy, Jews "survived [the Depression] with more modest losses."[15] The Depression's uneven impact on different occupational groups was clearly evident in the city's relief statistics. New Yorkers who worked in white-collar jobs were less likely to require federal assistance. Among New York's white population, Italians demonstrated the highest proportion of families on relief. Twenty-one percent of Italian youth reported that their families accepted relief, but significantly, the number of Italians whose fathers worked in unskilled labor was almost double that of other youth of foreign-born parentage. Only 12 percent of Jewish youth indicated that their families were on the relief rolls, a figure that can be largely attributed to Jewish white-collar tendencies. The authors of the Welfare Council survey concluded that both Jews and Prot-estants had "unusually large proportions of white-collar workers, who were less widely affected by depression conditions than men in industrial em-ployment."[16] Jews did not escape the hardships of the Depression, how-ever; many experienced unemployment, downward mobility, and persistent economic insecurity. Yet, because they were concentrated in certain sectors of the economy, Jews fared better during the Depression than many other groups.

Jewish families often struggled through difficult economic circumstances, but few reported complete financial devastation. "We were poor," Irving Howe remembered about his working-class Bronx family. "We were never really hungry but almost always anxious."[17] A Works Progress Administration (WPA) study of Jewish family circles in New York revealed a similar portrait of Jewish life in the 1930s. "The crisis struck a number of members of our [family] circle," reported the WPA authors, "but it did not have catastrophic effects on them. Their standard of living is considerably lowered, but they are not subjected to hunger."[18] In the minds of Depression-era Jews, the distinction between complete destitution and simply being poor seemed to be the issue of hunger. In a host of Jewish memoirs and recollections from the period, Jews reported living in diminished circumstances but drew the line between themselves and others who lacked food, clothing, or housing. Sydney Evans, who came of age in Brooklyn in the 1930s, interpreted his family's situation in comparative perspective. "We never experienced the deep depression that many people went through," Evans explained. "We always had food. We always had a place to live and we always had warmth. Somehow or another, we always had clothes, even though I remember some of the shoes I had which were more than hand-me-downs. It was the

Depression and I knew it [but] we were fortunate enough never to have experienced hunger."[19] Having read reports about the dust bowl and witnessed the construction of shantytowns, most Jews acknowledged that they had not felt the harshest effects of the Depression. "We didn't have too much money, but . . . I don't remember ever being hungry," Amram Ducovny recalled about his Brooklyn boyhood. "I do remember not having bicycles, clothes, etc., but compared to others in the Depression we did quite well."[20]

Jews entered the decade with particular occupational tendencies that worked to their advantage during the economic crisis, but lower rates of unemployment and relief applications represented the statistical measures of Jewish group experience—they did not always reflect the individual circumstances and communal perceptions of Depression-era Jews. Jewish working-class families, who bore the brunt of the Depression's hardships, hardly took comfort in the general white-collar profile of their ethnic group. Those who labored in the garment trades or other industries, a full one-third of the New York Jewish population, were utterly devastated by layoffs and unemployment.[21] Alfred Kazin, who grew up in a Brownsville neighborhood that housed thousands of Jewish blue-collar workers, recalled that, "It puzzled me greatly when I came to read in books that Jews are a shrewd people particularly given to commerce and banking, for all the Jews I knew had managed to be an exception to that rule. I grew up with the belief that the natural condition of a Jew was to be a propertyless worker like my painter father and my dressmaker mother."[22] In 1934, workers in traditionally Jewish industries such as clothing manufacture, building, printing, amusements, and other trades earned less than $1,200 a year, if they were employed regularly, and most were not. Half of those on the relief rolls had once held jobs in industry and manufacturing.[23] Jews, as a group, may have fared better than many other sectors of the American population, but the Depression highlighted the continuing class divisions within the Jewish community as it shattered the financial stability of thousands of Jewish working-class families.

The overall portrait of Jewish economic fortunes in the 1930s belies some of the particular realities of Jewish experience. In fact, the economic distinctions between blue- and white-collar may have been more significant in employment and relief statistics than within the Jewish community. Before the Depression, skilled manual laborers, classified as blue-collar, often had higher incomes than many Jewish small business owners who were listed as white-collar.[24] Among immigrant Jews, the economic and status divisions between modest retailers and skilled factory workers were not clearly drawn. In the late 1920s, even the politically leftist founders of the Workers Cooperative Colony, one of the most ideologically rigorous Jewish cooperative

3. *This Jewish-owned furniture store, like so many others in the city, became a casualty of the Depression-era economy. Courtesy of the American Jewish Historical Society, Waltham, Massachusetts.*

housing projects in the city, refused to exclude Jewish entrepreneurs from the category of "workers." The cooperative's directors restricted the housing project to "those who earned their living by the sweat of their brows." Elaborating the definition of that category, the directors insisted that, "small business owners were considered self-employed workers, but bosses, who lived off the labor of others, were not welcome."[25] The Jewish world had its own internal occupational scale. Within the Jewish community, proprietors of fledgling businesses often occupied the same economic levels as skilled factory laborers. The emerging cadre of clerks, accountants, office workers, and professionals were considered truly white-collar, as opposed to the petty merchants that dotted Jewish neighborhoods. In another category altogether were the factory owners, big business leaders, landlords, and "bosses" who earned the disdain of the Jewish working class. Both before and during the Depression, the Jewish community's internal divisions of class and status did not always correspond to the official listings of government statistics.

Unemployment calculations could be somewhat deceptive in the case of small merchants. To be sure, blue-collar factory workers were the hardest hit members of the Jewish community, but they were not the only Jews to suffer during the economic crisis. The Jews who owned small businesses, managed grocery and drug stores, sold furniture, or ran other retail establishments made up the bulk of the adult white-collar population. These Jews, although officially members of the white-collar class, often faced severe hardships and sometimes lost their businesses. For example, in the Jewish-dominated furniture industry, the number of wholesalers plummeted from 1,146 in 1929 to 730 in 1933; almost eight thousand retail furniture stores closed during the same period. The sharp reductions in the furniture industry mirrored similar declines in the other small-scale trades that comprised the backbone of the Jewish economy.[26] In the early twentieth century, thousands of Jewish immigrants had opened stores with minimal capital investments; many of them could not keep those establishments afloat in the Great Depression. Even before the Depression, chain stores had begun invading Jewish neighborhoods, threatening the success of modest retail businesses. In the midst of the Depression, chain stores heightened the economic pressure on independent Jewish merchants. In 1933, one young Jew who identified himself in a newspaper editorial as the "son of an entrepreneur," insisted that, "Although Mr. Woolworth does not acknowledge my father to be a competitor of his, nevertheless we are acutely aware of the presence of the aforementioned Woolworth and were I to have a dollar for every time I hear the term, 'I can get it cheaper at Woolworth's' then the depression as far as we are concerned would not exist."[27] Jewish retailers did maintain a distinct advantage over factory workers in the options available to them. With some luck and ingenuity, Jewish entrepreneurs had the chance to keep their businesses functioning. When customers could not afford new furniture, dealers might turn to reupholstery. When the purchase of new hats exceeded Depression-era budgets, haberdashers could begin reconstructing and cleaning old ones. Even if they were barely surviving, small shopkeepers could tread water longer than manual laborers, making them more likely to remain off the relief rolls and invisible within unemployment statistics.

There is a certain irony to Jewish economic experience in the 1930s. Jews were indeed comparatively fortunate in weathering the crisis, but they had never felt less confident about their financial futures or their security in America. The relative degree of Jewish economic success fueled resentment and anti-Semitism, increasing Jewish anxiety in the Depression years. So pervasive and widespread was the notion that Jews dominated the American economy that *Fortune* magazine felt the need to investigate the extent of Jewish business interests. In a detailed analysis that refuted charges of Jewish economic control, *Fortune*'s editors insisted that "Jewish participation [was] incidental or non-existent" in banking, finance, heavy industry, as well as in a host of other white-collar professions. The study concluded only that Jews

4. This Lower East Side clothing business survived the Depression by becoming an all-purpose establishment, buying and selling used clothes, cleaning and pressing garments, and accepting relief tickets as payments from its customers. Courtesy of the Richard A. Lyon Collection, Museum of the City of New York.

clustered in certain light industries, particularly clothing manufacture, trade, scrap metal dealership, and the entertainment and amusement businesses. *Fortune's* editors claimed that Jews were "clannish," crowding together in specific sectors of the economy but assured its readers that there was "no basis whatever for the suggestion that Jews monopolize U.S. business and industry."[28] The study's authors considered themselves to be supporting American Jews and combating dangerous misinformation, but Depression-era Jews did not find the article reassuring. The defensive posture of the argument, the sense that Jewish economic achievements needed to be justified and rendered less threatening to the non-Jewish public, underscored the uneasiness that

Jews felt in the 1930s. "What it amounts to is challenging the right of Jews to succeed in the economic field," declared one WPA writer, noting that the article revealed the prevalence of a "subconscious idea that Jews somehow do not belong, and therefore, have no right to play important roles."[29]

In the 1930s, New York Jews had good cause to fear economic resentment. At a time when Jews appeared to be weathering the Depression better than other groups, many Americans gave credence to charges of Jewish financial dominance. The entry of Jews into government employment stoked the fires of popular prejudice in the Depression years. In the mid-1930s, a growing number of Jews joined the ranks of New York's civil service employees. After his 1933 election, Mayor Fiorello LaGuardia implemented a merit system for selecting civil servants, an effort that effectively overturned the Tammany government's long tradition of Irish patronage.[30] LaGuardia's commitment to balanced ethnic representation in public service gave many Jews their first chance for government employment, an opportunity that Roosevelt's New Deal Administration would also offer Jews on a national level. In the midst of the Depression, the growing presence of Jews in both local and national civil service produced a backlash of hostility. A 1938 survey revealed that almost one-quarter of Americans believed that Jews held too many government jobs.[31] The *Brooklyn Tablet*, the borough's official diocese newspaper, insisted that Jews controlled the best employment positions, claiming that "in the professions, civil service, schools and public life they are represented out of all proportion to their numbers."[32] The widespread perception that Jews held an economic advantage and the vociferous public articulations of such sentiments fueled Jewish concerns about their security and belonging within Depression-era America.

For American Jews, accusations of favoritism and financial prowess seemed absurd at a time when job discrimination had become the foremost Jewish communal problem. During the Depression, "Christians only" want ads ran regularly in mainstream newspapers, including the *New York Times*. Even employers who did not run such advertisements often refused to hire Jewish workers. "They would give you an interview and ask your religion," recalled Jean Margolies, who grew up on New York's Lower East Side. "They wouldn't say that they didn't want you. They'd say, 'We'll get in touch with you,' and then you were out. . . . Many times it happened so I knew it must be that they didn't like Jews."[33] Certain employers, such as the city's telephone and gas companies, routinely rejected Jewish applicants. Insurance agencies, banks, and law offices also regularly refused to hire Jewish workers.[34] Although the public schools ostensibly offered legal guarantees of equal opportunity, prospective Jewish teachers were often identified and excluded through an oral examination designed to detect particularities of Jewish speech. Teaching, government jobs, and civil service presented the best conditions for Jewish employment, but such highly coveted positions were not plentiful during the Depression.[35] In the face of growing barriers to Jewish employment, some Jews concealed their religion or changed their names in the hope of securing work; others refused to "pass" as Christians for the sake of a job. As the poor economy hindered the ability of all Americans to find employment, Jews felt doubly beleaguered by the rising tide of job discrimination.

Even young Jews who remained in school, choosing not to test the lean job market, could not escape discrimination. In the interwar years, most elite private colleges imposed a quota system for Jewish admission, limiting Jewish enrollment to about 10 percent. Most New York Jews, unable to afford private colleges, attended the city's public universities where no quotas barred their enrollment. But if they chose to pursue professional training after graduation, Jews encountered formidable quota barriers. The number of Jewish medical students fell steadily throughout the Depression, at a rate far greater than the national average. New York's five medical schools imposed drastic limits on Jewish enrollment and the percentage of Jews in each entering class dropped sharply throughout the 1930s.[36] The *Fortune* survey found that although Jews comprised 50 percent of the nation's medical school applicant pool, only 17 percent gained admission.[37] A slightly better situation awaited aspiring Jewish lawyers since law school quotas in New York were not quite as rigid. During the Depression, Jews constituted more than half of New York law students, but only about 25 percent nationwide. Law school held greater appeal for many young Jews, in part, because it was considerably less expensive than either medical or dental training. But by the 1930s, many law schools had introduced "character" criteria in their admissions policies and the percentage of Jewish law students also began a steady decline.[38]

Jews who did graduate from universities and professional schools during the Depression could expect that discrimination would follow them into the workforce. In the mid-1930s, non-Jewish law firms seldom hired Jewish attorneys. "The doors of most New York law offices were closed, with rare exceptions, to a young Jewish lawyer."[39] Medical and dental offices also did not welcome newly minted Jewish graduates, so Jewish dentists and physicians set up their own independent practices. In this respect, Jewish professionals behaved very much like Jewish merchants, insurance agents, and accountants; they opened Jewish offices, with a largely Jewish staff, serving a primarily Jewish clientele. During the Depression years, employment discrimination contributed to the maintenance of an ethnic economy. The

Jewish community provided a relatively solid economic base capable of providing work for at least a portion of its members. The ethnic economy was by no means self-sustaining; thousands of Jewish lawyers, engineers, and professionals remained unemployed or underemployed throughout the Depression. Nevertheless, as historian Henry Feingold has explained, "Despite its contraction, the Jewish ethnic economy still had comparatively greater depth than that of other groups and was able to absorb some of its own unemployed."[40]

Once again, however, the relative security of the Jewish economy provided little reassurance to American Jews who faced the pressures of the economic depression at a time of rising anti-Semitism and employment discrimination. Troubled by the specter of young, well-educated Jews unable to earn a living, Jews worried particularly about the fate of the next generation. New York Jews watched as sons and daughters with high school, college, and professional degrees searched for part-time work or joined the ranks of the unemployed. The unemployment of youth was certainly not unique to the Jewish group; the Depression hit America's young people particularly hard. But the combination of bleak job opportunities, university quotas, and employment discrimination created a sense of foreboding among American Jews. The deteriorating prospects for Jewish employment, unfolding against an international climate of fascism and Nazism and the growing strength of American anti-Semitic movements, enhanced Jewish insecurity and informed Jewish responses to the daily challenges of economic survival. Jews began to wonder if the political power of anti-Semitism, the pervasiveness of employment discrimination, and the economic stringencies of depression might combine to reverse the progress achieved by a generation of immigrant Jews, creating a cadre of educated but unemployable Jewish youth and undermining the Jewish future in America. Unemployment and lack of job opportunity were national problems during the Great Depression, but the vicissitudes of the economic crisis had specific manifestations for American Jews who were negotiating a complex maze of economic, social, and cultural forces.

The organized Jewish community recognized that Jewish economic and employment needs required particular attention. Since many employment agencies refused to accept Jewish applicants, Jewish communal leaders initiated their own programs to help Jews find jobs. Even before the Depression, several Jewish employment agencies existed throughout the city, sponsored by organizations ranging from the Ninety-second Street YMHA to the Jewish Board of Guardians to the Brooklyn Jewish Federation.[41] In the first decades of the twentieth century, such agencies assisted new immigrants looking for

5. *At this employment bureau, as in many others in the city, job listings regularly specified that applicants be "Christians only." Courtesy of the Richard A. Lyon Collection, Museum of the City of New York.*

work and provided a range of vocational services for Jewish job-seekers. When the Depression came, Jewish employment offices suddenly faced an avalanche of clients. In 1933, four New York Jewish employment agencies reported a combined total of twenty thousand applicants registering for job placement; they were able to find work for only four thousand.[42] With individual agencies taxed to capacity, Jewish social workers suggested that Jewish employment needs might be better served through a coordinated communal effort. In 1934, New York's Federation of Jewish Philanthropies created a central Jewish employment bureau. The Federation Employment Service was a joint venture supported by the then separate Brooklyn and New York Jewish Federations along with several of the city's other private

Jewish agencies. Designed to "administer employment services of a place-ment, guidance, and research kind for Jews resident in New York city," the Federation Employment Service dedicated itself to "economic planing for the Jewish people."[43]

The creation of the Federation Employment Service (FES) testified to the tenor of concern about employment and economic status within the Jewish community. Worried about job discrimination and the swelling numbers of Jewish unemployed, Jewish leaders felt the need to formulate a communal response to the problem. The Federation's elite members sponsored the FES; its board of directors included established leaders from the German-Jewish community, such as international banker Paul Felix Warburg and prominent philanthropist Rebecca Kohut.[44] The Business Men's Council, which repre-sented the Federation's most affluent members, contributed to the FES by mining the resources of the ethnic economy and "stimulating employment opportunities among the industries in which they have influence." Unlike some immigrant-aid ventures of the early twentieth century, the FES was not strictly an organization founded by German-Jewish leaders in order to serve an immigrant population. By the 1930s, patterns of Jewish communal leader-ship had shifted; East European Jews also served on the FES board and its professional staff was largely American-born and college-educated. The per-sistence of Jewish joblessness, particularly among well-educated and profes-sionally trained youth, exposed the vulnerability of all Jews to the precarious Depression-era economy. Employment discrimination had become such a far-reaching problem that Jewish organizations, led by both German and East European Jews, felt compelled to act. Many young Jews came to Jewish employment agencies because they had either experienced or feared dis-crimination on the job market. The FES reported that applicants often wanted "to know particularly those fields which are closed or open to Jews because of anti-semitism."[45] Designed as a strategy to combat practical problems of Jewish unemployment, the FES reflected the deep-seated and widely shared communal fears about the Jewish future in the American economy.[46]

The Federation Employment Service developed a thorough, scientific approach to job placement and vocational counseling. Led by associate direc-tor, Irwin Rosen, the FES conducted detailed studies of the educational back-grounds, employment patterns, and job preferences of its applicants. A Harvard University graduate and experienced Jewish caseworker, Rosen had coordinated the Ninety-second Street YMHA employment bureau before tak-ing over the FES.[47] Overseeing the bureau during the worst years of the Depression, Rosen encountered an unfortunate combination of rising num-bers of applicants and shrinking job opportunities. Since he could find work for only a small percentage of applicants, Rosen emphasized the importance

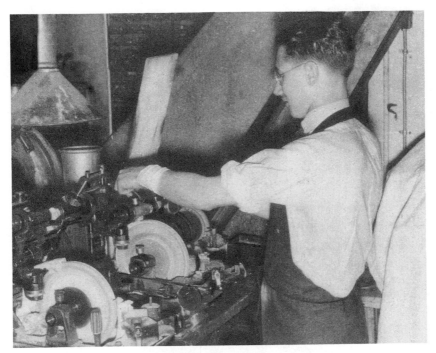

6. *The New York Jewish Federation provided training for Jewish job-seekers. The caption accompanying this photograph in the Federation's magazine declared, "A real break—apprenticed to a good trade, lens-grinding. Jobs are scarce, but Federation agencies have been resourceful in searching out opportunities in industry." From* Federation Illustrated *(July 1936).*

of vocational preparation. He instituted classes in bookkeeping, accounting, and stenography and implemented psychological testing to determine the suitability of applicants for particular occupations.[48] Despite his best efforts, Rosen operated the bureau at a time when job prospects were increasingly bleak. By the winter of 1932, enrollment in the Ninety-second Street Y's vocational training programs had ballooned to more than two hundred students per class. During the worst year of the economic crisis, overcrowding and the poor job market forced Rosen to close registration temporarily. At that time, he estimated that the odds of finding a job had become one in twenty and conceded the unlikelihood of placing the flood of Jewish applicants.[49]

Rosen could not manufacture jobs for Jews, but his meticulous statistical calculations of the FES clientele did help to identify the central problems of Jewish employment, particularly those of Jewish youth. (The appendix offers a thorough analysis of the FES survey.) In one eight-month period from

7. *The Federation Employment Service trained men and women for different careers. The caption under this photograph reported, "Through Federation agencies many girls find places as clerical workers, and in stores and industry. But their number is but a fraction of those who still await their chances." From* Federation Illustrated *(July 1936).*

September 1934 to May 1935, almost eight thousand Jews came to the Federation Employment Service hoping to find a job. Eighty-five percent of the applicants ranged from eighteen to thirty-five years old. Most were the American-born children of immigrants and came from working- and middle-class Jewish families. The unemployed Jewish population that registered with the FES had generally not grown up in poverty: only one-sixth lived in the five lowest-income neighborhoods of the city and one-third made their homes in the five highest rent districts. Jewish applicants to the FES had obtained a relatively high level of education. More than 99 percent had completed at least eight years of schooling, and 68 percent had pursued academic, commercial, or technical training beyond the high school level.[50] Their parents worked in skilled labor or small business, but they came to the bureau seeking white-collar jobs.[51] This was precisely the group that the relief and employment statistics declared were faring best economically, but they had arrived at the FES unable to find work. "A superior type of applicant seeks employment through our agency," Rosen explained, "and is met with the dilemma that positions become increasingly inferior."[52]

The collective client profile of the FES revealed the problems that most concerned Jewish communal leaders during the Depression. Despite the economic crisis, young Jews continued to aspire to professional and white-collar careers, but such positions were in short supply and almost half of all Jewish youth looking for work failed to find jobs.[53] The Depression prompted a communal discussion about the possibility that American Jews were becoming a maladjusted and "abnormal" economic group. The editors of *Fortune* magazine had argued precisely that point when they claimed that Jews displayed "a curious industrial distribution, [a] tendency to crowd together in particular squares of the checkerboard."[54] Several years before the article appeared, Jewish leaders had already contemplated the issue and worried that Jewish occupational preferences might prove detrimental in an age of economic contraction. "Unlike Americans as a whole, the Jewish group does not possess that balanced economic distribution which will enable economic gains and losses, strains and tensions to be spread evenly throughout their number," declared one Jewish social service worker, pointing out the infinitesimal number of Jews in agriculture and the shrinking Jewish presence in manual trades.[55] Jewish communal leaders who studied occupational patterns noted with dismay that young Jews were gravitating toward a single, already overcrowded, sector of the economy. As it turned out, Jews of the post–World War II era benefited greatly from their occupational preferences, but in the midst of the Depression, some Jews began to doubt the economic path they had chosen.

In the turmoil of the Depression, many social workers and community leaders attempted to guide young Jews away from overcrowded white-collar fields. "Sound vocational guidance should be effective in redirecting Jewish workers into new occupations and into those jobs where less competition . . . exists," declared one Jewish social worker.[56] In 1935, the vocational guidance department of the Jewish Social Service Association proudly reported that "many of the hundreds of boys eager to become doctors and lawyers, and many of the hundreds of girls wanting to be teachers or private secretaries have been diverted from overcrowded fields to training for occupations which offer them a chance of a better future."[57] Jewish agencies often believed that they provided sound advice to young Jews by encouraging them to avoid professional pursuits and highly coveted white-collar jobs. "Rising generations of Jews will find it increasingly difficult . . . to climb freely as their fathers did by means of the urban businesses, trades and professions," warned one Jewish social worker. "We ought, therefore, to provide for them new places and escapes through a more balanced distribution."[58]

The question of how or whether to attempt to change Jewish occupational patterns elicited a multitude of communal responses. Most Jewish social workers advocated offering Jews instruction to broaden their career opportunities, not suggesting factory work, but recommending more modest positions in accounting, stenography, and other small-scale trades. The Depression crisis did evoke more radical proposals, however. Some voices within the community called for a redistribution of Jews into manual labor or agricultural work. The Jewish Agricultural Society, which had sponsored farming projects since the late nineteenth century, accelerated its campaign during the Great Depression, touting agriculture as one answer to Jewish unemployment. "It is perhaps time to reopen the question of agriculture as an opportunity . . . for the young people who are casting around for a career."[59] Although some Jewish poultry and dairy farms did function successfully through the Depression, most American Jews never seriously considered turning to farming. Other suggestions about reviving the "dignity of labor" included the recommendation that young Jews reenter the manual occupations that had employed many of their parents, an idea that also failed to elicit any sustained interest. The dearth of white-collar positions kept many young Jews out of work, but most preferred to continue searching for employment rather than embrace such drastic solutions to their economic problems.[60]

In fact, the majority of Jewish communal workers argued that it was both futile and foolish to attempt any radical reconstruction of the Jewish economic profile. "I am not entirely sympathetic with the present vogue for decrying Jewish 'middle-class and professional leanings,'" insisted social worker Ben Selekman, "for it seems to me that the idealization of physical work as such belongs to a passing era. . . . Before training too many of our Jewish youth for unwanted manual occupation[s], let us make sure . . . that they offer the only or even the most promising way out in America."[61] Irwin Rosen harshly criticized plans for redirecting Jews to manual trades, emphasizing that by persisting in white-collar occupations, Jews had "allied themselves with what must be considered the relatively good employment possibilities." Since industrial laborers fared much worse than white-collar workers during the Depression, he argued, "there could hardly be any logic in recommending redistribution of Jews" into factory and industrial work.[62]

"Any achievement of such distribution would materially lower the present economic level of the Jewish people and would certainly direct many of them into occupations below their employment level."[63] Some Jewish leaders had suggested that eliminating Jewish overcrowding in white-collar positions might reduce anti-Semitism, but most members of the Jewish community disagreed. Morris Waldman, secretary of the American Jewish Committee, maintained that Jewish occupations were the targets not the causes of anti-Semitism, adding that "we cannot at all be certain that anti-Semitism resulting from economic competition will be materially modified by shifting the competition from one occupation or profession to another."[64]

The best response to Depression-era employment problems, according to most social workers, involved combating anti-Semitism and job discrimination whenever possible while trying to help Jews withstand the economic crisis. Irwin Rosen acknowledged that young Jews were not likely to find work, and he joined the chorus of experts encouraging youth to remain in school. In 1932, he advised job applicants "to return to or continue with school since the opportunities for profitable employment in business are largely non-existent at the present time."[65] Rosen and others who defended the Jewish white-collar profile and urged Jews to stay in school witnessed the wisdom of their claims in the postwar era. But in the turmoil of the Depression, as Jewish leaders struggled to determine the most prudent path for Jews to follow, they could not have envisioned the successes of the next decade. In truth, the ongoing debate among social workers and communal leaders had little impact at all on Jewish occupational choices. While the experts argued about the best prospects for young Jews, the next generation continued an unabated pursuit of higher education and white-collar careers.

The heated discussion about employment patterns revealed, above all else, Jewish fears about the future. Communal leaders worried not only about Jewish economic fortunes but, more broadly, about Jewish security and acceptance in America. On the most basic level, the setbacks of the Depression raised serious doubts about the fate of the next Jewish generation. Joblessness and economic adversity unsettled New York Jews, but the climate of discrimination and prejudice informed Jewish responses to Depression-era unemployment. Defending the need for Jews to maintain their own employment agencies, one social worker insisted that the effort would be necessary "so long as the Jewish community feels and understands that Jews throughout the world are going through a period of grave economic insecurity."[66] Jews interpreted their own economic challenges as distinct from those of other groups, for they encountered the Great Depression against the backdrop of national and international developments that lent particular meaning to their search for employment and financial stability. Even as a host of Depression-era surveys revealed the comparative good fortune of American Jews, Jews did not feel economically, socially, or politically secure.

The economic profile of New York Jews, their less frequent appearances on the relief rolls, and their relatively lower levels of destitution offer some perspective on Jewish experience in the Depression years. The daily challenges facing Jews looking for work and the responses of the organized Jewish community to their employment problems testify to a more complex Jewish economic reality, not always apparent in numerical calculations and occupational status. The particular character of the ethnic economy, the battle against discrimination, and the broader framework informing Jewish economic circumstances complicate the collective portrait of Depression-era Jewry. Against the canvas of these larger economic and cultural forces, Jewish families and households navigated their course through the rough waters of the Great Depression.

# 2

## A Family Affair

*The family was a whole greater than all the individuals who made it up.*
—Alfred Kazin, *A Walker in the City*

Stanley Katz was only five years old on Black Thursday, the fateful October day when the stock market crashed. The Katz family spent the Depression years in Brooklyn, in a working- and middle-class neighborhood in East New York. Stanley's father, a cloakmaker in the garment industry, found only occasional piecework during the Depression and managed to secure part-time employment as a night watchman. In the mid-thirties, his parents opened a dry-cleaning store where his mother worked as a seamstress, usually doing the sewing from home. Both Stanley and his older brother held jobs intermittently throughout their adolescence. Stanley found a position as a stock boy in a department store and attended school at night. Although there were hard times, the family never applied for government assistance. They moved from one apartment to another several times during the Depression, depending upon fluctuations in income, but the collective earnings of the family of four sustained the Katz household through the ups and downs of the economic crisis.[1]

New York Jews negotiated the challenges of the Great Depression not as individuals but as families. "Our parents clung to family life as if that was their one certainty," Irving Howe remembered.[2] Like other immigrant groups, Jews viewed the family as an economic and social unit with shared resources and responsibilities. Personal choices about work, education, and social life depended upon the needs of the family as a whole. Collective family strategies were not new to the Depression era. As immigrants, Jews had relied on family support networks to mediate adjustment to American life, sharing wage-earning and household responsibilities and easing the social and cultural transitions of immigration.[3] As they adapted to the American environment, both parents and children depended on the family economy; husbands, wives, sons, and daughters contributed to the maintenance of the household and determined the priorities of its members. By the 1930s, immigrant Jewish families had settled comfortably in America, established a solid economic footing, built social and cultural organizations, and were raising a generation of American-born children to adulthood. The Great Depression disrupted the economic and social progress of New York Jews and renewed the importance of family collectivity. In a decade of economic hardship and frustrated expectations, the family provided stability for New York Jews, albeit not without occasional discord and strife.

The Depression had no uniform effect on the families of any ethnic group and no single consequence within Jewish families. Some Jewish families suffered severe financial hardships, while others remained virtually untouched by the economic crisis. Many middle-class households, or families with one or two steady wage earners, managed to survive the Depression with only minor budgetary adjustments. By eliminating luxuries, cooking at home rather than eating in restaurants, or limiting recreation and entertainment expenses, many Jewish families handled the Depression by modestly altering their lifestyles. Even working-class families initially responded to the Depression in the same way that they had approached other economic downturns. Having endured the hardships of migration and the periodic slack seasons of the garment industry, many Jewish immigrants interpreted the Depression as "yet another crisis they would have to get through."[4] Although the Depression turned out to be longer and more severe than they had ever expected, working-class Jewish families had years of practice in handling economic adversity. Jewish factory workers had never known prosperity in the 1920s, and their families had mastered the art of stretching

*Table 2. Nativity of Parents of New York City Youth in 1935*

|  | Total | Catholic | Jewish | Protestant |
|---|---|---|---|---|
| Number of subjects | 9041° | 4392 | 2835 | 1606 |
|  | Percentage Distribution | | | |
| White | 96.1 | 98.9 | 100.0 | 81.1 |
| Both parents native | 24.7 | 28.9 | 8.8 | 43.0 |
| One or both parents foreign-born | 71.4 | 70.0 | 91.2 | 38.1 |

°208 subjects failed to report their religious affiliation.
Source: Nettie Pauline McGill and Ellen Nathalie Matthews, *The Youth of New York City* (New York: MacMillan, 1940), 12.

scarce resources. Most New York Jews faced some degree of economic stringency and uncertainty during the Depression years, but families that endured protracted unemployment and had no regular income struggled most painfully with financial survival and with difficult decisions about work, housing, and schooling.

In the 1930s, the typical Jewish family consisted of immigrant parents and American-born children. The 1935 Welfare Council survey reported that the city's Jewish youth were overwhelmingly native-born, but more than 90 percent had foreign-born parents (see table 2). Since the mid-1920s, restrictive quotas had severely limited the number of Jewish immigrants arriving in the United States.[5] Without a steady influx of immigrants, native-born Jews began for the first time to outnumber immigrants within the Jewish population.[6] During the 1930s, most young Jews continued to live in their parents' homes through adolescence and young adulthood, so that Old World and American values cohabitated (and often clashed) within Jewish households.[7] Despite the pressures brought to bear on the family unit during the economic crisis, household cooperation remained the norm within Jewish families and provided a basic means of confronting the challenges of the Depression.

Since the immigrant period, Jewish wives and mothers had shouldered responsibility for the economic well-being of their families, and they remained at the center of Depression-era Jewish households. Although Jewish wives worked for wages less frequently than their non-Jewish counterparts, many Jewish women returned to the labor force when economic need demanded it. Immigrant Jews inherited a cultural tradition that supported married women working. In Eastern Europe, Jewish wives had frequently contributed income to the family. The popular image of the full-time male

Talmud scholar whose wife supported the family was more myth than reality; only a small percentage of Jewish men in Europe were religious scholars and very few Jewish wives actually shouldered the family's economic burden alone. Nevertheless, the Jewish cultural *ideal* celebrated Jewish women who worked as storekeepers or small businesswomen in order to enable their husbands to pursue religious study. Because Jews came from a culture that legitimated married women's work, immigrant Jewish families were often more comfortable with the role of married women as breadwinners.[8]

At the same time, immigrant Jews rapidly accepted American norms of gender behavior in marriage. The American ideal prescribed that the husband should be the sole wage earner while his wife scrupulously maintained the home. Although immigrant Jews did not immediately embrace the model of American domesticity, patterns of work for married women did change quickly in American Jewish families. Jewish women in America typically abandoned wage employment once they married. As early as 1911, only 1 percent of Jewish wives worked for wages as opposed, for example, to the 36 percent of Italian married women in the workforce.[9] Immigrant Jewish wives contributed to the family economy by taking in boarders, managing small family stores, or working as seamstresses from home, but few sought employment outside the home. Jewish families generally chose to send unmarried daughters rather than wives to the factories.[10] During the Depression, patterns established during the immigrant period continued to influence the work-related decisions of Jewish families. In the 1930s, most Jewish wives did not regularly work for wages, but cultural traditions that validated married women's economic contributions may have paved the way for Jewish women to enter the workforce in times of financial distress.

When husbands lost their jobs or the family needed extra income, Jewish women sometimes sought paid employment. The work of married women was usually described as supplemental, both by family members and by the working wives themselves. "I didn't have good jobs, or make a lot of money," one Jewish woman explained about her Depression-era employment, "but I always had a job. If I didn't help out, we couldn't have managed at all."[11] Jewish wives frequently viewed their employment as "helping out" rather than as a legitimate occupation. When asked if she had worked during the Depression, Rebecca Augenstein initially answered that she had not but later added that she had held a part-time job in a bakery. Augenstein lived with her husband and small children in the Bronx and like many Jewish wives, she helped keep the family afloat when her husband lost his job in the fur industry. Augenstein worked half the day until her children returned from school, earned meager wages, and clearly did not regard her job as full-fledged employment. She admitted, however, "I needed that 85 cents an hour very badly at that time."[12] In her account of Jewish immigrant women's lives, Sydney Weinberg observed that "daughters remembered, above all, their mothers 'managing' in hard times, when 'managing' frequently meant earning enough money to keep the family together."[13] During the 1930s, Jewish wives moved in and out of the labor force, taking jobs when finances were strained. Although women may have viewed their paid labor as supplemental, their contributions remained crucial to family stability during the Depression years.

By the 1930s, Jewish families had begun to accept and internalize American cultural norms that scorned married women working outside the home. "My husband never wanted me to work," one Jewish woman explained, "but it was a necessity so I had to."[14] During the Depression, New York Jews struggled to balance the need for women's wages with the desire to attain middle-class respectability. Even the Socialist *Jewish Daily Forward*, the leading Yiddish daily paper and the voice of the working class, wavered in its support for married women working. Some *Forward* articles, notably written by women, argued strongly in favor of a woman's right to remain in the labor force after marriage. "Women have learned to be independent people," wrote one female *Forward* reporter. "They do not consider marriage as a medium to liberate them from work."[15] Other editorials, however, portrayed married women working for wages as a step backward. Deploring the depths to which impoverished Jewish wives had sunk in order to support their families during the Depression, one *Forward* author lamented that "poor Jewish women now look for all kinds of ways to make a living. They peddle; they take in boarders; they raise other people's children. Still others return to the factory. Fifteen years ago, they . . . dreamed that they would ultimately 'find their destined mate and be free of the factory.' Now they have their mates, but after fifteen years' time, they must go back to the factory."[16] In this article, as in many similar statements from the period, the need for married women to work during the Depression came to symbolize the unfulfilled expectations of a generation of immigrants. The image of the full-time housewife whose husband supported the family exerted a powerful influence even within families in which husbands were not the sole breadwinners. Many Jewish families simply could not afford to conform to middle-class notions of proper gendered behavior in marriage. Feeling the weight of cultural norms, most Jews justified married women's work as a temporary necessity during difficult financial periods but never considered it an ideal situation.[17]

Jewish concerns about married women working for wages mirrored the debate taking place throughout the country in the 1930s. During the Depression, working wives faced growing hostility from critics who accused them of taking jobs from men. A 1936 Gallup poll reported that 82 percent of Americans believed that wives should not work if their husbands were employed.[18] Disapproval of married women working outside the home gained government support in the so-called married persons clause contained in Section 213 of the National Economy Act of 1932. The legislation, which prohibited more than one family member from working in the federal civil service, reflected a nationwide condemnation of the employment of married women.[19] Throughout the Depression, women were accused of working only for "pin money" and robbing men of jobs. In fact, the American workforce had become so highly sex-segregated, with certain types of employment designated as "women's work," that men and women seldom competed for the same jobs. Moreover, during the Depression, the gendered division of labor favored female-dominated sectors of the economy. Women concentrated in light industry and clerical work, occupations that fared better and recovered more rapidly during the Depression. Because of the uneven effects of the economic crisis on different types of industry, women were sometimes able to find jobs more easily than men.[20] Despite ongoing objections to their labor force participation, married women joined the American workforce in growing numbers during the Depression years. In 1930, married women constituted almost 29 percent of all female workers in America, but by 1940, their numbers had grown to 35 percent.[21] Still, even among the lowest income families, only one in four wives worked at any given time during the Great Depression, demonstrating the pervasive disapproval of married women working.[22]

During the Depression, the Jewish community conducted its own internal debate about whether married women should work. Pearl Bernstein, who held a government job during the Depression, remembered that in New York "women had to work because many of their fathers, husbands, and sons didn't have jobs and they happened to have jobs."[23] The *Forward* noted that a young woman could "find a job more quickly than a boy her age."[24] The Jewish community may have been slightly less critical of wives working for wages. The Yiddish press carried some articles that denounced any restrictions on the work of married women. One female *Forward* reporter insisted, "It is time to recognize that women are people with the same rights and privileges as men. Married women have exactly the same right to hold their jobs as married men."[25] Wholehearted support for the fundamental right of married women to work could be heard within the Jewish community, particularly in Socialist circles, but the rhetoric of equality seldom translated into popular sentiment or behavior. Jews walked a fine ideological line between Socialist-inspired support for gender equality and a genuine desire to conform to American middle-class standards of conduct. Economic hardship may have derailed their mobility and expectations, but most New York Jews still aspired to the American family ideal which dictated that wives abandon paid labor after marriage.

When economic necessity demanded that Jewish wives contribute income to the household, they usually chose jobs that were the least disruptive to the ideal of American domesticity. Factory jobs and other full-time employment carried a stigma for married women, so Jewish wives often performed less visible wage-earning labor. Stanley Katz remembered that during the Depression his mother began working at home as a seamstress. "She had a small sewing room [in the apartment] and a Singer sewing machine." Working out of the home, she earned extra money which Katz explained "was an important supplement to the income of the family." Ida Barnett and her husband struggled to make a living during the Depression years and she regularly worked alongside her husband in the family's Bronx candy store.[26] For many women, the experience of working in the family business offered an acceptable alternative to other forms of wage labor. By working at home or in the family business, Jewish wives were able to earn money for the household while maintaining, as much as possible, their domestic roles.[27]

More often than they worked for wages, Jewish wives sustained the family economy through careful supervision of the household budget. "You had to buy just so much, had to be careful how to spend the money," explained Tillie Spiegel. During the Depression, Spiegel's husband had steady employment as a clerk in a government office and the couple lived on the Grand Concourse, a stylish, upper-middle-class Bronx neighborhood, but nevertheless she prudently monitored expenditures. "I cooked dairy," Spiegel elaborated. "I never skimped on my kids . . . [they also] had steak, meat, liver . . . you had to be economical, that's all."[28] The tasks that Jewish women performed as household managers varied widely depending on the family's economic fortunes. In middle-income households, women could afford to feed their families well-balanced meals as long as they handled the budget carefully. In her memoirs, Kate Simon recalled that during the Depression, "my father was never out of a job; we had fresh rolls and generous helpings of meat and chicken, and my mother bought her soup greens fresh and perky." Food remained inexpensive throughout the Depression so that even lower-income families were able to provide regular meals. In Simon's working-class home, her father's steady earnings kept food on the family's table. She reported a much different scenario, however, at a friend's home where the father had long been unemployed. At her friend's table, she ate "two- or three-day-old bread that was bought cheaply at a local bakery and the improvisations on bones, stock of wilted soup greens, beans, and homemade noodles." The mother "saved a little [of the stock] each time to use as the base for the next invention, which might be a stew of carrots, onions, and potatoes, strengthened by another bone or two wheedled from the local butcher."[29]

In times of economic distress, Jewish wives had to become resourceful household managers, learning to shop for and cook foods that were both substantial and inexpensive. Rebecca Augenstein remembered that during the Depression, she "learned to cook things that were nutritious and that lasted." Taking a lesson from "how my mother fed us in Europe," Augenstein described the content of her family's diet: "There was a lot of potatoes; eggs were a very nutritional thing, beets—you made a borscht that lasted . . . and [served] chopped meat and chicken only when we had enough money . . . and only for Shabbat, Friday night to bring the Sabbath in."[30] Jean Margolies remembered that her mother refused to buy the cheapest grade of food that local markets sold at reduced prices. "She couldn't afford to give us nice portions," Margolies explained about her mother's marketing strategy. "She said instead of buying cheap grade that was already half rotten, she'd get more quality and we'd all get small portions and that's how she managed." When Margolies' father died, her mother worked tirelessly to feed the family on an extremely limited income. "She would shop every day for fresh milk and vegetables. . . . She always did her own baking. She even used to churn her own butter." Although the family ultimately applied for government assistance, Margolies remembered that "relief was only enough for bare necessities" and that it was her mother's ability to extend scarce resources that sustained the family during the worst years of the Depression.[31]

Federal relief investigators were often incredulous at women's ability to devise household strategies that stretched the family dollar. One investigator, assigned to review the welfare application of the Berger family, did not believe that the Jewish family of four could possibly manage on the five dollars a week that they claimed constituted the household food budget. Although the investigator stated that "there seemed to be little more than potatoes" when he examined the kitchen cupboard, he asked Mrs. Berger to keep a daily record of her food expenses. Three weeks later, having reviewed the list that the Bergers presented, the investigator reported that "the family seems to have been living on a diet which excludes milk, meat, or fish. They use potatoes, evaporated milk, canned fish."[32] After reviewing the evidence, the relief investigator questioned the truthfulness of the Bergers' statement and turned the case over to the staff nutritionist for a final decision. Rejecting the Bergers' application, the nutritionist claimed that "the family could not have lived on this budget for any length of time without seriously impairing their health."[33]

Such encounters between trained investigators and Jewish housewives revealed the wide gulf that existed between professional attempts to regulate the family diet and the daily realities of stretching the food budget. No one was less welcome in Jewish households than the federal relief investigator. "The investigators would open the ice-box in each apartment they visited and say things like: What are you doing with butter? You should only have oleo."[34] Women learned from experience and ingenuity how to feed their families on limited budgets, but social workers attempted to provide them with scientific instruction in matters of household economy. Like federal investigators, workers in Jewish agencies emphasized the importance of preparing meals that were both inexpensive and well-balanced. Promoting a scientific approach to home economics, Jewish agencies taught women shopping and preparation techniques that maximized cost-efficiency and nutrition. The Jewish Social Service Association outlined the successful managerial prowess of one woman who served her family of five balanced meals on a budget of $8.75 a week: "Potatoes and one green vegetable in season, dried or fresh fruit, dark bread, whole-grain cereals and milk—at least a pint per person—are served daily. She uses unsweetened evaporated milk for cooking. She prepares inexpensive cuts of meat or fish three or four times a week. On other days, peas, beans, egg or cheese dishes substitute for meat."[35] The efforts of Jewish social workers reflected their growing awareness that women's control of the family diet was a matter of great importance. Yet, despite their best intentions, social workers' scientific approach had little impact on Jewish women who learned their shopping and cooking techniques from daily necessity and proven experience.

In addition to the judicious purchasing and preparation of food, Jewish women also found other ways to extend the family dollar. Jean Margolies recalled that her mother scrupulously monitored the family's use of electricity. "My mother was very careful. She made sure that we turned the lights off early at night. . . . She was frugal; she had to be."[36] Many families tried to reduce their electricity consumption in order to save money, but attempts to restrict the use of lights sometimes caused discord among family members. Louis Kfare, who shared a small Bronx apartment with his brother and sister-in-law, remembered that his sister-in-law became angry when he kept the lights on too long. "I was an avid reader," Kfare recalled, "so if I burnt a light too long, it was expensive; it cost too much money . . . I used to go to the library to do my homework; I couldn't do it in the house because I had to burn lights; lights [were] expensive . . . so I developed a sort of dislike for the house."[37]

During the Depression, families depended upon small savings garnered from cost-conscious efforts such as turning off lights, reducing the cost of clothing, or walking longer distances rather than paying for the subway. When relief investigators questioned the Berger family, Mrs. Berger "explained that she watches every penny; that her husband takes his lunch with him and that her boy walks to school because they do not have the carfare to give him."[38] Jean Margolies reported that in order to save five cents, her mother regularly restocked the icebox by carrying the heavy ice to the apartment on her back. Ice delivery cost ten cents, but the same product could be purchased "cash and carry" for only a nickel.[39] In order to clothe her family inexpensively during the Depression, Lillian Gorenstein scoured Coney Island's bargain stores for cloth remnants that she then stitched into garments, "all by hand, since I had no sewing machine." In the worst years of the crisis, her husband, Saul, used cardboard inserts to preserve old pairs of shoes. Only after Saul Gorenstein found a secure government job did the family begin resoling shoes and purchasing more expensive clothing.[40] Jewish women's daily efforts to stretch limited resources carried their families through the difficult years of the Depression. Whether working for wages, feeding the family, or extending the household budget, immigrant Jewish women provided vital, though often unrecognized, contributions to the family economy.

While immigrant mothers worked to sustain the household, their children also bore their share of the family's responsibilities. During the Great Depression, more than 90 percent of New York Jews under the age of twenty-five lived in their parents' homes. Through high school, college, and young adulthood, Jewish youth generally remained part of their parents' households and constituted an integral part of the family economy.[41] Long before the Depression, Jewish families had depended on the economic contributions of all family members, but the economic crisis heightened the family's financial interdependence. Older children often sacrificed full-time education to search for employment while younger siblings looked for part-time work after school. The WPA's study of Jewish family circles in New York surveyed the employment histories of sixty American-born children belonging to one family circle. By the age of seventeen, 80 percent of the girls and a slightly greater percentage of the boys had begun working; by the time they were fourteen, 40 percent of all the children earned some family income.

While many of the children worked only part-time, the WPA study concluded that "even in America, the children set out to search for work while they are still very young. . . . It is a fact that tens of thousands of school children help the butcher, the laundryman and the grocer in their free time."[42] Jewish youth often combined employment with the pursuit of education. Nathan Belth attended college during the 1930s but also helped to support his family through the lean years of the economic crisis. "My family was in a bad way during the Depression," Belth explained. "The kids grew up to take jobs and to get work early. Earning a living was essential at a very early age."[43]

Jewish families attempted to keep their children in school, even if only part-time, but economic survival sometimes required difficult decisions about work and schooling. In many households, families made choices about which children would pursue education and which would search for employment. In the 1930s, most Jews attended secondary school and child-labor laws forbade young children from entering the workforce, but some Jewish families could not afford to allow all of their children to attain the same level of education. Typically, as one young Jewish woman explained, "It's the older ones in every family that have to help out."[44] In the immigrant period, older children generally went to work while younger family members remained in school. During the Depression, the same general pattern prevailed, but the overall level of schooling attained by Jewish children was considerably higher. Virtually all young Jews completed the eighth grade, and more young Jews received high school educations in the 1930s than in the immigrant period, mirroring the general increase in high school attendance throughout the country: the abysmal job market kept both Jewish and non-Jewish children in school during the Depression years.

In many cases, daughters abandoned schooling to look for work so that sons could continue their educations. The combination of birth-order and gender expectations generally determined work and educational patterns within Jewish families. The Welfare Council survey documented several cases in which Jewish daughters worked while their brothers furthered their educations. One case history reported: "A family of five, the oldest a Jewish youth of 20 and an 18-year-old girl, were the children of a Polish Jew, who owned a grocery store in lower Manhattan. The boy was in his last year in college, while the girl was a clerk at $15 a week in a dress factory."[45] Women were more likely to pursue education if they had older siblings. The third of five children, Anna Kfare described a typical situation: Her two older sisters worked in the millinery industry while the two younger brothers remained in school. With two sisters earning regular wages, Kfare completed the eighth grade but then enrolled in a commercial school, "because that was a lead to earning a living." After getting a job, Kfare pursued her education at night, like many Jewish youth, earning a diploma from Morris Evening High School in 1935. The demands of full-time work clearly derailed her intellectual aspirations however. "I went to high school at night," she explained. "I thought I would go to college . . . but I was missing some credits . . . and I was working and so I gave up."[46] In the opening decades of the twentieth century, immigrant Jewish families had expected their daughters to contribute to the family economy, usually by working in the garment industry. During the Depression years, Jewish daughters retained their role as family wage earners, but they generally worked in white-collar, clerical jobs rather than in the factories.

Jewish daughters often shouldered the financial burden in order to keep their brothers in school, but young Jewish men also found their educational and career paths disrupted by the need to find employment. Louis Kfare worked full-time at a factory job while attending high school at night. In order to save the five-cent subway fare, he walked from work to Morris Evening High School. He arrived at school so exhausted, however, that he had trouble staying awake in class, and after five months, his instructor recommended that he postpone further study until his economic situation improved.[47] If their families could manage without their financial contributions, or if other family members could provide the additional income, Jewish sons had the chance to attend both high school and college. Most young men obtained their educations by juggling scholastic work with at least some part-time employment. Even for Jewish sons, who generally received preference for schooling within Jewish families, the balancing act between educational aspiration and household obligation was not an easy task.

The Great Depression heightened economic cooperation within families, increasing the need for young Jews to contribute to, and to benefit from, the support of the family economy. As historian Judith Smith has observed, "The effect of widespread unemployment in the depression years was to renew economic interdependency within the family."[48] Because financial circumstances made it difficult for them to live on their own, most Jewish youth remained within their parents' homes during the Depression. For example, with the onset of the Depression, the Jewish residence clubs that provided housing for single women suddenly shifted from capacity occupancy to an unprecedented number of vacancies. "The four clubs for Jewish girls [in New York], which had waiting lists in 1929, showed only about 60 percent occupancy at present," one study reported in 1933, adding that, "the directors suggest that because of financial difficulties many girls were returning to their families."[49] The Clara de Hirsch Home for Working Girls, which had offered housing to single Jewish women in Manhattan since 1897, encouraged young women to return to their families during the Depression. As Bess Spanner, the home's director, explained in 1933, "It may sound incongruous to say that some of the best work we did this past year was in the number of girls we did not admit. We refused admission to any girl whose family needed her support, or who had lived at home until the date of the application. . . . We advised every girl whose family was in need to return and contribute there what she was paying for board elsewhere."[50]

Most Jewish family members required little encouragement to maintain their family connections. New York Jews relied on family support networks to carry them through difficult periods. Jewish families generally went to great lengths to keep financial problems to themselves, shunning both Jewish agency and government assistance whenever possible. Irving Howe reported that in the Bronx Jewish neighborhood where he grew up, relief was "suspect as both gentile and bourgeois. Many people in the East Bronx would have starved—and perhaps some did a little—rather than go on 'relief.'"[51] The overall Jewish occupational profile along with a reticence to accept federal aid resulted in a comparatively small number of Jews on the relief rolls. Nevertheless, many Jews did accept both home and work relief.[52] Like other Americans, Jews usually considered federal assistance a last resort and were often ashamed about having to turn to the government. Ida Barnett and her husband applied for home relief in 1934 "in order to get food for the family." The couple desperately needed assistance at that time, but as Barnett explained, "We tried to keep it quiet . . . you have a certain pride. . . . We didn't want our neighbors to know that we were on home relief. Maybe they were too, but it wasn't common knowledge. . . . We felt a little embarrassed."[53] Years after the Depression, Boris Ourlicht remembered his shame about being "a kid on relief." "One of my worst recollections is that it was my job at home to keep the surplus food stamps, issued by the Home Relief Office, and take them down to the store for trading in. It was a very embarrassing period of time for me; I was ashamed, in a way, because I felt it was demeaning."[54] The demoralizing effects of accepting welfare never completely disappeared, but the implementation of work relief removed some of the stigma associated with taking government handouts. As the Depression wore on, federal welfare became more widely accepted and most people knew someone who took home relief or held a WPA job. Nevertheless, Jewish families continued to apply for government assistance only when all of their other employment and budgeting options had failed and after they had exhausted the networks of family support.

Like other American families, Jews devised several strategies to avoid taking relief. During periods of unemployment and economic hardship, Jews looked to their extended families for support. Families in Jean Margolies's Lower East Side neighborhood often had difficulty paying the rent. "Maybe they'd pay one month and then they didn't have any work, so they couldn't pay the second month . . . and then they'd borrow from some relatives. . . . They didn't want to go on any home relief."[55] When there was no money to borrow, families whose financial circumstances had deteriorated sometimes moved in with relatives. Judith Smith has suggested that the Depression forced greater numbers of families to share living quarters. "In times of particular need," she explained, "children of immigrants fell back on the strategies that they knew from first-hand experience could extend scarce resources."[56] During the 1930s, immigrant traditions of extended kin networks remained intact and helped multigenerational families weather the challenges of the Depression. "When my father's grocery store in the West Bronx went bankrupt in 1930 and he became a 'customer peddler' trudging from door to door," recalled Irving Howe, "we were really poor, crowded into a small apartment with aunts, uncles, and grandmother in order to save rent."[57] Merging households was not always a permanent measure, but often a temporary solution during trying economic times. Doubling-up with relatives helped Jewish families survive seasonal unemployment or unexpected financial setbacks. As a safety net in hard times, sharing household space provided a prudent economic strategy for Depression-era Jewish families.

For some Jews, changing living quarters was a regular occurrence in the 1930s. Forced evictions provided the most visible evidence of tenant movement, but more often families used frequent moves as a form of financial management. During the Depression, many Jewish families moved from one apartment to another, sometimes relocating with changing financial fortunes, and other times moving simply as a money-saving measure. New York's vacancy rates soared during the Depression, rising to more than 9 percent in the Bronx and parts of Brooklyn and to more than 15 percent in the city's poorest neighborhoods.[58] Because landlords needed tenants, changing living quarters could be profitable for Depression-era families. "Most people moved a lot," Sydney Evans recalled. "In those days it paid to move. They usually gave you two to three months free rent to get you into the apartment." During the Depression, the Evans family moved at least five times in a seven-year period. "I moved five different times in Brooklyn and twice in the Bronx; that was almost once every year and a half," he remembered. "For practical purposes, instead of paying a year and a half's rent, you paid a year and three months because three months you got almost free. That was part of the practicality of living during those times."[59]

Many Jewish families engineered their moves to fit changing economic circumstances. "When my father was down financially, we moved to a less expensive apartment," Evans added, "and when he made more money, we moved up to a better apartment."[60] Although living quarters changed frequently, Jewish families often confined their moves to a relatively small geographic area. "During the Depression, we made three moves all within three blocks," Stanley Katz recalled, explaining that his family remained in East New York for the duration of the Depression, but once his father's finances improved, the family moved from a smaller apartment to a six-room duplex with a backyard garden.[61] In cases of downward mobility, family relocation could be both a more frequent and painful experience. Ida Barnett and her husband were never financially secure in the 1930s, and she could not recall just how many times they had changed their address during the Depression. "We moved from apartment to apartment," Barnett elaborated. "My kids went to a half a dozen schools."[62] When financial necessity forced Irving Howe's family to move from the West to the poorer East Bronx, Howe explained that the relocation "came to no more than a few miles, but socially the distance was vast. We were dropping from the lower middle class to the proletarian—the most painful of all social descents."[63] When the situation became desperate, as social worker Harry Lurie describes it, the Depression forced Jewish families into "harmful reductions in the standard of living, the giving up of desirable living quarters, and the return to overcrowded and undesirable neighborhood conditions."[64]

Although some Depression-era families were constantly moving, struggling to stretch scare resources, and barely treading water, thousands of Jewish families survived the economic crisis without ever facing such desperate circumstances. In fact, many Jews managed to retain a comfortable lifestyle in the midst of the Great Depression. They kept their children in school, sometimes hired housekeepers, and were able to afford carfare and occasional recreation. Such amenities were not reserved for the wealthy. A secure civil service job, a relatively stable business, or steady white-collar employment assured family members of a degree of financial security. Because prices for almost everything were drastically slashed in the 1930s, a regular income allowed Jewish families to maintain a comfortable standard of living. It was not uncommon for New York Jews of modest means to continue taking summer vacations during the Depression. Even with meager earnings, immigrant Jews had indulged in the affordable retreats offered in the Catskills and at the Jersey Shore. Although the summer vacation was often one of the first luxuries to be surrendered, resorts worked hard to accommodate families on limited budgets. Grossinger's and other Catskill retreats announced "rates in step with the times" and offered their customers reduced travel fees and three meals a day. Several Jewish resorts survived the economic crisis by instituting special family packages designed to lure cost-conscious city dwellers to the mountains. The number of Jewish vacationers decreased sharply during the Great Depression, but reduced prices allowed Jews of modest but secure financial means to afford brief family getaways.[65] Of course, even those Jews who enjoyed relative stability during the Great Depression understood that they were only a lost job or a business failure away from faltering.

Jewish families across the economic spectrum felt the weight of persistent insecurity. For immigrant families that had only recently gained a foothold in America, the setbacks of the Depression were particularly unsettling. Even families spared the harshest consequences of the Depression could not be certain about their fate or about their children's future. In households without a steady income, undoubtedly the most severe economic casualties of the Depression, the sense of uncertainty was part of the fabric of daily life. "With my mother every morsel of life was paid for in fear," Alfred Kazin reflected about his Depression-era family. "You calculated the price of everything before you bought it, and even if you bought it, you could not enjoy it for thinking how much it had cost you."[66] At best, the Depression brought only ongoing anxiety about employment, income, and the vagaries of the business cycle, but in the worst cases, it left New York's Jewish families scrambling to survive.

Struggling Jewish households depended upon the collective resources of the family unit, but family cooperation did not always translate into family harmony. The Depression certainly renewed the importance of the family economy, but unemployment, economic hardship, and unfulfilled expectations often sparked frustration, conflict, and strife within New York's Jewish households. When family members remained out of work for long periods or when finances grew particularly strained, the family cooperation that sustained New York Jews through difficult periods sometimes disintegrated.[67] The Jewish Social Service Association (JSSA) reported that among the more than eighteen thousand clients that it served in 1935 were "men and women whose courage has crumbled under the prolonged strains of unemployment; children bewildered and suddenly unmanageable in homes where family discord has supplanted a normal orderly life; restless and rebellious young people through with school and with no good way to use the empty hours."[68] Although the JSSA may have overdramatized the desperation of its clients, there is little doubt that the Depression disrupted the lives of many Jewish family members. From unemployed husbands who felt powerless to support and control their families, to youth who became frustrated by the lack of job opportunities, to households plagued by bickering and conflict, the Depression had the potential to destabilize Jewish family life.

Perhaps the most compelling evidence of Depression-era family strife was offered by the Jewish Conciliation Court, a legally sanctioned New York arbitration court where litigants appeared free of charge, agreeing to abide by the decisions rendered by a board of volunteer judges—usually a rabbi, a lawyer, and a layperson. Established in 1920, the court was created to settle the disputes of immigrant Jews in an atmosphere that respected Jewish law and custom.[69] During the Depression, the Jewish Conciliation Court suddenly found its calendar filled with domestic cases. In 1933, Louis Richman, the executive secretary of the conciliation court, reported that, "due to economic distress, the pressure on the calendar of the Court has been greater than in any previous year. Cases of non-support of parents by their children, wives by their husbands, and general misunderstandings in families, have been presented to the Court in greater numbers than the years previous." By 1933, one-third of the cases brought to the conciliation court involved family quarrels.[70] Court officials noted with great concern the unprecedented level of discord within Depression-era Jewish families. "Disputes between husband and wife and between parents and children are recurring with greater frequency than ever before," officials at the Jewish Conciliation Court told the *New York Times*, attributing the sharp rise in family conflict to deteriorating economic conditions.[71]

The domestic disputes brought before the conciliation court usually involved multigenerational, often lower-income families, who sought third-party arbitration because they were unable to resolve their disagreements among themselves. "Six children will not give enough [monetary] support to their elderly father" declared the *Jewish Daily Forward*, reporting a typical case brought before the court.[72] The *Forward* regularly covered the proceedings of the conciliation court, providing a chronicle of Jewish family conflicts in the 1930s. The decade's most common complaints involved parents suing their children for nonsupport. In 1935, the court heard the testimony of a mother who explained that her four sons had taken good care of her in the past. However, as the *Forward* reported: "Once they married, they forgot that their mother must also live. They would have forgotten her entirely, but her tears had an effect on two of her sons. One gave her ten dollars a month; another one also gave her ten dollars a month. The two brothers had a talk with the third son and he also began giving a few dollars a month. However, the fourth son said that he couldn't give his mother a cent. . . . He [had] a wife and four children and he had a mother-in-law who [was] like a mother to him."[73] After further questioning, the judges determined that given the generous funds the fourth son had offered to his mother-in-law, he could certainly afford to contribute at least five dollars a month to his mother's support. Many cases involved such squabbles between children who could not amicably share responsibility for their elderly parents.[74] Court officials always demanded that children contribute to their parents' support, designating the amount required according to the incomes and family responsibilities of each sibling.

Domestic disputes brought before the court included not only nonsupport of parents, but also wives arguing with husbands about family finances. "When money becomes scarce," one court official observed, "love has a habit of flying out the window."[75] After months of bickering, one Jewish wife had permanently expelled her husband of twenty years from the home because he no longer provided a regular income. "I am a watchmaker," the husband told the court. "Some weeks I make enough to live on and at other times not even enough for that." After deliberation, the court set a minimum weekly payment to be met by the husband.[76] The disputes that came before the Jewish Conciliation Court probably did not reflect the condition of most New York families. The tremendous increase in the court's domestic caseload, however, provides an important barometer for measuring the Depression's impact on Jewish families. Unemployment and financial uncertainty may have motivated some families to pull together, but they also fueled family tensions. As one recent author observed, "To read some of these [cases] is to taste, without the sugarcoating of today's fad for nostalgia, the bitter flavor of the depression."[77]

According to most Depression-era reports, the family member who suffered most acutely was the male breadwinner. One of the most powerful symbols of the decade was the portrait of the unemployed and demoralized husband and father. For Jewish husbands, like their non-Jewish counterparts, unemployment meant more than loss of income; it also brought a sense of personal failure. Kate Simon recalled that the homes of many of her friends "held as prisoners abashed, unemployed fathers."[78] The *Forward*, which reported the plight of the unemployed man with regularity and emotion, explained: "Not only do [their] feet become swollen looking around and inquiring for work; [unemployment brings] a total upheaval within men's minds and hearts. [A man's] hope extinguishes more and more with every time that he hears, 'No, we don't need any workers.' He becomes discouraged to look for a job. He begins to look at himself as a good-for-nothing, a ne'er-do-well, and it seems to him that everyone looks at the jobless as useless."[79] In their classic work, *Middletown in Transition*, Robert and Helen Lynd concluded that men experienced more dramatic role displacement than women during the Depression. Because so much of men's status derived from their occupations while women's identities centered around the home, unemployment more drastically disrupted men's lives.[80]

Although not applicable to all cases, the Lynds' observation accurately described the experiences of many unemployed Jewish men. The Jewish Social Service Association offered the following case history of one jobless Jewish man as typical of its clientele: "After I lost the last job, I used to pretend to the neighbors I had night work. . . . About eleven o'clock, I'd take my hat and go away as if I was going to work. After everybody had gone in, I'd come back. . . . But after a while I couldn't even pretend. . . . It's fifteen months now since I've had a job—fifteen months with thirty days in a month and twenty-four hours in a day."[81] Jewish men, like other American males, struggled to maintain their sense of pride when they lost their jobs. Irving Howe recalled that while his father was unemployed, his mother worked to support the family while also "helping my father to overcome his shame at having failed in business."[82] Reflecting on his working-class Brownsville neighborhood, Arthur Granit remembered, "With the depression, Brownsville was assailed on all sides. The men began to lose their jobs and appear wheeling baby carriages. Soon they began to shop for their wives and argue with the peddlers. And as times grew worse, the long, fascinating noses of our Jews got closer to the ground."[83] Even men who retained their jobs carried the burdens of financial responsibility and job insecurity. "My father doesn't know I know it," one Jewish daughter revealed, "but he's scared he's going to lose his job. . . . The other night I was awake, and he was sitting at the table talking to himself."[84] As the designated family breadwinner (regardless of other household wage earners), Jewish men may have shouldered a heavy share of the Depression's economic and psychological burdens.

Protracted unemployment not only disrupted men's status as workers but also threatened their role as authority figures within the family. "You could hardly call us a family now," one Jewish father told a JSSA caseworker. "My whole family is going to pieces. . . . My girl, Rose, keeps out some of her money for clothes and carfare. . . . Our boy, Meyer, he's ready for high school. . . . But now he's nervous and angry. And the younger children behave badly. I tell you we're a family of wrecks."[85] Once they lost their position as breadwinners, Jewish men sometimes commanded less authority within the household. Jewish social workers frequently reported that unemployed Jewish men had become despondent and unable to control their children's behavior.

Such assessments must be qualified, however, since immigrant parents had begun exercising less control over their American-born children long before the Depression. As Irving Howe explained, "The more we native-born boys and girls made our way into American spheres of school and work, the more our parents grew uncertain about their right to command."[86] The growing independence of American-born adolescents altered but did not completely overhaul parent-child relationships. For example, second generation Jewish children continued to contribute to the household, although many began to keep some of their earnings for themselves, rather than giving their unopened pay envelopes to their parents.[87] Although the combination of unemployment and greater dependence on children's wages may have diminished Jewish men's authority, the Depression was not entirely responsible for the loss of parental control. Moreover, patriarchal authority remained intact despite the growing independence of youth and the uncertainty of male employment. Mirra Komarovsky's 1940 study, *The Unemployed Man and His Family*, revealed that even without a job, most men retained their roles as family decision-makers.[88]

During the 1930s, the number of Jewish men who deserted their families declined sharply. Desertion had been one of the most pressing family problems of the immigrant generation, arousing so much concern that in 1911 the Jewish community created the National Desertion Bureau, a Jewish agency devoted to locating missing husbands. The bureau handled as many as twenty-five hundred desertion cases per year, working with the *Jewish Daily Forward* which published the photographs of deserters in a regular feature entitled, "The Gallery of Missing Husbands."[89] The *Forward* chronicled the desertion problem throughout the early twentieth century, but in the 1930s, the newspaper began reporting a different story, noting the steadily declining numbers of desertion cases. The director of the desertion bureau indicated that, not only were fewer Jewish men leaving their families during the Great Depression, but that the economic crisis had brought many Jewish husbands back to their homes.[90] Without secure employment options and regular income, the director explained, men had neither the resources nor the desire to leave their families. As the *Forward* sarcastically observed, "The wife has credit with the butcher and grocer."[91] Legal divorce was an expensive and impractical option in the poor economy; indeed, the national divorce rate plummeted from 1.66 per 1,000 in 1929 to 1.28 by 1932.

Although some evidence suggests that desertion, often called the poor man's divorce, became more common in America during the Depression precisely because legal divorce was too costly, such was not the case within the Jewish community. According to the *Forward* and the National Desertion Bureau, the lower incidence of Jewish desertion was one of the few positive results of the Great Depression.[92]

For the most part, Jewish families stayed together during the Depression. The pressures of the crisis strained many familial relationships, but family strife did not obviate the need for cooperative household strategies. The Depression took its toll on both parents and children, reversing some of the gains that immigrants had won and hindering the ability of young Jews to start their own lives on solid footing. Most Jewish families proved resilient to the challenges of the Depression, pooling collective resources, trying to keep children in school, and enduring sporadic setbacks and conflict. The economic crisis effectively prolonged the maintenance of the immigrant nuclear family, keeping children within the home and the family economy intact. Even as financial pressures and internal disputes plagued Jewish households, the family remained the first line of defense in times of economic contraction. For all the political, social, and economic upheaval of the decade, the experience of family shaped the Jewish encounter with the Depression at the most fundamental level.

The family provided anchor for young Jews as they made their way into an increasingly complicated and confusing world. The Depression arrived just as young Jews were gradually leaving the world constructed by their immigrant parents and building new forms of identity as native-born Americans. The doubts, frustrations, and setbacks of the Depression era had particular meaning for Jews who came of age in the 1930s. As much as young Jews continued to rely on their families, they interpreted and negotiated the challenges of the Great Depression on their own terms.

# 3

## Starting Out in the Thirties

*The depression had a personal meaning for each one of us—at home, in school, in our interests and aspirations. We were a part of a generation that had known fantastic prosperity in the Twenties, only to see near-starvation all around us in the Thirties. We knew what breadlines were, CCC camps for youths who couldn't be prepared for non-existent jobs, and apple-sellers on almost every street corner. A vast percentage of us came to the College hoping to become teachers, because an appointment to a civil service position meant security. Many of us settled later for any kind of job.*
—Irving Rosenthal, "Rumblings of Unrest and Empty Stomachs"

The Great Depression was a formative experience for Jews growing up in the 1930s. When the Depression arrived, young Jewish men and women stood at a crossroads between the vibrant immigrant world of their parents and the search for a new American way of life forged against the backdrop of New York's urban landscape. Raised to believe in America as a land of opportunity and security, young Jews of the 1930s encountered instead a society of limited possibilities, growing anti-Semitism, and social and political turmoil. "This was a time profoundly disorganizing in its effects upon the young," remembered Irving Howe. "We were adrift and needed definition, meaning, platform, and anchor."[1] Howe represented the significant minority of Jewish youth who looked to leftist politics for solutions to the decade's social and economic ills. Radical politics were one manifestation of the curious combination of desperation and idealism that characterized the Depression era. Most young Jews of the 1930s did not turn to political radicalism, but virtually all struggled with the uncertainty and anxiety of the age. The children of Jewish immigrants reached adulthood at a time when America's future seemed in doubt and the situation in Europe was even more ominous. Confronting bleak job prospects, facing employment discrimination and university quotas, encountering the growth of anti-Semitism at home, and watching the rise of fascism abroad, this generation of native-born Jews came of age in an increasingly insecure world.

Jewish youth had been brought up with the hopeful expectations of immigrant parents. Jewish parents instilled lofty ambitions in their children and invested heavily in their achievements. "It was not for myself alone that I was expected to shine," reflected Alfred Kazin, "but for [my parents]—to redeem the constant anxiety of their existence."[2] No matter how much immigrant families struggled, they trusted that the future would be brighter for the next generation. By the 1920s, many Jewish families enjoyed their first taste of economic stability. With their children able to remain in school longer, immigrant Jews firmly believed that their sons and daughters would reap consistently greater rewards in America. Then the Depression came. The stalled mobility and frustrations of the thirties forced immigrant parents to doubt their expectations for the future and called into question their children's own hopes for American success. For young Jews who had grown up believing in their potential for educational and economic advancement, the Depression cast a large shadow, leaving them disappointed, disillusioned, and searching for some security. As Jewish men and women made the transition from adolescence to young adulthood, the Depression influenced their choices about work and schooling and their decisions about marriage and family planning. Jewish youth of the 1930s did not abandon the hopes of a generation of immigrant Jews and continued to pursue long-term educational and occupational goals, but the Depression created formidable stumbling blocks in the Jewish path to the American Dream.

Most young Jews spent at least part of the Great Depression in school. New York's neighborhood high schools provided a foundation for Jewish teenagers growing up in the 1930s. During the Depression, school attendance increased throughout the nation due to the scarcity of jobs and the enactment of a 1936 compulsory education law that raised the age of required schooling from fourteen to sixteen years old. As early as 1930, 60 percent of America's teenagers attended high school. In New York City, high school enrollment almost doubled in the early thirties.[3] Depression-era Jews tended to stay in school longer than their non-Jewish counterparts. The Welfare Council found that young Jews completed high school and college courses at two times the rate of other ethnic groups. Moreover, because New York Jews tended to live in certain neighborhoods, Jews constituted as much as three-quarters of the student body in some city schools. Young Jews constructed a social world in the city's high schools, one grounded in the context of an American education but also rooted in the ethnic character of their neighborhoods. Jewish youth attended schools populated largely by fellow Jews and with a growing number of Jewish teachers. Almost half of all new teachers joining New York's public schools in the Depression years were Jewish.[4] Because of the large concentration of Jewish students and teachers in neighborhood high schools, most Jewish youth first experienced the realities of the Depression in a Jewish context.

Jews attended high schools that both consciously and unconsciously underscored Jewish identity and concerns. To be sure, neighborhood schools were not uniformly Jewish in student population or personnel and witnessed their share of ethnic tensions. Many Depression-era Jewish students recalled being embarrassed by their accents and feeling the pressure to speak a "'refined,' 'correct,' 'nice' English" that did not come naturally to the children of immigrants.[5] Although, as Irving Howe insisted, "the educational institutions of the city were still under the sway of a unified culture, that dominant 'Americanism,'" most young Jews encountered American culture in an environment filled with Jewish students and teachers.[6] Students at Brooklyn's largely Jewish Abraham Lincoln High School remembered that one of their teachers peppered his speech with "frequent Yiddish gems of worldly wisdom." At Thomas Jefferson High School, principal Elias Lieberman reminded the 1933 graduating class that even as they faced an economic crisis at home, "there is a water shortage in Jerusalem and a sad dearth of decent human regard for the feelings of others in Germany."[7] Jewish high school students came to understand the turmoil of the thirties through the filter of Jewish ethnicity and learned to evaluate their Depression-era experiences in Jewish terms.

As they observed developments at home and abroad, Jewish high school students internalized the insecurity of the age. In one high school yearbook, students confessed that "we find it more difficult than ever to adjust ourselves to a world which is, itself, maladjusted."[8] Depression-era teachers worried about their students' futures, wondering openly, "What will life do to them? Will they successfully survive the cruel blows that the present depression will lavish on them?" Gabriel Mason, the Jewish principal at Lincoln High School, noted that the Depression had exacted a psychological toll on his students. "If our youths, a golden decade ago, were blasé, indifferent, imprudent, and materialistic," young Jews of the thirties were "serious, resourceful, courageous, self-reliant, and idealistic." Teachers attempted to instill hope in their students, sometimes managing only familiar clichés, reminding graduating students that they were "the only ones who can untangle the sorry mess in which the world now finds itself."[9] School administrators recognized that their students worried most about finding jobs after graduation and New York high schools joined the chorus of organizations trying to lead youth to the best employment prospects. By the mid-thirties, the yearbook at Lincoln High School included not only the usual class photographs, but also a section of "Graduate Opportunities" complete with interviews and profiles about various careers options.[10]

In their own statements about the future, Jewish students alternated between idealism and despair. Depression-era class yearbooks from predominantly Jewish high schools were filled with standard graduation fare, proclamations that "we are the ones who captain our fate. . . . We must go out into the world, out into life's arena, out to win our fortunes." The Dollars and Sense Club at Lincoln High School insisted in 1934 that "at some time in our lives we have made plans to beat the Stock Market and make our first million."[11] Such statements of optimism and hope stood side by side with sobering reflections about the prospects after high school. "No matter how eager we may have been to get out of school," one graduating senior at Thomas Jefferson High School admitted, "now that the time is here . . . we are downhearted. It is just a passing cloud to some. To others it goes a little more deeply, but to those who are not going to college (not by choice but by necessity) . . . the downheartedness will linger."[12] As they prepared to finish high school, young Jews could not ignore the serious obstacles awaiting them. Even their more lighthearted expressions reflected anxiety about the future. Graduating seniors at Lincoln High School jokingly combined economic concerns with class rivalry, commenting in their yearbook's last will and testament that "we would cut [sophomores] off with a schilling but for the fact we haven't got a schilling."[13] The city's high schools "gave New York a good part of whatever morale it managed to keep in the Depression years," but they also harbored young Jews full of doubt and uncertainty.[14]

Jewish teenagers of the 1930s found many ways to boost their spirits in the midst of the Depression. Although most lived with constant fears about employment and security, they enjoyed many diversions from the pressures of the economic crisis. Throughout the Depression, the children of immigrants inhabited the streets and playgrounds of the city. They knew the realities of the Depression, but also the distractions and escapes of New York's urban pleasures. For those without even a nickel to spare, there was always stickball in the streets, basketball in neighborhood gyms and playgrounds, and excursions to the beaches of Coney Island and the Rockaways. New York Jews who grew up in the 1930s recalled the city's streets and amusements as vividly as they remembered the hardships of the Depression. "We had no money and we were *always* playing ball," one Brownsville native explained about his Depression-era youth.[15] Sports provided a popular outlet, especially for boys. Jews played on high school and club teams, at the local YMHAS, in city parks, or wherever they could find a basketball. Sports were not the sole province of Jewish men. One WPA writer observed that Jews of both genders demonstrated an appetite for athletics, noting that "the young men and women of this race swim, dive, smite the ball, pummel the punching bag, gallop about the tennis courts, and romp through gymnastics, in numbers that fairly defy an estimate." When summer arrived, Jews flocked to the New York beaches, an inexpensive venture even for the Jewish poor. "On a normal hot Sunday or holiday these public beaches hold more than a million and a half persons," calculated a WPA survey. "It is by no means stretching the probability to say that more than half of these have come from the Jewish quota of the population."[16] Young Jews explored American culture through the retreats of public recreation and the affordable attractions of dance halls, clubs, and movies. In the bleakest moments of the Depression, New York's urban pastimes provided refuge and entertainment as well as an education in American life far beyond what formal schooling provided.

Jewish communal leaders, like other social workers of the period, worried about the "unwholesome" lures of city life, concerned that crime, delinquency, and reckless behavior might appeal to teenagers in a time of crisis. Jewish periodicals and social work conferences devoted unprecedented time and attention to the many dangers awaiting Jewish youth in Depression-era America. Communal leaders made a concerted effort to direct Jewish play and recreation to the organized activities of settlement clubs and YMHAS. Officials at the Ninety-second Street Y insisted that "the greatest contribution being made in these trying times is the YMHA gym facilities" where teenagers could be supervised and instructed as they enjoyed sporting and social events. Through physical education programs, dances, and lectures, Jewish social workers attempted to keep young Jews off the streets and involved in constructive projects. Jewish youth exhibited little interest in the character-building exercises of social reformers, but they did not hesitate to take advantage of

8. *Outings to Coney Island and other inexpensive urban pleasures provided diversion and enjoyment for New York Jews in the midst of the Great Depression. Courtesy of the Brooklyn Historical Society.*

their recreational provisions. Attendance at New York Y's and community centers soared during the Depression. Unemployment left Jews with increased leisure time and Jewish centers offered many opportunities for diversion. Most young Jews joined the city's YMHAs in order to use the gymnasium and pool facilities.[17] In 1937, the New York Jewish Federation reported that "the past year saw settlements, Y's, and community houses thronged day and night." In a one-year period, monthly attendance at the city's community centers averaged almost half a million, leading Federation leaders to boast about the "rich, varied program" available to Jewish youth.[18] Communal leaders constantly extolled the virtues of organized recreation as a means of building physical and moral fiber and keeping Jewish youth out of trouble. Young Jews displayed little enthusiasm for the intent of such efforts but eagerly embraced Jewish community programs because they offered an accessible and inexpensive outlet for enjoyment in the midst of the Depression.

The diversions available to New York Jews provided no permanent escape from the pressures they faced during the Depression. By the time they

9. *This photograph of a boy on the Lower East Side captures the somber mood of Jewish youth in the Great Depression. The photograph was submitted to the Citizens Housing Council Photo Contest in 1939. Courtesy of the Citizens Housing Council of New York, Inc., Museum of the City of New York.*

reached their late teenage years, Jews assumed increasing responsibility for family income and, if they could afford it, for their own education. Virtually all Jews under the age of twenty-five lived in their parents' homes and whatever their aspirations for the future, most maintained an obligation to the household. As schoolchildren, Jews had often held part-time employment or performed odd jobs in order to contribute to household expenses. But once they approached their final high school years, decisions about work and education grew more complicated. Especially in families where finances were strained, economic need and the good of the family unit often required personal sacrifices from Jewish youth. The WPA Yiddish Writers' Group reported that "a considerable number of the youth [in New York's Jewish family circles] had to give up college because of the crisis; others who had intended to study and become professionals have, for the same reasons, been forced to renounce their aspirations."[19] As they became young adults, Jews juggled a complex set of responsibilities, balancing personal goals with family obligation, educational pursuits with financial ability, and hopes for the future with the demands of the present.

After high school, some young Jews went to college; others looked for work, and a great many did both at the same time. Harold Kase graduated from Evander Childs High School in 1930. After his father's business failed, Kase knew that "the family just couldn't afford to send me to college." Like many young Jews, Kase began working during the day while attending college at night. "I found a job in a kosher butcher shop on Tremont Avenue near the Grand Concourse," he recalled. "I delivered orders and I plucked chickens. I received the munificent salary of $8 a week plus tips when I delivered the orders. I did this for two years, and from the earnings and the tips I was able to meet the tuition payments and the expenses to go to school."[20] During the Depression, New York Jews were overrepresented in the city's evening high schools and colleges. Many Jewish students enrolled in night school in order to work during the day, but even those attending day sessions often worked to support themselves and their families. At least 50 percent of all full-time Jewish college students in New York held some kind of job during their educational careers.[21]

Whether or not they attended college, Jewish youth retained economic responsibilities. The Depression heightened the need for Jewish sons and daughters to contribute to the family economy, but finding a job had never been more difficult for young Jews than during the 1930s. The Depression devastated America's youth and diminished their chances to secure even the most meager jobs. The Russell Sage Foundation estimated that by 1934, half of all Americans under the age of twenty-five were unemployed.[22] The majority of young men and women in their late teens who looked for work during the Depression failed to obtain employment.[23] As a white-collar group, Jews had more job opportunities than manual laborers or agricultural workers, but overt hiring discrimination often counterbalanced their favorable economic profile. In a decade characterized by "Christians Only" classified ads, Jewish youth frequently discovered that employers in a severely depressed economy preferred not to hire Jews. In New York, about half of all Jewish youth seeking employment failed to find jobs, remaining out of work at twice the rate of the overall adult population.[24] During the height of the crisis, securing even a part-time job could be a formidable task. Many Jewish youth held a series of temporary positions, sporadically testing the job market while they remained in school. As high school and college students or as prospective full-time workers, young Jews searched for whatever work could be found in the midst of the Depression.

For Jews making supplemental contributions to household or educational expenses, the futility of the job search could be disheartening and frustrating, but Jewish youth whose families depended on their earnings faced much greater pressures. In a 1931 article published in *The Day*, Diana Silver, leader of a Jewish women's club, recounted the particular burdens facing young Jewish women who were often expected to be family wage earners. Describing the mounting stress placed on Jewish daughters, Silver explained:

> I was speaking recently to several out-of-work girls of my circle, and members of a club of young Jewish women that I lead. One of my friends had just lost her job. She joked about finding another one, until one girl cried out, 'Don't talk that way! You'll soon see how it is—You leave in the morning, walk all day, and see everyone else walking all day—thousands of people looking for one job, any job. And then you come home at night, and your folks say, "Well?" and you yell at them. Then you start sitting around. And after two months of that, you get bluer and bluer, and you yell and cry at everything.'[25]

Lack of employment frequently led to bickering and strife within Jewish families. "It isn't only the looking [for a job] that kills you," the young woman elaborated. "It's your mother and father . . . you feel like a bum when you have to tell [your parents], 'Nothing doing.'" Persistent unemployment often exacerbated tensions between parents and children. "Your father gets after you and says that other girls have jobs. And if you haven't, why don't you stay home instead of spending money on lunch and carfare?"[26] The impediments facing young job-seekers placed an additional strain on Jewish families already struggling with unemployment and economic insecurity. Particularly in households suffering most acutely from the Depression, the demands and the uncertainty of finding work weighed heavily on Jewish parents and their children.

The burdens of finding employment and providing income fell on both Jewish sons and daughters, but their experiences varied considerably according to gender. Although high school enrollment remained common for Jewish youth of both sexes, men and women embarked on divergent paths by the time they reached their late teenage years. Jewish families continued to depend heavily on the economic contributions of their daughters, preferring to keep sons in school whenever possible. Even families that could afford to allow daughters to attend high school expected them to earn money for the household. Jewish parents generally disapproved of factory work for their children. They considered clerical jobs the best way for young women to make a good living, often insisting that their daughters pursue vocational training rather than continue general education. After high school, thousands of Jewish women enrolled in commercial schools; many left high school at the age of sixteen in order to train for a commercial career. The Welfare Council reported that almost three-quarters of New York's young Jewish women had studied bookkeeping or stenography, frequently forfeiting higher education to search for clerical jobs.[27] Their brothers were more likely to have the chance to pursue an advanced degree. College enrollment among Jewish men was double that of Jewish women. The children of immigrants, both men and women, attended college at a very high rate, far disproportionate to their numbers, but Jewish men still received preference in higher education.[28]

Nevertheless, Jewish women went to college more frequently than other American women their age, pursuing higher education 2 to 3 times more often than their non-Jewish counterparts. By 1934, Jewish women comprised over half the female students enrolled in New York's public colleges.[29] During the Depression, thousands of Jewish women attended municipal colleges hoping to prepare for a teaching career. Considered the most secure and desirable Depression-era job for either sex, teaching was the premier professional goal among Jewish women. Families that could manage advanced education for their daughters considered it an investment that would benefit the entire family. Sending Jewish women to college remained part of household economic strategies. While attending college, Jewish women usually worked part-time to support themselves and their families. Those who eventually became teachers continued to lend financial support to their parents' households, sometimes even after they married.[30] Like their brothers, Jewish women who pursued education balanced their studies with their economic obligations to the family.

The vast majority of New York Jews able to attend college enrolled in the city's public universities. Lacking the financial resources to pay costly tuition and barred from admission to private universities by restrictive quotas, the sons and daughters of Jewish immigrants flocked to New York's free colleges. During the 1930s, Jews constituted from 80 to 90 percent of the student body at City College, Hunter College, and Brooklyn College.[31] The strong Jewish presence transformed the city's universities into bastions of Jewish youth culture in the 1930s. In the midst of the Great Depression, thousands of young Jews made the daily journey back and forth from their parents' homes to the urban campuses of New York. The city's colleges became the primary locus for the difficult economic struggles, heated ideological battles, and heightened political activism that characterized a generation of Jewish students.

New York Jews remembered college "as refuge for many of us in the Depression," a place to go "as much for lack of anything better to do as with any particular goal in mind."[32] After all, Jewish young adults had virtually no job opportunities, and college gave them at least a chance to prepare for a civil service exam. At the same time, college was no escape from the realities of the Depression. On the contrary, most Jews barely managed to afford the expenses of higher education. Although tuition was free at the city's colleges, students still had to find money for subway fares, books, and meals. Many Jews worked full-time to support their families and attended night classes, leaving little extra for the cost of education. Ida Levinson "did all sorts of work" while attending Hunter College, holding office and sales jobs and waiting tables. With part-time earnings, she paid college expenses and also provided income for her family.[33] Louis Weiser carefully monitored his spending habits while in school. "I managed to buy books one term and then sell them the next term and I'd walk as much as I could."[34] Morris Freedman, a City College student in the late thirties, recalled that "the round-trip subway fare then was only a dime, and although for fifteen cents one could get on campus a memorably generous and highly seasoned chopped liver sandwich, I was pressed to raise even this daily quarter, especially after I had paid for books."[35] Throughout their college years, Depression-era Jews struggled to afford the free education offered in New York City schools. Their level of desperation came to light in 1932 when New York's Board of Education proposed the imposition of tuition and other fees throughout the municipal college system. Students immediately initiated vigorous protests. From City, Brooklyn, and Hunter Colleges, student delegations descended on City Hall to voice their opposition to the proposed hikes, successfully pressuring officials to revoke the plan. The activist climate on campus gave momentum to the strident protests, but so too did the realization that any increase in fees would put an end to the college careers of most students who could scarcely afford a university education even with free tuition.[36]

New York's campuses nurtured the political radicalism of Depression-era youth. The educational initiation of Jewish college students included constant encounters with the economic and political problems plaguing New York City. They witnessed massive unemployment, breadlines, labor strikes, and evictions on every corner. "No sequestered nooks here! No protected oasis of learning," declared the Brooklyn College yearbook.[37] As they watched the apparent collapse of American society and the crisis sweeping through

Europe, many young Jews concluded that the old order was becoming unhinged and looked to leftist ideology for solutions. "Among young people the one political idea, perhaps the one idea, that had real power was radicalism."[38] The radical campaigns on college campuses derived from many sources. Students protested the imprisonment of the Scottsboro Boys, led the fight for free speech, supported the pacifist movement, and took the Oxford Pledge. They voiced opposition to fascism in Europe, criticized the New Deal, and defended striking workers. College students also initiated many battles on their own turf, fighting for student rights, denouncing ROTC training on campus, and resisting any attempts by city officials to impose tuition fees. The political spectrum among young Jews ranged from liberalism, considered the most tame of positions, to the various strands of socialism and communism that gave tone and substance to the political culture of New York campuses. The political fervor of the decade existed precisely because of the many competing movements, ideologies, and issues swirling around Jewish students in their college years. The heated discussions that took place in the Alcoves of City College, conducted with equal intensity on other city campuses, have assumed almost mythical status because of the "activism, fanatical intelligence, [and] emotional investment" of the participating students. No matter what their individual political persuasions, young Jewish men and women could not help but imbibe the political passions of the age.[39]

Yet, despite the overwhelming Jewish presence in left-wing movements and campus protests, only a minority of young Jews became devoted radical activists. Most Jewish youth sympathized with and occasionally participated in radical activities but remained preoccupied with the burdensome tasks of pursuing education and finding jobs. Even Irving Howe, among the most dedicated activists of the era, acknowledged that the spirit of radicalism did not overtake all of his peers. "Many of the boys and girls growing up in my neighborhood tried to pretend that all was normal, the Depression had not struck . . . expectations of a future still made sense. They looked for work. They hoped for a modest career, maybe as accountants or schoolteachers."[40] Despite the radical climate of City College, recalled Meyer Liben, "most of us finished our classes and went home [and] were not involved in the radical movement."[41] Juggling part-time or full-time jobs with schoolwork, many college students attended occasional protests and meetings but were too busy to lend undivided attention to activist campaigns. "The bulk of students, who were poor, were strenuously engaged in getting an education, posting good marks, and generally preparing themselves for getting on in the world. They may have had radical and Marxist sympathies, but they did not have

10. *This demonstration at City College was prompted by the expulsion and suspension of several students who led a mass protest when the university's president welcomed a delegation of Italian students to campus. The protesters accused the president of supporting fascism and denounced his decision to take action against student activists. Courtesy of the Archives of the City College of the City University of New York.*

much time to be activists."[42] Heightened political consciousness, ideological ferment, and protest movements were part of the constant current of life for Jews coming of age in the Depression. Political awareness colored not only their college experiences but their perceptions of America and its future. Movements for social change held enormous power for young Jews in the 1930s, but Depression-era Jews seldom let their leftist sentiments impede their increasingly difficult quest for economic security and stability.

There were also lighter moments for young Jews. During their educational careers, many Jewish students followed college and professional sports with the same interest and passion they devoted to political events. In the 1930s, the City College basketball team emerged among the elite championship clubs in the city, coached by Nat Holman who worked simultaneously as athletic director at the Ninety-second Street YMHA. Basketball was a Jewish sport in the 1930s. "Only a total of five Gentiles were able to crash the solid lines of Jewish players for C.C.N.Y. (or for that matter N.Y.U. and St. John's) from 1929 to 1935," related one WPA report.[43] The attraction of college sports went beyond rooting for the home team. For Depression-era Jewish students, the experience of winning, particularly with a virtually all-Jewish team, symbolized the triumph that young Jews craved but seldom attained in the 1930s. "The City College basketball team taught us the meaning of victory," explained Liben. "Our victories were important beyond the actuality of the score; immigrants or (mostly) sons of immigrants, we triumphed over the original settlers . . . became Americans, became winners, understood what it meant to belong, the way we never belonged as critics of society." The "world of Victory" inhabited briefly at college games was far from the world that young Jewish men and women encountered in their daily lives.[44] College athletics provided a symbolic temporary diversion for New York Jews, not to mention an inexpensive means of entertainment. "The basketball season has begun," announced a City College student magazine.

VARSITY BASKETBALL TEAM -- 1937-38

Top Row (l. to r.)   Nat Holman (Coach), Louis Daniels, John J. Foley, Alfred Soupios, Harold Kaufman, David Siperstein, Harold Padow (Manager).
Middle Row (l. to r.)   Joseph Adler, Louis Lefkowitz, Emanuel Jannon, David G. Paris, Bernard Fliegel (Captain), Morris Goldstein, Isadore Katz, Arthur J. Rosenberg.
Bottom Row (l. to r.)   Jack Carpien, Isadore Schnadow, Harry Sand, Martin Kaufman.

*11. In the 1930s, Jews predominated as members of the City College Basketball Team. The team's coach, Nat Holman, also served as athletic director at the Ninety-second Street YMHA. In the most desolate moments of the Depression, New York Jews avidly followed the progress of the college's successful Jewish teams. Courtesy of the Archives of the City College of the City University of New York.*

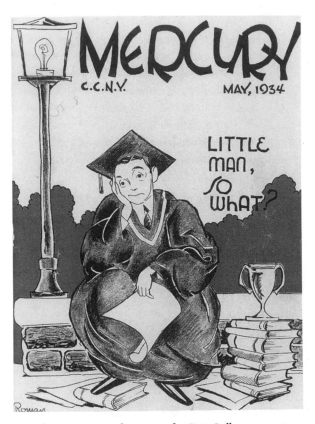

12. *This cartoon on the cover of a City College magazine captured the mood of prospective graduates who found themselves with college diplomas but few job opportunities. Courtesy of the Archives of the City College of the City University of New York.*

"Now all the fellows who have girls and no money have a place to bring their girls on Saturday night."[45] Even as they were conducting fiery political campaigns, battling economic and educational obstacles, and combating war and fascism, young Jewish men and women took pleasure in the small triumphs of a winning Jewish team.

Jewish young adults emerging from college needed whatever diversions they could muster, for the future appeared increasingly grim. The usual platitudes and optimistic fanfare of college graduations faded in the wake of the Depression. Instead, the predictions and proclamations from commencement speakers resonated with uncertainty and somber reflection. The annual yearbooks from City College became chronicles of the deflated hopes of a generation of young Jews. Graduating seniors explained that "the 1933 class has seen times and conditions change to a great extent since its entrance into the College. Four years ago we rode on a crest of prosperity and today we battle the vicissitudes of the depressed and practically moribund world."[46] For all the turmoil and anxiety experienced by Jews during their college years, the prospect of graduation into a society of mass unemployment was even more daunting. In 1937, a class that had both entered and exited City College in the midst of the Depression expressed the dark mood of its graduates. Preparing for final commencement exercises, the 1937 yearbook predicted, "Silently, the class will walk in the stadium for its final meeting as a class. Just as silently will the boys meet again on the line outside the employment office."[47]

Many Jewish college graduates did indeed gather outside New York employment offices. Despite having obtained an education, young Jews, like other American youth, faced extremely limited job opportunities. Few Depression-era youth immediately reaped the benefits of their educational efforts. In the 1930s, high school graduates remained unemployed at approximately the same rate as youth with less schooling and even those with advanced degrees did not fare much better.[48] Every June during the Depression, the *Forward* carried articles describing the bleak prospects awaiting the year's fresh crop of college graduates.[49] "You'd never guess to look at me now that I'm a college graduate, would you?" one young Jewish man rhetorically asked a caseworker at the Jewish Social Service Association. "I worked my way through. I got my degree and lost my job the same day. That was two years ago. Since then I've been kicking around, just gradually going to pieces. . . . Twenty-one and done for."[50] While the JSSA tended to embellish its case reports, the frustration of Jewish youth remained a very real product of the Depression decade. Well-educated Jews became increasingly bewildered by their inability to find work. One twenty-year-old Jewish man lamented, "I studied with great eagerness, always receiving the highest distinctions. I finished public school, high school, and even college." But like others in his situation, he discovered that education did not lead to opportunity. "For weeks, I have looked, groping through the want-ads in the newspapers, hoping I will find something to do, but [there is] nothing of the kind. I am tired and desperate from roaming the streets."[51] By the early 1930s, many applicants at the Ninety-second Street Y's employment department had become so despondent that in the job preference section of the application, they simply wrote "anything." The department's director, Irwin Rosen, noted the psychological toll of persistent unemployment, observing that

Jewish job applicants were becoming "sadder and wiser" as the Depression wore on.[52] "The problems of obtaining employment, the uncertainty of job[s], the general difficulty of getting ahead, have in large measure sobered the youth," Rosen explained.[53]

Young Jews who had grown up with expectations of great success found themselves hoping just to obtain some sort of stable job after graduation. The quest for secure employment along with financial pressures led some Jews to abandon aspirations for graduate or professional school. Reminiscing about his colleagues in Brooklyn College's 1933 graduating class, Roland Baxt lamented, "Some of my friends were going to be the greatest lawyers, doctors, teachers, historians" had the Depression not interfered with their plans.[54] Certainly many young Jews pursued postgraduate studies, in part because there were few jobs to be found. But professional status offered little security during the Depression. For example, thousands of Jewish lawyers hovered at the poverty line in the 1930s, leading some Jews to choose safer options. "I may have harbored some thoughts of becoming a lawyer," explained William Stern, who later became youth director for New York's Workmen's Circle, "but I got out [of college] during the Depression. And everybody wanted something secure. . . . Security was so important in those days."[55] Recalling the mood of the era, Louis Weiser insisted that "the biggest factor in anyone's life was security."[56] A term invoked repeatedly by Jewish men and women growing up in the Depression, security became the watchword of the age, summarizing the persistent fears and nagging doubts of a generation.

The Great Depression brought, above all else, the perception among young Jews that they might never rise above their parents' level of success. Jewish children had been raised with an ethic of achievement and a firm belief in their potential to advance in American society. Jewish parents had stressed the rewards of education, but Depression-era Jews did not benefit from their greater schooling in the 1930s. One Depression-era graduate of New York University earned a journalism degree only to return to work in his father's poultry market. "This place was built by my father twenty years ago," he lamented. "I never thought I'd end up here. I used to pass by on the other side of the street."[57] In the midst of the Depression's setbacks, a few voices within the Jewish community even called for Jewish parents to temper the pressure that they placed on their children to succeed. In 1932, one young Jewish woman wrote a newspaper article, "Must We All Be Wonder Children?" Criticizing the high expectations of Jewish parents, she asked, "Why must Jewish parents give their children untenable wings which too often leave them maimed and hurt?"[58] Given the barriers to success in the

1930s, lofty ambitions for career advancement seemed unrealistic and perhaps damaging to Jewish youth. An editorial in *The Day* insisted that the Depression might prove beneficial by bringing an end to parental pressure: "The cult of success, or perhaps security, often came between immigrant fathers and children of the first generation here. It was an unwritten law in every family that sons—and where there were no sons, then daughters—must succeed. It began with high marks in school, medals, honors. Later there had to be glory and rewards in the workaday world. . . . The depression will give many Jewish parents a new set of values in life. In this, the growing generation of youth are fortunate."[59] Such statements reflected the frustrations of the times, but during the Depression, immigrant Jewish parents continued to encourage their children to pursue education and upward mobility. Second-generation Jews remained in high school and college, partly because they had no viable employment options and partly because they, too, believed in the promise of education. "The psychology of individual striving had been called into question," explained Irving Howe, "but it had a strong grip even upon those who rejected it."[60]

The economic crisis produced no reversal of Jewish educational trends or occupational patterns, but unrealized expectations fed the anger and consternation of Jewish youth. During the worst period of the Depression, Irwin Rosen reported a "discipline problem" in his vocational training classes due to "the large number of restless and dissatisfied young men."[61] The Depression left young Jews with no jobs and an abundance of free time to nurture their doubts and frustrations. As the Jewish Social Service Association recognized, the "plight [of Jewish youth] is all the more distressing because they are at the age when a belief in themselves and a hope for their future would seem their rightful portion."[62]

The Depression elicited a running dialogue about the plight of Jewish youth. Jewish social workers, communal leaders, and the Jewish press expressed profound concern about helping young Jews find jobs and boosting their morale during the crisis. Jewish professionals agreed that community centers and Jewish agencies should systematically address the problems of Jewish youth. To that end, they organized leisure-time activities to provide a refuge for unemployed young men and women. During the Depression, the gyms and pools of YMHAS were filled, not only with teenagers, but with young adults who remained out of work. Well-intentioned Jewish communal workers sponsored a host of recreational and educational programs designed to fill increased leisure time and to help Jewish youth weather the emotional vicissitudes of the crisis. They believed that young Jews who were "mentally and emotionally sick as a result of the depression" would "regain confidence in themselves . . . and take on new life in the gymnasium."[63] At the same time, while Jewish centers attempted to occupy the free time brought on by unemployment, organizations like the citywide Federation Employment Service set out to assist Jewish youth in the job search. Sound vocational guidance, argued Jewish professionals, could help the young Jew determine how to "improve himself in his vocation and how he may meet discrimination which confronts him when he goes out into the world to look for a position."[64] For their part, young Jews gladly took advantage of the Jewish community's recreational programs and employment bureaus but paid little attention to the message delivered by Jewish professionals. The problem of youth, so widely debated during the Great Depression, reflected the fears of Jewish adults for their children but seldom represented the sentiments of young Jews.

The protracted discussion about the dilemmas of Jewish youth testified to the cleavage between the generations. Jewish professionals repeatedly complained that young Jews were not particularly receptive to their efforts. "As I observe the young people in this fourth year of the depression [1934]," one communal worker complained, "I am appalled by their cynical acceptance of things as they are. They are not avid for tools of understanding: they reject opportunities for vocational preparation, seeing, as they do, that fitness is no guarantee of work."[65] For all their good intentions, Jewish social workers were attempting to manage the problems of youth in an era that defied programmatic control. "I hated all abstract talk of youth and the problems of youth," declared Alfred Kazin. "I was youth, afraid to go home without a job. . . . *I* was youth—out of college for the year, useless, driven as an alley cat."[66] While professionals criticized the younger generation for their lack of direction, unwillingness to reevaluate occupational choices, and tendency toward political radicalism, Jewish youth devised their own responses to the Depression. They embraced leftist ideologies and hoped to create a new social and economic order. They looked for diversions in athletics, music, and movies. To the dismay of their elders, they even joked about their predicaments. City College's humor magazine, the *Mercury*, provided an ongoing satiric commentary on Depression-era Jewish experience, including comic portrayals of politics, job discrimination, and the quota system (see fig. 13). While communal agencies put forth a concerted effort, young Jews steered their own course through the Depression, guided by the economic, cultural, and political realities of the decade.

Scarcity of employment and fears about security and stability changed the way that Jewish youth approached the future. Like other American youth, Jewish men and women responded to the uncertainty of the Depression not

"Stop! I wanna go to Princeton!"

*13. The serious obstacles facing Jews in the Great Depression were often treated with humor and cynicism by Jewish youth. In this cartoon, City College's humor magazine offered a tongue-in-cheek commentary on Jewish quotas in universities. Courtesy of the Archives of the City College of the City University of New York.*

only by adjusting political allegiances and career aspirations but also by rethinking decisions about marriage and childbearing. During the Depression, the national marriage rate dropped precipitously, falling from 10.1 marriages per thousand people in 1929 to 7.9 during the worst year of the Depression in 1932.[67] Unemployment, lack of financial resources, and monetary obligations to the family forced many Americans to postpone or cancel marriage plans. In the Welfare Council survey, 32 percent of men over the age of 21 and 21 percent of women over the age of 18 indicated that the Depression had interfered with their marriage intentions.[68] Jewish youth tended to marry at an even lower rate than their non-Jewish counterparts, a statistic that the Welfare Council attributed to their remaining in school longer. Although more than 12 percent of non-Jewish youth under the age of 25 had married by 1935, only 8 percent of young Jewish men and women had chosen to marry.[69] Marriage rates plummeted across the nation during the worst years of the Depression, but Jews demonstrated a particular tendency to avoid marriage in the wake of the economic crisis.

Financial instability interfered with the courtship and marriage plans of Jewish youth. Dating patterns changed when young men could no longer afford to take their girlfriends "out" for the evening. "You can't have dates without money," one young man told the Welfare Council.[70] Yet other young Jews devised many ways to do just that. One Jewish man explained that he managed to entertain his girlfriend on a limited budget. "I courted her for about a year's time, taking her out to places, to parks, for boat rides, movies, sometimes just going for coffee and dessert in a restaurant—we never went in for regular meals."[71] Although many Jewish youth remembered going dancing, seeing movies, watching sporting events, or attending free (often WPA-sponsored) concerts and plays, economic realities often kept dating from leading to marriage. "A lot of fellas didn't make a living," Jean Margolies recalled, so marriage seemed impractical.[72] By the mid-thirties, Louis Kfare had begun dating one young Jewish woman regularly, and they had considered marriage. However, Kfare explained, "I realized that how could I have a wife, with what? I was earning peanuts. . . . How will I support a wife? How will I pay rent?" Kfare conceded that the couple probably could have managed somehow, "but I was too yellow, too scared."[73] Given the dearth of employment opportunities and the lack of job security, many young Jews believed that it was impossible or at least inadvisable to start their own families.

Obligations to the family also contributed to the postponement of marriage. The *Jewish Daily Forward*, which covered the declining rate of Jewish marriage with great concern, chronicled in some detail the many economic constraints that kept young Jews from marrying. In 1933, during the worst period of the Depression, the *Forward* reported, "Nowadays there are thousands and thousands of families where only one family member earns anything and brings a few dollars to the household. The ten or fifteen or thirty dollars a week that one [family member] earns must maintain the whole family. If that one is a boy or a girl of marriageable age, he or she cannot think about getting married."[74] Even when they were not the only wage earners in the family, many young Jewish men and women described similar feelings of household obligation. "My father is out of work and I must help out my family with my earnings," one young Jewish woman explained. "I have a young man who I would like to marry, but under such circumstances, I can no longer think about getting married."[75]

Of course, young Jews did marry during the Depression years. After 1932, the marriage rate gradually rebounded. Alfred Kazin remembered that despite economic conditions, "many of my friends were getting married and moving in with the wife's family."[76] For young Jews who married during the Depression, living with the family provided a much-needed economic boost.

When Roland Baxt married in 1937, he had graduated from college and obtained a WPA job and his wife was a high school graduate who worked as a salesperson. Although they were both employed, Baxt explained, "We lived at her family's home for a couple of years until we had more income to afford an apartment."[77] The combination of family obligations, lack of secure employment, and uncertain future prospects delayed many wedding plans, but postponement rather than cancellation of marriage characterized the experience of most young couples.[78]

Just as Jewish couples deferred marriage because of poor economic conditions, so too did they postpone having children. The national birthrate fell from 21.3 live births per thousand people in 1930 to 18.4 by 1933.[79] But the Jewish birthrate dropped even more precipitously than the national average. Since the early twentieth century, Jewish fertility had been low in absolute numbers as well as in comparison to other American ethnic groups.[80] The economic crisis and the decrease in marriages during the 1930s only accelerated that trend. In 1930, Jews had 69 births for every 100 births among white Americans. Between 1920 and 1940, the decline in Jewish fertility was twice that of the native white population.[81]

The Yiddish press carefully monitored the falling Jewish birthrate and expressed great concern about the Depression's effect on young Jews considering parenthood. "In the past, women used to have as many children as 'God had given,'" declared one *Forward* reporter, nostalgically altering the history of Jewish fertility. The Depression, he lamented, "has terrified parents about having children. Now, when one has only a few children, it is difficult to give them a means of support."[82] Like other Americans, young Jews adjusted their decisions about childbearing according to changing economic circumstances. Although Jewish family size had been decreasing before the onset of the Depression, the economic crisis prompted more Jewish couples to postpone parenthood and to have fewer children.

As the lower birthrate indicates, young Jews demonstrated a greater tendency to control their fertility through contraception and family planning. By the 1930s, many Americans had begun to look more favorably on contraception and birth control. A 1936 Gallup poll reported that 63 percent of Americans approved of the teaching and practice of birth control; a *Ladies Home Journal* survey revealed that 79 percent of American women supported the use of contraceptives. Moreover, birth control became more widely available due to both the growing commercialization of contraceptives as well as a 1936 Federal Appeals Court decision that removed all previous federal bans on their distribution. By 1938, more than three hundred birth control clinics were operating across the nation.[83] The country as a whole grew more accepting of birth control during the Depression years, but American Jews relied on contraception and family planning to a greater extent than other Americans. One Jewish demographer observed that, "Jewish fertility levels basically followed over time the general fluctuations of the total whites, but patterns of response . . . were relatively earlier, sharper, and faster as appropriate to a nearly perfectly contracepting population."[84] A study of the Bronx women attending Margaret Sanger's Birth Control Clinical Research Bureau in 1931 and 1932 confirmed such assertions. The clinic, which served a largely white-collar population, reported that its Jewish clients used contraception far more frequently than women of other religious groups.[85] Corroborating previous findings about the prevalent use of birth control among Jews, the authors of a 1939 study concluded that "urban American Jews constitute the most ardent birth-controlling group in the population. Regardless of economic or educational status the Jews seem overwhelmingly to be of the opinion that contraception is the thing."[86]

Within the Jewish community, the birth control movement received both support and condemnation during the Depression years. For the most part, American Jews advocated the use of contraception as a means of family planning. In the late thirties, the Men's Club of the Brooklyn Jewish Center organized a symposium to discuss the issue; ultimately the club advocated "a more civilized attitude toward birth control."[87] Like other Americans in the 1930s, Jews were particularly interested in controlling conception during the economic crisis. In 1933, the National Council of Jewish Women opened the first birth control clinic operating under explicitly Jewish auspices. Located in Brooklyn, the "Mother's Health Clinic" provided advice and information about birth control to a very select population. The clinic served only married women referred to the office by a social agency when they were unable to pay for medical services elsewhere. In addition, the National Council of Jewish Women indicated that the clinic provided contraceptive information only when the health of the woman was at stake. Despite the limited clientele that it served, Jewish sponsorship of the clinic represented a significant endorsement of birth control within the community.[88]

American Jews generally supported the birth control movement, but the sharp decline in the Jewish birthrate during the Depression motivated some critics to condemn the widespread use of contraception among young Jewish couples. Rabbi I. L. Bril, who had once occupied the pulpit at the Jewish Center of University Heights, offered one of the most scathing attacks on Jewish birth control. "Birth control is no solution of our economic life," Bril argued, equating the Jewish use of contraception with "wholesale suicide." He not only assailed birth control as a selfish response to the economic crisis, but blamed young Jewish women in particular for the drop in the Jewish birthrate. In 1932, Bril declared, "I am not so sure that those who preach and practice birth control are actuated altogether by unselfish motives. The desire for ease, for greater luxuries is very often the motivating reasons for not wanting children. Many women prefer a dog or cat to a child. Very many marriages go on the rocks because they are childless, because the wife refuses to have children."[89] Bril's harsh condemnation of birth control, however, represented a minority opinion in a Jewish community that widely practiced contraception.

Young Jewish couples of the Depression-era not only had fewer children, but they also expressed a desire to modify the family patterns constructed by their immigrant parents. The Depression did not erode traditional notions about marriage nor dramatically alter gender roles within the Jewish family. Yet young Jews who had been reared and educated in an American environment brought a variety of new expectations to their marriages and families. Jewish sons and daughters had come of age in a culture that celebrated romantic love and envisioned the family not only as an economic unit but also as a source of personal happiness and fulfillment.[90] Unlike their parents, young Jews were guided by attraction and romantic feelings when choosing their mates. "So far as I knew, love was not an element in my parents' experience," Alfred Kazin recalled, noting that immigrant couples "always had the look of being committed to something deeper than *mere* love. Their marriages were neither happy nor unhappy; they were arrangements."[91] Like other Americans their age, young Jews looked for love and companionship even as the Depression forced them to view marriage pragmatically.

The younger Jewish generation also expressed attitudes about gender roles in marriage that differed somewhat from those of immigrant parents. Jews who had grown up during the height of the American women's movement brought new sensibilities to their relationships. On a practical level, young Jewish men and women understood that economic pressures placed new demands on both husband and wife. Moreover, Jewish youth often claimed to hold more progressive views about women and to reject the subservient role assigned to women in the traditional Jewish family. In 1931, the Yiddish newspaper, *The Day*, sponsored an essay contest directed toward Jewish youth, offering ten dollars to the contributor who best discussed the question of whether a "fifty-fifty marriage" was preferable to a traditional marriage arrangement. *The Day*'s editors explained that in a "fifty-fifty marriage" both the husband and wife worked for wages and provided equal economic contributions to the family. (Sharing household responsibilities was never mentioned.)[92] Almost half of the contest entrants advocated a marriage of equals. "The men have as their ideal a girl with the ability to handle two life jobs—career and home," reported the editors.[93] One young man's letter demanded, "Why cannot the woman with her newly found economic freedom help her husband in productivity so that their aims and ideals may be mutually attained?"[94]

Yet, while many letters supported a "modern" approach to marriage, most indicated that the "fifty-fifty" arrangement should be temporary, terminating once the couple had children. The young man who had argued fervently in support of a marriage of two employed partners added that "I am not speaking of the mother. The proper care of a child consumes all the time and energy that a mother can give."[95] The prize-winning essay, written by a young Jewish woman, unequivocally rejected the traditional Jewish marriage arrangement in which the woman "was merely a puppet" with no outlet for independence. She also acknowledged the difficult economic constraints weighing on Jewish couples and advocated shared economic responsibility within the family, but only until the birth of children. "The man may not be in a position financially to establish and keep up a home so that the woman is forced to continue working to assist him," she explained. "This may be a very satisfactory arrangement for a short time but, certainly, to keep it up would be to defeat the fundamental purpose of marriage,—that of bringing into the world, and rearing children."[96]

Young Jews, *The Day*'s editors insisted, had "respect for women's integrity as an individual over and above her biologic role" and approved of a childless married woman working, but they retained traditional notions about motherhood.[97] Given the hostility toward married women working for wages, the views expressed by Jewish youth in the contest were rather progressive. Nevertheless, although most of the entrants described their attitudes as a modern rejection of their parents' values, they reflected less a departure from immigrant family models than an acceptance of middle-class American norms. Much like the opinions expressed by an older generation of Jews, most of the contest letters portrayed married women's work as a temporary necessity. The younger Jewish generation may have articulated a new respect for women's abilities and independence, but they continued to embrace the ideal of American domesticity that viewed the employment of wives and mothers as an aberration. Like their immigrant parents, American-born Jews interpreted the family compromises required by the Depression as temporary deviations from the American ideals to which they aspired.

The emerging generation of Jews did not radically revise gender roles in marriage, but as they responded to the constraints of the Great Depression, they did significantly alter the overall patterns of Jewish life. Jews coming of age in the Depression years remained in school longer, delayed marriage, and limited the size of their families. Young Jewish men and women did not relish the choices foisted on them by the Depression. They were as much lost as driven during their adolescence and young adulthood, often bewildered, frustrated, and disappointed by the lack of opportunities available to them in America. The Depression disrupted the expectations of success that young Jews had inherited from their immigrant parents. Forced by circumstance to temper their hopes for the future, Jewish youth adjusted their occupational goals and reevaluated their approach to starting their own families. The decisions made by young Jews in the turmoil and frustration of the Depression permanently changed the collective profile of American Jewry. A decade or two later, when optimism returned to the Jewish scene, patterns established in the Depression era would characterize middle-class American Jewish life.

From the perspective of hindsight, it is clear that Jewish youth weathered the economic crisis in a comparatively fortunate position. They stayed in school when there were no jobs to be found; they maintained a white-collar occupational profile that proved enormously beneficial in the post–World War II economy; and they began to construct marriage and family patterns suited to middle-class suburban life. But young Jews of the 1930s did not know that their educational attainments and employment preferences would be so generously rewarded in post–World War II America. Charting an unknown course in a decade of cultural, political, and economic transition, Jews coming of age in the Great Depression envisioned their futures in the most uncertain terms.

During the Depression years, Jewish youth initiated transformations in the basic structures of American Jewish life. Yet, even as they approached the unprecedented challenges of Depression-era America, as they journeyed to college and pursued occupations far removed from the world of their parents, they also returned daily to the distinct ethnic neighborhoods of New York City. The city's diverse Jewish neighborhoods provided an intimate and vibrant foundation that bolstered New York Jews as they confronted the Great Depression.

# 4

# The Landscape of Jewish Life

For most of the Great Depression, Louis Kfare lived in the South Bronx and in nearby Hunts Point. As a young man in his early twenties, Kfare journeyed daily across the borough to the West Bronx where he delivered groceries for a local store. The distance between his home and work amounted to only a few miles, but the differences in class and culture were vast. The modern elevator apartments of the West Bronx contrasted sharply with the modest brick buildings inhabited by Kfare and his South Bronx neighbors. Kfare cherished his job in the "fancy neighborhood" where he could hope for generous tips from middle-class West Bronx residents. He might even have the chance to retrieve empty milk bottles left outside apartment doors and return them for a two-cent per bottle deposit fee, a lucrative opportunity for a working-class young man in the midst of the Depression. Every working day, as he traveled from one neighborhood to another, Louis Kfare came to understand the diversity of Depression-era Jewish experience, given concrete expression in the urban geography of New York City.[1]

New York neighborhoods provided the fabric of community for Jews in the Great Depression. There was a provincialism to this world in the 1930s. Most Depression-era Jews, even the American-born children of immigrants, did not yet completely define themselves as New Yorkers. "We were of the city, but somehow not in it," explained Alfred Kazin. "I saw New York as a foreign city."[2] Jews were more likely to regard themselves as part of a particular neighborhood, as residents of Brownsville or Flatbush, the Grand Concourse or the East Bronx. The name of each district alone conjured up a certain image, signifying poverty, radicalism, or middle-class comfort. In each of the city's ethnic enclaves, Jews lived among friends and neighbors of similar background and class orientation. "Our life," Irving Howe recalled about his youth in the 1930s, "was shaped by the fact that in New York the Jews still formed a genuine community reaching into a dozen neighborhoods."[3] The neighborhood remained the primary association for New York Jews and the principal locus for the many different Jewish encounters with the Great Depression.

By the time the Depression struck, most New York Jews had moved out of the city's immigrant neighborhoods. The Lower East Side and Harlem, once hubs of Jewish life, had given way to new Jewish districts in Brooklyn, the Bronx, and upper Manhattan. Working and middle-class Jews migrated to new areas of the city, settling in neighborhoods that reflected their economic status and cultural preferences. As they relocated, New York Jews preserved a sense of ethnic community by continuing to live among other Jews. The intracity Jewish migration followed a clear pattern of concentrated dispersal, creating pockets of Jewish life throughout New York's boroughs. As one *Forward* reporter explained, "90 out of every 100 Jews . . . seek a Jewish [apartment] house, situated on a Jewish block, in a Jewish neighborhood."[4] During the twenties, new Jewish districts grew rapidly, fueled by the postwar building boom and increased Jewish prosperity. By 1930, almost three-quarters of Jewish New Yorkers had moved to new neighborhoods with predominantly Jewish populations.[5] The Depression halted the rapid neighborhood expansion and intracity migration of the 1920s, leaving most Jews living in the districts where they had settled during the interwar years.[6] There was a degree of physical movement within Depression-era neighborhoods: protracted unemployment forced some Jewish families to move to poorer sections of the city, whereas Jews with capital to invest took advantage of the depressed market to purchase real estate. But no new Jewish neighborhoods took shape in the 1930s. Instead, working-class Jewish districts constructed before the Depression became poorer and harbored growing numbers of Jewish unemployed. Middle-class Jewish neighborhoods maintained rela-

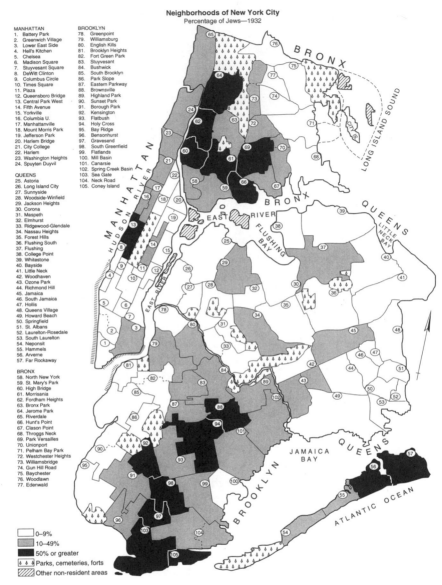

## Neighborhoods of New York City
### Percentage of Jews—1932

**MANHATTAN**
1. Battery Park
2. Greenwich Village
3. Lower East Side
4. Hell's Kitchen
5. Chelsea
6. Madison Square
7. Stuyvesant Square
8. DeWitt Clinton
9. Columbus Circle
10. Times Square
11. Plaza
12. Queensboro Bridge
13. Central Park West
14. Fifth Avenue
15. Yorkville
16. Columbia U.
17. Manhattanville
18. Mount Morris Park
19. Jefferson Park
20. Harlem Bridge
21. City College
22. Harlem
23. Washington Heights
24. Spuyten Duyvil

**QUEENS**
25. Astoria
26. Long Island City
27. Sunnyside
28. Woodside-Winfield
29. Jackson Heights
30. Corona
31. Maspeth
32. Elmhurst
33. Ridgewood-Glendale
34. Nassau Heights
35. Forest Hills
36. Flushing South
37. Flushing
38. College Point
39. Whitestone
40. Bayside
41. Little Neck
42. Woodhaven
43. Ozone Park
44. Richmond Hill
45. Jamaica
46. South Jamaica
47. Hollis
48. Queens Village
49. Howard Beach
50. Springfield
51. St. Albans
52. Laurelton-Rosedale
53. South Laurelton
54. Neponsit
55. Hammels
56. Arverne
57. Far Rockaway

**BRONX**
58. North New York
59. St. Mary's Park
60. High Bridge
61. Morrisania
62. Fordham Heights
63. Bronx Park
64. Jerome Park
65. Riverdale
66. Hunt's Point
67. Clason Point
68. Throggs Neck
69. Park Versailles
70. Unionport
71. Pelham Bay Park
72. Westchester Heights
73. Williamsbridge
74. Gun Hill Road
75. Baychester
76. Woodlawn
77. Edenwald

**BROOKLYN**
78. Greenpoint
79. Williamsburg
80. English Kills
81. Brooklyn Heights
82. Fort Green Park
83. Stuyvesant
84. Bushwick
85. South Brooklyn
86. Park Slope
87. Eastern Parkway
88. Brownsville
89. Highland Park
90. Sunset Park
91. Kensington
92. Flatbush
93. Holy Cross
94. Bay Ridge
95. Bensonhurst
96. Gravesend
97. South Greenfield
98. Flatlands
99. Mill Basin
100. Canarsie
101. Spring Creek Basin
102. Sea Gate
103. Neck Road
104. Coney Island

Legend:
- 0–9%
- 10–49%
- 50% or greater
- ♦ ♦ ♦ Parks, cemeteries, forts
- ▨ Other non-resident areas

*14. Jewish neighborhoods of New York City. Adapted from J. B. Maller, "Neighborhoods of New York City—1932," Jewish Social Service Quarterly 10, no. 4 (June 1934).*

tively secure standards of living, given Depression-era conditions, but their populations ranged from Jews with steady employment and regular income to those barely clinging to financial stability. The challenge for the "middle-middle-class" was keeping its foothold on an increasingly shaky Jewish economic ladder. In Brighton Beach, a struggling middle-class area, one former resident remembered sensing "the anxiety of everyone to keep his place on the balance."[7] With Jewish neighborhoods becoming relatively frozen in terms of class composition, Jewish districts came to embody their residents' level of security or desperation in the Great Depression.

When the Depression arrived, Jews were living in several distinct, ethnically coherent communities throughout the city, each responding differently to the challenges of the economic crisis. Class was the primary but not the only factor determining Jewish residential choices. Jewish districts reflected the gradations of economic status within the Jewish community as well as the various political ideals, cultural allegiances, and religious preferences of New York Jews. Certain sections of the city emerged as hubs of communism, others as centers of Orthodoxy or Zionism, still others as the homes of the established Jewish elite or the new middle class. One *Forward* reporter, intimately acquainted with the subtle distinctions of New York neighborhoods, explained, "There are Ghettos for foreign born Jews and Ghettos for native born Jews. Ghettos for poor Jews and Ghettos for middle class and for rich Jews, for Russian Jews and for German Jews. The East Side is one kind of Ghetto, Washington Heights another kind, West Bronx a third, Riverside Drive a fourth. . . . Brooklyn has a dozen different kinds and styles of Ghettos of its own."[8] New York Jews constructed neighborhoods that gave concrete expression to the economic stratification and internal diversity of the community. When the Depression came, the city's Jewish quarters did not share a common fate. Just as individual Jews experienced the economic crisis differently, depending upon their occupation, class, and family structure, so, too, the Depression painted an uneven stroke across the New York Jewish world.

Within the Jewish community, the Lower East Side bore the brunt of the Great Depression. The East Side had been the center of Jewish life at the turn of the century, but thirty years later, it housed only a small percentage of New York's Jews. During the twenties, Jews abandoned the East Side's cramped quarters for more spacious and modern housing, leaving behind immigrants and their children who lacked the financial means to move to better neighborhoods. In 1925, the Lower East Side retained only 15 percent of the city's Jewish population and that number declined sharply through the next decade. By the Depression era, the Lower East Side was the poorest of all Jewish neighborhoods and one of the most disadvantaged in the city. Only Harlem outranked the East Side in numbers of families receiving federal assistance.[9] Jean Margolies, who grew up on Broome Street and attended Seward Park High School during the 1930s, described her East Side neighbors as "very, very poor." At a time when most Jewish families lived in modern housing, the Margolies family, like many East Side residents, shared a two-room apartment with no private bathroom.[10] During the Depression years, the Lower East Side ceased to represent the core of the Jewish community and instead became the home of its least fortunate members.

Despite its poverty, the Lower East Side survived as a Jewish neighborhood, still housing many Jewish institutions, associations, and local businesses. Moreover, the East Side emerged as a nostalgic center for New York Jews, a living reminder of an idealized immigrant world as well as a mirror of the past that reflected the extent of Jewish progress. Religious schools took their young, American-born Jewish students on field trips to the East Side to catch a glimpse of a fading Jewish culture.[11] At the height of the Depression, New York's Graduate School for Jewish Social Work sponsored a photographic study of the Lower East Side designed to record "a passing picture of Jewish communal life." Commenting on New York's poorest Jewish neighborhood, the photographers insisted that although, "every one had his problems, . . . the east side was like a happy family."[12] As the Depression devastated the district, Jews no longer living on the East Side constructed a glorified image of the neighborhood that obscured the reality of its grinding poverty.

New York Jews who had abandoned the Lower East Side elevated the area to an almost mythical status, but for the Jews who inhabited the neighborhood during the Depression, the experience was not so romantic. In his scathing 1930 Communist critique, *Jews Without Money*, Michael Gold presented a dismal account of Jewish life on the Lower East Side. "As fast as a generation makes some money, it moves to a better section of the city," Gold explained, leaving the poorest members of the Jewish community to occupy the dilapidated tenements and battle the filth and disease of the deteriorating neighborhood. For Gold, the East Side represented the worst of urban existence, "a world of feebleness and of stomachs, livers, and lungs rotting away," where Jews lived in tenements that were "nothing but junk-heap[s] of rotten lumber and brick."[13] During the 1930s, as the Lower East Side assumed nostalgic power for Jews who had moved elsewhere, the residents left behind became the most severe casualties of the Great Depression.

Among Jewish neighborhoods, Brooklyn's Brownsville district ranked second only to the Lower East Side in the number of families receiving federal welfare during the Depression.[14] Almost as poverty-stricken as the

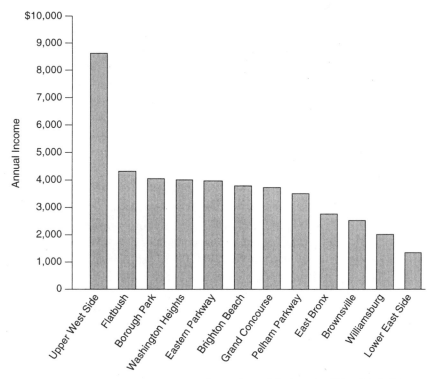

15. *Estimated median family incomes of Jewish neighborhoods of New York City, 1930. From* New York City Market Analysis *(1933).*

East Side, Brownsville evoked none of its nostalgic sentiment, at least not until long after the Depression had faded into distant memory. The Brownsville community had begun to take shape after the turn of the century, when Brooklyn emerged as a viable residential choice for New Yorkers seeking better housing. The construction of bridges and subway lines provided easy access to Manhattan, allowing immigrant Jews to leave East Side tenements. Brownsville gradually became a working-class community, populated by garment workers and small business owners. More than any other New York neighborhood, Brownsville was a Jewish district. Jews constituted more than 80 percent of the Brownsville population, lending the community a rich ethnic flavor. "I thought the entire world was Jewish. . . . I didn't realize that I was a minority," recalled Lillian Elkins, who grew up in Brownsville, the daughter of factory workers.[15] Brownsville nurtured a vibrant Jewish culture with a multitude of synagogues (more than eighty-three in less than two square miles), as well as dozens of religious schools, Yiddish cultural organizations, left-wing movements, political clubs, and union activities.[16] A densely populated neighborhood, Brownsville was almost a city unto itself. The depth and extent of Jewish life earned Brownsville the title Brooklyn's Lower East Side—crowded, poor, and teeming with activity.

Brownsville's wealth of Jewish culture was matched by its material poverty. During the Depression, the neighborhood's preponderance of blue-collar workers made Brownsville a bastion of unemployment. Alfred Kazin, whose father worked as a painter in Brownsville, recalled that "from the early 'thirties on, my father could never be sure in advance of a week's work."[17] Almost half of Brownsville's Jews lived in tenement housing and struggled to find even part-time employment; in one survey, more than 73 percent of the neighborhood's boys described their families as impoverished.[18] Growing up in Brownsville during the Depression meant teetering on the brink of destitution and inhabiting the bottom rung of the Jewish world. Capturing the essence of Brownsville life, Kazin explained, "We were the end of the line. We were the children of immigrants who had camped at the city's back door, in New York's rawest, remotest, cheapest ghetto . . . we were Brownsville—*Brunzvil*, as the old folks said—the dust of the earth to all Jews with money, and notoriously a place that measured all success by our skill in getting away from it."[19] Years after the Depression, some former Brownsville residents recalled the isolation and sheer poverty of their neighborhood. Others described the sense of security that derived from "living in a world all Jewish, where no alien group imposed its standards." In a more moderate assessment, one Brownsville Jew reflected, "it wasn't as Utopian as some recall, nor was it as grim as others remember."[20]

Brownsville provided both an intimate and vibrant Jewish community as well as "the challenge of the gutter."[21] A neighborhood of active, crowded streets, offering an unparalleled range of Jewish political, religious, and social expression, Brownsville had its share of vitality during the Depression. Pitkin Avenue, known as the Fifth Avenue of Brooklyn, housed dozens of small Jewish businesses, and its street corners were regular gathering places for local residents looking to occupy spare time or take in the political speeches routinely given by neighborhood orators. Brownsville retained the vigor of a strong working-class community, as its residents suffered crippling unemployment, struggled to support their families, and were often forced to turn to government agencies for assistance. As one Jewish philanthropic organization declared, Brownsville was the home of "some of the most unfortunate dependent classes," and its residents shared a certain sense of desperation in the Depression years.[22] Like the Lower East Side, Browns-

16. *Pitkin Avenue, known as the "Fifth Avenue of Brook-*
*lyn," was a hub for Jewish businesses, a center of neighbor-*
*hood social life, and a frequent setting for informal political*
*gatherings. Courtesy of the United States History, Local*
*History and Genealogy Division, New York Public Li-*
*brary, Astor, Lenox and Tilden Foundations.*

ville was a neighborhood occupied by New York's poorest Jews, those hit
hardest by the Great Depression, but it remained a rich and tightly knit
working-class Jewish community.

   To the east of Brownsville stood East New York and Canarsie, which contained large working-class Jewish populations and shared many of Brownsville's economic woes during the Depression years. Although none could
match its vibrant Jewish culture, these Brooklyn districts replicated Browns-

ville's working-class composition and substandard living conditions. Kazin called Canarsie "the great refuse dump . . . a place so celebrated in New York vaudeville houses for its squalor that the very sound of the word was always good for a laugh. CAN-NARR-SIE! They fell into the aisles."[23] In Canarsie and East New York, poverty and radicalism usually went hand in hand. Like Brownsville's Jews, residents of East New York demonstrated an affinity for left-wing politics and activism that grew stronger when economic conditions deteriorated, particularly during the worst years of the Depression. The streets of these working-class neighborhoods, crowded with Jews who had no regular jobs and nothing but spare time, reflected the economic privation that engulfed poorer Jewish districts and nurtured the radical culture prominent in many New York neighborhoods.

To the north of Brownsville and just across the bridge from the Lower East Side was Williamsburg, a district known more for Orthodoxy than radicalism, but also one of the hardest-hit working-class Jewish communities. In the late-nineteenth century, Williamsburg had been the province of wealthy German Jews, but by the Depression era, affluent and upper-middle-class Jews had been enticed to newer Brooklyn districts, leaving Williamsburg to Jewish workers. A 1936 study conducted by the Jewish Welfare Board found that two-thirds of Williamsburg's residents labored in the garment industry or worked in retail trade, giving Williamsburg far fewer white-collar employees than was the Jewish norm. That occupational profile proved detrimental to Williamsburg's Jews in the Great Depression. The percentage of families on welfare was 50 percent higher in Williamsburg than within the borough of Brooklyn as a whole.[24] Like their neighbors on the Lower East Side, in Brownsville, and in East New York, the Jews of Williamsburg battled through hard economic times. All of these districts shared a common problem: their occupants depended heavily on jobs in the needle trades that were decimated by the Depression. The concentration of Jewish workers in particular neighborhoods, which began during the 1920s, gave working-class Jewish neighborhoods a similar profile in the Depression years. At the same time, each district maintained a particular character. During the 1930s, the Williamsburg community emerged as a center of Orthodoxy. At least fifty synagogues, several Yeshivot, Talmud Torahs, and leading Orthodox organizations such as Agudath Israel and Young Israel made their homes in Williamsburg. Many of its neighborhood institutions barely escaped financial ruin but kept themselves afloat, often without paying their staff and teachers for months, even years, at a time. Throughout the Depression, Williamsburg remained an Orthodox stronghold as well as a struggling working-class neighborhood.[25]

Within a few miles of Brooklyn's working-class districts lay several middle-class Jewish enclaves. Despite the setbacks of the economic crisis, many

New York Jews maintained middle-class status, achieved in those years with only a steady white-collar job. Every Jewish resident of the borough understood the neighborhood boundaries that distinguished the gradations of class and economic status in Brooklyn. Middle-class Jews made their homes to the west of the working-class sections of Brownsville and East New York. Where Brownsville ended, Eastern Parkway began, offering its residents "wide and tree-lined" streets that contrasted sharply with the crowded avenues of Brownsville. Eastern Parkway, as Alfred Kazin observed, was the province of "middle-class Jews, *alrightniks*, making out 'all right' in the New World."[26] The Brooklyn Jewish Center, one of New York's largest and most expensive synagogues, was erected on Eastern Parkway by Jews eager to apply middle-class standards to Jewish religious and cultural practice. Its elaborate facilities testified to the comparative economic comfort of Eastern Parkway's Jews and their level of security and financial status in the Great Depression.

Only a short distance to the south of Eastern Parkway lay Borough Park, which had once been Brooklyn's most elite neighborhood, but by the Depression, wealthy residents had moved to other New York districts. In the 1930s, Borough Park could be classified as a solidly middle-class area, home to the "moderately successful businessman."[27] Its residents fared very well during the Depression, boasting one of the highest median household income levels in the borough and recording a relatively low percentage of welfare recipients. Borough Park also fostered a rich and varied Jewish culture and supported a YMHA, several philanthropic and Zionist organizations, as well as religious institutions representing different movements. The area gained a reputation for its middle-class versions of both Zionism and Orthodoxy. Borough Park became one of the first communities to be designated "modern Orthodox," a description reflecting the acculturated religious observance of its middle-class population.[28]

Flatbush was Brooklyn's most affluent neighborhood in the Depression years. A relatively new section of the city, Flatbush's tree-lined streets and spacious housing attracted successful Jews who had moved out of Brooklyn's older neighborhoods. With a yearly median income of more than $4,300, Flatbush was an upper-middle-class district that, not surprisingly, recorded Brooklyn's lowest percentage of families on home relief.[29] Like other Jewish neighborhoods, Flatbush maintained a Jewish culture that reflected the needs and desires of its residents. The area housed modern synagogues that were equipped with gymnasiums and recreational facilities, as well as a successful Jewish Communal Center. In their ethnic institutions, Flatbush Jews expressed their Jewish identity in a manner commensurate with their class status and aspirations.[30] The spacious community centers of Eastern

*17. This modern apartment house, located on a tree-lined section of Eastern Parkway, reveals the comfortable surroundings enjoyed by middle-class Jews during the Great Depression. Courtesy of the Brooklyn Historical Society.*

Parkway, Bensonhurst, and Flatbush contrast sharply with those of poorer Jewish neighborhoods. In East New York, the local YMHA was housed in a loft above a fish store, whereas the Jewish Communal Center of Flatbush maintained an elaborate structure, complete with gymnasium, social halls, clubrooms, and the most up-to-date recreational provisions.[31] In the apartments they occupied, the stores and businesses they frequented, and the communal facilities they supported, New York Jews displayed their internal differences of class and culture. Alfred Kazin claimed that the Jews of Brooklyn's affluent neighborhoods were so different from the Jews he encountered in Brownsville that "they were still Gentiles to me."[32] In the borough of Brooklyn alone, the distinct Jewish neighborhoods told multiple stories of Jewish experience during the Depression.

The Bronx offered a similar diversity of Jewish neighborhoods and Depression-era experience. Financially secure Bronx Jews made their homes in the western section of the borough, on the Grand Concourse, an area that the WPA *New York City Guide* called "the Park Avenue of middle-class Bronx residents."[33] It was this neighborhood, the West Bronx, where Louis Kfare delivered groceries and marveled at the luxurious apartment buildings and comfortable standard of living enjoyed by its residents. Grand Concourse Jews were not wealthy, but they were a successful, primarily white-collar group that weathered the Depression without severe setbacks. One WPA writer reported that Grand Concourse residents were "manufacturers and tradesmen, doctors, dentists, lawyers, engineers, school teachers, salesmen, and minor executives. They are the envy of the Jewish poor."[34] Debby Kirschenbaum, who lived with her husband and two children on the Grand Concourse, recalled that most of her neighbors were "professional men" who did "not have much difficulty in the Depression."[35] Half of the residents paid rents between fifty and seventy-five dollars per month, placing them firmly in the middle-class.[36] Jews represented almost three-quarters of the population on the Grand Concourse and gave the area a distinct ethnic flavor. Like other comparable New York neighborhoods, the Grand Concourse supported a multitude of Jewish institutions, including several large synagogues representing Orthodox, Conservative, and Reform Jews. A vibrant community throughout the 1930s, Grand Concourse residents remained economically secure during the Depression years. To live in the West Bronx meant to enjoy the best the city had to offer and to be spared the Depression's harshest blows.[37]

Residents understood the wide gulf that existed between the West and the East Bronx. Irving Howe recalled that "in my part of the East Bronx . . . it was rare for a building of red or tan brick to break the monotony of muddy browns and grays. . . . If you wanted to see a 'modern' building—one that had an elevator, parquet floors, and French doors—you had to take a trolley across the borough to the newer sections of the West Bronx."[38] West and East Bronx residents defined themselves according to which side of the borough they occupied. "It was not really the Bronx we lived in," one young Jewish writer sarcastically explained, "it was the West Bronx, and if you don't think it makes a difference, just try living in the West Bronx and having people ask you where you live, and if you can just calmly say 'The Bronx' (leaving out the West part of it), without having to swallow four times, you're good."[39] There was more than status associated with residing in the West Bronx; there was also a very real difference in levels of economic security and survival. Unlike their more fortunate residents to the west, East Bronx residents endured protracted unemployment and extreme financial hardships, experiencing "the collapse of American industry far more severely

18. *Middle-class Jewish residents of the Bronx made their homes in spacious apartments like this one located on the corner of Grand Concourse and 170th Street. Courtesy of the Bronx County Historical Society, Bronx, New York.*

than the merchants and professionals of the Grand Concourse neighborhoods."[40]

A predominantly working-class neighborhood with a large number of factory workers, the East Bronx housed almost half of the Jewish population of the Bronx. The director of the Bronx Council House, a settlement house and Jewish Federation agency, described the neighborhood as "a poor community trying to recover from the depths of the Depression . . . [where many] people were on relief, or WPA, or NYA, or sending their children to CCC camps."[41] A move to the East Bronx in the middle of the Depression meant that a family had lost its financial base. Historian Lucy Dawidowicz recalled that in the 1920s her family had bought a house in "a developing section of the Bronx." However, she explained, "by 1937, my parents could no longer keep up the payments on the mortgage, despite the help that Roosevelt's New Deal gave to small homeowners. The bank foreclosed on the house and that summer we moved to a dismal apartment in a dilapidated East Bronx neighborhood."[42] The East Bronx covered a large geographical area, encompassing a variety of different Jewish sections and class subgroups. "An inexperienced eye moving across the East Bronx would have noticed little difference between one part and another," Howe explained. "That eye would have been mistaken, for the immigrant world had its intricate latticing of social position." Several distinct neighborhoods of different economic status existed within the area known as the East Bronx. The residents who lived in Park Versailles and near Crotona Park were predominantly middle-class. One historian also described Hunt's Point, which housed most of the area's small synagogues, as a "middle-middle-class" population.[43] The eastern corner of the East Bronx housed the poorest Jews and was considered the worst part of the neighborhood. Howe remembered that even when the Depression forced his family to move to a working-class section of the East Bronx, his father insisted, "'At least we're not on Fox Street.' Fox Street he regarded as our private Bowery, the bottom in poverty."[44]

More than any other section of the city, the East Bronx was a haven for political radicalism. A tightly knit Jewish community, East Bronx residents lived amid a Jewish culture that permeated the streets, schools, and local businesses. "In the early thirties . . . the East Bronx was still a self-contained little world," Howe recalled, "lacking the cultural vivacity that had brightened the Lower East Side of Manhattan a decade or two earlier but otherwise, in custom and value, not very different. Yiddish was spoken everywhere." The secular Jewish culture of the neighborhood contained a healthy dose of radicalism that became part of the rhythm of daily life in the East Bronx. Socialists, Communists, and union activists found a receptive audience in Bronx communities. "Radicalism in our part of the city seemed more than marginal exotica. . . . It had a place and strength of its own . . . almost everyone seemed to be a Socialist of one sort or another."[45] The area surrounding Pelham Parkway was the center of East Bronx radicalism, where Jewish cooperative housing projects provided political leadership and organization. The housing projects had been built by Jews representing different ideological positions and occupational groups. The Sholem Aleichem apartments were founded by Jews committed to the preservation of secular Jewish culture; the Worker's Cooperative Colony was a Communist stronghold, while still other cooperatives represented trade unions and rival cultural and political movements. These communities, populated by working and lower-middle-class Jews, provided residents with the benefits of modern housing within an ideological setting. Their pervasive secular Jewish culture with an emphasis on radicalism lent the Bronx cooperatives a distinct political character. Located in pockets of the North Bronx and Pelham Parkway, the left-wing districts became radical strongholds and vital centers of grassroots Jewish activism. During the 1930s, these radical communities not only gave tone and substance to Jewish neighborhood life, but also sparked some of the Depression's most vigorous neighborhood protests.[46]

By the 1930s, the Bronx and Brooklyn combined to house almost 80 percent of the city's Jewish population. In the Depression era, Manhattan was home to only 16 percent of New York Jews, who lived in small, select pockets of the borough.[47] The Lower East Side, as previously indicated, remained a vibrant but impoverished Jewish neighborhood throughout the Depression years. Other Jewish enclaves in Manhattan included Yorkville, an affluent Jewish district on the Upper East Side, where the modern Orthodox synagogue, Kehilath Jeshurun, made its home. The Upper East Side remained a very small Jewish community in the 1930s, housing no more than 4 percent of New York's Jews.[48] Washington Heights was a more heterogeneous middle-class district. In the 1920s, Washington Heights had attracted successful Jews who wanted to move out of Harlem. They were joined in the thirties by German Jewish refugees who created a unique cultural subcommunity, known sarcastically as the "Fourth Reich." By the time the Depression struck, more affluent Washington Heights residents had begun leaving the area, relocating in Manhattan's most elite Jewish neighborhood—the Upper West Side.[49]

The Upper West Side was New York's only truly affluent Jewish neighborhood, earning its reputation as "the gilded ghetto." An area that prospered and expanded throughout the Depression years, the West Side epitomized the Jewish quest for success. As early as 1922, Mordecai Kaplan noted that "the Jews of the well-to-do class constitute the predominant element of the population in [the] West Side section of the city," adding that "they are conspicuous by their vulgarity and flashiness."[50] Populated largely by East European Jews who had attained rapid economic success, the Upper West Side nurtured a fashionable brand of Jewish culture. With all the trappings of their prosperity, West Side Jews built a thriving Jewish community. By 1929, the area housed ten synagogues, many of them large and ornate, and supported scores of kosher butchers, bakeries, and restaurants. During the Depression years, the area surrounding Central Park West demonstrated few visible effects of the economic crisis. West Side residents earned a median income of $8,700 and almost two-thirds lived in apartments where rentals ranged from 100 to 200 dollars a month.[51] Many garment manufacturers resided on the West Side and although they suffered some economic declines during the Depression, many managed to maintain a comfortable living. There were some West Side Jews whose financial losses forced them to move to less expensive areas; the Upper West Side lost approximately 10,000 residents in the thirties.[52] Yet, the Jewish population of the West Side actually increased throughout the decade, as a significant number of Jews continued to achieve financial success despite the Depression. Although the economic crisis adversely affected many of the area's synagogues and Jewish institutions, most West Side Jews weathered the Depression with few sacrifices. Even at the height of the Depression, Jews on the West Side had the resources to take extended summer vacations and send their children to expensive summer camps.[53] On Manhattan's Upper West Side, the Great Depression was a dramatically different event than it was only a subway ride away in the less fortunate Jewish districts of New York City.

New York Jews did not share a common fate in the Great Depression and their neighborhoods gave physical expression to the divisions of class and culture that shaped Jewish experience in the Depression. From the impoverished neighborhoods of Brownsville and the Lower East Side, to the distinct working-class sections of Brooklyn and the Bronx, to the many middle-class enclaves that dotted New York boroughs, Jews encountered the Depression through the lens of their neighborhood streets and institutions. Indeed, the internal class variations within the Jewish community had never been more apparent than during the difficult years of the Great Depression.

New York's Jewish neighborhoods reflected the class composition of the Jewish community, but at the same time, the city's Jewish districts were more than geographical divisions of class and economic status. Jewish neighborhoods also provided a foundation and sometimes a safety net for Jews as they encountered the Depression. The sense of community, constructed differently in each neighborhood, shaped the rhythm and tone of Jewish life in the 1930s, offering Jews a sense of security in hard times. In New York's upper-class and solidly middle-class Jewish districts, the Depression's impact was seldom visible on neighborhood streets. Although they often felt the effects of the Depression and adjusted household budgets accordingly, the residents of economically secure districts generally did not require the financial support networks of the local community. In poorer sections of the city, where the Depression dealt its harshest blow, Jews relied heavily on the inner resources of the neighborhood. Neighbors often behaved like extended family, offering emotional and material aid to one another in times of economic distress. Jewish neighborhoods were genuine communities, nurturing a shared culture and providing informal networks for economic assistance and personal support.

For New York Jews, the neighborhood was an intimate and familiar community. Describing his Bronx neighborhood, Louis Kfare remembered, "The butcher, the baker, you knew everybody. You knew everybody on the floor. You knew everybody in the next building." Congregating at corner

19. *In Jewish neighborhoods, the streets were regular gathering places for men, women, and children. Such gatherings provided New York Jews with a genuine sense of community. Courtesy of the American Jewish Historical Society, Waltham, Massachusetts.*

stores (which housed the only telephones in some neighborhoods), young Jews sometimes earned a few pennies by calling local residents to the phone. "I used to hang around at the corner drugstore and when there was a phone call, you used to find the person. You'd get a nickel, three cents. If they were rich, you'd get a dime."[54] Being part of the neighborhood community meant not only knowing local residents by name, but also claiming the streets, parks, and corner stores as familiar territory. In New York's working-class districts, Jews made the streets a second home. "All the bank corners on Pitkin Avenue were gathering places," recalled Alfred Kazin. "The men would stand around for hours—smoking, gossiping, boasting of their children, until it was time to go home for the great Sabbath meal."[55] For the younger generation, the streets provided an instant community. The streets "were our salvation and sometimes our primary home," remembered one Brownsville youth.[56] "*Our* life every day was fought out on the pavement and in the gutter, up against the walls of the houses and the glass fronts of the drugstore and the grocery," Kazin explained.[57] "Back in Brownsville when you stepped out of your house there were forty or fifty kids on a corner. There were *always* some friends. You were surrounded by kids."[58] Middle-class Jews inhabited less congested streets, but their neighborhoods also expressed, consciously or unconsciously, the sense of Jewish community.

One WPA writer noted that on the Grand Concourse, "Saturday afternoon is the perfect time to watch a Jewish crowd pass in endless procession."[59] For New York Jews in the 1930s, the neighborhood was more than a geographical space; it was a community of familiar people and places "within the shadow of which we found protection of a kind."[60]

When New York Jews faced unemployment and financial setbacks, they turned first to the familiar support networks of their communities. Once family and extended kin resources had been expended, Jews looked to their neighbors for help. "It was a tough time," Jean Margolies nostalgically recalled about her Lower East Side community, "but people were close . . . family, even neighbors, they helped each other."[61] Irving Howe explained that in the East Bronx, "all through the years of the Depression our neighborhood clung to its inner supports of morale, its insistence upon helping its own in ways that were its own—which meant keeping as far as possible from the authority of the state."[62] Although many Jewish families did apply for government assistance, they still relied on neighborhood ties to help them extend scarce resources. Particularly in the city's poorer sections, Jews counted on the intimate networks of friends, family, and neighbors to sustain them during periods of hardship.

Most neighborhood assistance took place on a personal, informal level. During the 1930s, New York's Jewish enclaves were tightly knit communities where residents established close relationships with their neighbors. The intimacy of the community fostered an environment in which neighborly help was routine. When a family could not pay the rent or faced an eviction, neighbors sometimes joined forces, collecting nickels and dimes for rent money. The federal relief officials who reviewed the Berger family's application for additional welfare funds discovered that the family had survived by borrowing money from friends. "Mr. Berger says that the last time he applied for supplementation he was ashamed to say that he had borrowed money in order to manage," explained the investigator. "He says that he borrowed from a friend, $10 or $15 at a time as he needed it for rent, and then paid it back when he got his check. He now owes two friends $15 each. He pays a little on these debts and then borrows again when the need for rent or utility bills becomes acute."[63] Because many families in working-class Jewish neighborhoods had little money to spare, financial assistance was not always an option. But Jews regularly came to the aid of struggling families in other ways, by caring for children whose parents were working or by preparing occasional meals for neighbors. Moreover, community support was not always confined to the city's poorest neighborhoods. Although Tillie Spiegel's family was financially secure and lived comfortably on the Grand

Concourse during the Depression, she explained, "I used to feed a man that worked for the WPA. . . . I gave him lunch every day for months. . . . I tried to help as much as I could."[64] During the Depression, personal assistance between friends and neighbors took place throughout the city among many ethnic groups; the residential clustering of New York Jews simply laid the groundwork for the formation of intimate and interdependent Jewish communities where helping neighbors in need was a way of life.

Jewish businesses were also integral to the neighborhood community. In Jewish districts, local merchants and business owners generally knew their customers well. Jews who regularly patronized neighborhood grocers and retailers counted on receiving a liberal credit line. Rebecca Augenstein lived on Vyse Avenue near Bronx Park South during the 1930s. After her husband lost his job in the fur industry, the family was forced to accept home relief until he received a WPA position. Augenstein recalled that her neighborhood grocer was extremely generous in allowing her to buy on credit: "At the very beginning, before my husband started to work and earn a little money, the grocer said to me, 'You can "trust" all you want.' And so it was. I bought food to eat. He used to have a *tzetl* [list]. . . . Everything that I bought when I didn't have the money to pay, he used to mark it down. . . . Then, when we got the [relief] check every month, I went to the grocery and he took off what I owed him."[65] Relief investigators often discovered that families survived by living on credit. The relief record of the Berger family contains the following report: "Investigator visited the grocer to whom the Bergers owe a debt of $25. The grocer says that he extended credit to them because they are the type of family who try their best. He knows that they would not apply for assistance unless their need was great."[66] Especially during periods of unemployment, Jews depended on the ability to buy on credit. Arthur Granit recalled that in Brownsville, Jewish men "went to the corner grocery to borrow on the bills so that they could have carfare to go looking for jobs."[67] For Jews struggling under financial pressure, the credit line at the neighborhood store often provided a vital means to stretch the household budget when jobs and cash were scarce.

The Depression put thousands of independent merchants out of business, but those that survived remained an important part of the economy in Jewish neighborhoods. The spread of chain stores, such as A & P and Woolworth's, did present formidable problems for small merchants. By the 1930s, chain stores had moved into many Jewish neighborhoods and they had the resources and mass buying power to undersell independent store owners. Louis Kfare remembered that members of his Bronx community used to wait for the advertised specials at the local A & P. "It meant a lot when you could buy three pieces of soap for what you used to pay for two pieces. And the chicken was so much cheaper at A & P than it was at the kosher butcher."[68] Unable to buy in mass quantities and restricted by the New Deal's National Recovery Administration codes that regulated retail prices and employee schedules, independent shopkeepers struggled to keep their doors open. Even store owners who managed to stay afloat were often forced to limit customer credit. Increasingly squeezed by the pressure to maintain a cash flow while trying not to alienate customers who patronized their shops because of the ability to buy on credit, many small store owners lost their businesses.[69] During the worst years of the Depression, the number of retail purchases bought on credit declined as chain stores expanded and small stores reduced credit privileges or closed altogether.[70] These factors combined to threaten the survival of the neighborhood Jewish merchant and the loyalty of local customers. Yet, despite chain store expansion, the local merchant retained a central role within the neighborhood economy. The safety net offered by neighborhood grocers and retailers steadily weakened during the 1930s, but it had not collapsed entirely.

The granting of credit declined but did not disappear during the Depression. In her study of Depression-era Chicago, historian Lizabeth Cohen maintained that, "as the corner grocer offered less credit than usual or closed down entirely, customers were forced to turn elsewhere. Loyalty to the local storekeeper of one's ethnicity had once been greatly valued, but now people felt that he or she had let them down, just when they needed help most."[71] To be sure, thousands of small New York merchants suffered and many disappeared during the 1930s, but they continued to be an important neighborhood presence. The New York Jewish community, whose size and depth was unparalleled in other cities, supported a network of independent ethnic shopkeepers. New York Jews still counted on the neighborhood merchant, particularly in hard times. Many customers continued to shop at small grocery stores solely because they offered credit. That pattern seemed to extend to other Jewish communities as well. In Washington, D.C., some Jewish residents claimed that "the Jews are patronized because they give on credit whereas the chain stores do not."[72] National retail figures also suggested that buying on credit remained a significant, though declining, practice. The percentage of total retail sales for which credit was granted in grocery and combination stores declined nationally from 49 percent in 1929 to 43 percent in 1933; the figures for meat markets during the same years showed a decline from 39 to 32 percent. The trend toward chain store shopping and decreasing credit purchases was unmistakable, but independent ethnic merchants had not completely lost their place in the neigh-

20. *The expansion of chain stores constituted one of the greatest threats to independent Jewish merchants in the Great Depression. Grocery stores like this A & P had the resources and buying strength to undersell small store owners. Courtesy of the Berenice Abbott Collection, Museum of the City of New York.*

borhood economy. Although many Jews did look to the local A & P for better prices, those who needed credit still depended on the economic cushion available in the corner grocery store.[73]

If they were fortunate, Jewish tenants might also receive similar consideration from their landlords. Sympathetic landlords or those who had become friends sometimes allowed their tenants to delay paying rent. Rebecca Augenstein remembered the extraordinary kindness displayed by her landlord during the difficult years of the Depression. Augenstein explained that her landlord came to the apartment one day and found her very upset because she could not afford to buy a Boy Scout uniform for her son. She recalled, "He said to me, '*Host geveynt mayn kind?*' [Have you been crying, my child?] So I said, 'Yes,' and he said to me, '*Far vos host du geveynt?*' He said, 'Why did you cry?' and I said, 'My son, every boy in Boy Scouts has a uniform. He is the only one that has no uniform.' You know what he said to me, '*Gib mir nit di dire gelt.*' 'Don't give me the rent. Go out and buy that

21. *Neighborhood Jewish merchants faced formidable financial challenges in the Great Depression but remained a vital part of the local Jewish economy. This store advertised its willingness to accept relief tickets in both English and Yiddish. Courtesy of the American Jewish Historical Society, Waltham, Massachusetts.*

child a uniform. This is much more important. . . . As soon as you'll have, you'll pay.'"[74] Such acts of kindness were not the rule, but they did occasionally occur. Jean Margolies also remembered that her family's landlord was a friend, giving her brothers Bar Mitzvah gifts and celebrating her elementary school graduation.[75] Nevertheless, the landlord-tenant relationship in Jewish neighborhoods was frequently stormy, culminating in rent strikes and eviction resistance. In fact, the Depression is best remembered for the contentious disputes that erupted between Jewish landlords and Jewish tenants.

New York's Jewish neighborhoods functioned in a variety of ways during the Depression. They expressed the class divisions and cultural distinctions within the Jewish community, tangibly revealing the range of Jewish experience. The economic crisis had a vastly different impact in the city's working-class neighborhoods than it did in the more secure middle-class districts. By necessity, poorer Jewish sections relied more heavily on the support networks within their neighborhoods. Yet, because Depression-era Jews of all classes resided within particular sections of the city and supported a plethora of local ethnic institutions and businesses, their neighborhoods fostered strong and varied expressions of Jewish community, identity, and culture.

In the 1930s, the security provided by the neighborhood was particularly important to Jews facing an increasingly uncertain world. Beyond Jewish districts lay a city "brimming with politics and confusion" but often "brutal and ugly" in the midst of the Great Depression. Eager to embrace "that alien territory" beyond their neighborhoods, young Jews, in particular, yearned to discover the "truly American streets" outside Jewish districts.[76] The neighborhood supplied a firm foundation for New York Jews as they sought a wider world and immersed themselves in the broader social, economic, and political concerns of the Depression decade.

Jewish neighborhoods of the thirties provided a sheltering and protective environment, but they could also be expansive and highly politicized. During the Great Depression, New York's Jewish neighborhoods performed a dual role, offering the support networks of an intimate, self-contained community while also nurturing an ethnically based political culture that led from neighborhood streets to New Deal America.

# 5

## From Neighborhood to New Deal

*The way anywhere . . . led through the rival meetings on Pitkin Avenue. . . . From blocks away you could hear the Communist voice on the bank corner shouting into the great dark crowd, and some wistful Socialist voice on the opposite corner crying in rebuttal.*
—Alfred Kazin, *A Walker in the City*

*My father would take me up on Pitkin Avenue on Sunday morning. By ten A.M., the sidewalks were jammed with people having political discussions. A liberal Democrat was about as right as you got.*
—Anonymous, cited in Jonathan Rieder, *Canarsie*

The Jewish political landscape of the 1930s defies neat categorization. Jews, like other Americans, were caught up in the explosion of political ideas and movements that swept the United States during the Depression. With the country on the verge of economic and social collapse and people struggling to keep their households afloat, many Americans began searching for a new political order or at least looking for ways to repair the old one. Political campaigns emerged from various corners of the Jewish world in the 1930s. While Jewish college students engaged in political debates and campus demonstrations, Jewish neighborhoods erupted with rent strikes and cost-of-living protests. As the New Deal gained momentum and Roosevelt appointed Jews to prominent positions in government, Communist organizer Ben Gold guided a resurgent furriers union and longtime Socialists Sidney Hillman and David Dubinsky led the Amalgamated Clothing Workers and International Ladies Garment Workers' Union into the newly formed Congress of Industrial Organizations (CIO).[1] The dynamism of Jewish politics in the Depression decade derived precisely from the many distinct arenas of activity and the diversity of political ideas. Jewish radicalism flourished in the 1930s, in forms ranging from orthodox Marxism and Trotskyism to the more moderate brands of socialism. At the same time, an emerging coalition of liberals and New Deal Democrats joined forces in the mid-thirties, gradually garnering the support of most Jewish Socialists and eventually building a lasting marriage between Jews and the Democratic Party. Amid all the political energy and innovation of the decade, as New York Jews participated in movements from communism to New Deal liberalism, they wove new textures and patterns into the fabric of ethnic politics.

Political fervor was hardly new to Depression-era Jews. The political groundswell of the 1930s followed decades of vibrant Jewish political activity. Since the early twentieth century, New York Jews had cultivated a complex political culture, nurturing a constellation of political viewpoints. There was no solid Jewish voting bloc before the Great Depression; immigrant Jews cast votes for candidates across the political spectrum. But party loyalty had never been at the heart of Jewish politics. Most East European Jews shared a leftist perspective informed loosely by socialism and fortified by the Jewish labor movement's deep roots within the garment industry. Within the broad fellowship of the Left that encompassed much of the Jewish world, there had always been a range of competing movements and ideologies. Communists, Socialists, and anarchists, as well as liberals and social democrats, contended for the allegiances of New York Jews. None of these movements ever claimed more than a small group of devoted ideological followers, but the leftist tradition possessed a power and vitality within the Jewish community that extended beyond issues of party allegiance. For New York Jews, politics had never been limited to supporting a particular candidate or party, but rather involved a legacy of labor militancy and union activity, a lively dialogue of street-corner debates and evening lectures, and a running political commentary provided by the city's many Jewish newspapers. Long before the Depression's surge of political activity, politics suffused the lives of New York Jews. The challenges, innovations, and realignments of the Great Depression gave new dimensions to an already rich and varied ethnic political culture, reviving the Jewish tradition of grassroots political protests, reinvigorating Jewish radicalism, while also creating for the first time an overwhelming Jewish loyalty to a single American political party.[2]

There are a multitude of stories to be told about Jewish political life in the Depression era. This chapter concentrates specifically on the particular dynamics of neighborhood Jewish politics. Although organized party politics flourished in the 1930s, they may not be the most useful yardstick for measuring the evolving Jewish political culture of the Depression decade. For all the national developments that influenced Jewish politics in the 1930s—the resurgence of radical movements, the progress of labor unions, the rise of individual Jews in the New Deal Administration, and the new Jewish allegiance to the Democratic Party—national politics and party affiliation reveal only one aspect of Jewish political behavior. For Depression-era Jews, the neighborhood remained the center of life and a crucial arena of political activity. In some respects, neighborhood politics addressed the most immediate and basic needs of New York Jews. Faced with mounting pressures to pay rent, purchase food, and ward off the threat of eviction, Jewish neighbors rallied to fight for cost-of-living reductions and to terminate evictions. Neighborhood campaigns were often sporadic and situational, but they also reflected and even shaped broader political agendas of the Depression decade. On the neighborhood level, radical movements gleaned popular Jewish support, political clubs vied for power, and government welfare programs addressed the economic demands of local residents. Within the neighborhood, the political process involved a broad Jewish constituency, spanning gender and age boundaries. Neighborhood politics also reflected the internal clash of Jewish class interests, most notably in the battle between Jewish landlords and tenants. The cauldron of neighborhood politics provides a particular lens on the epoch's political changes, revealing the grassroots appeal of radicalism and the New Deal's role in altering Jewish political sentiments. A focus on neighborhood politics shifts attention from the ideological pronouncements of political parties and the actions of individual leaders to expose the more subtle transformations in Jewish political identities.

The Great Depression marked the height of political radicalism within American society and within the Jewish community. When the Depression arrived, New York Jews were already well acquainted with radicalism and left-wing movements. Young Jews of the 1930s were likely to have grown up

surrounded by neighborhood demonstrations, labor strikes, and political debates. When the deepening economic crisis and social disruption of the
Depression revived leftist politics across the nation, Jews displayed a particular affinity for radicalism. Membership in the Communist Party peaked in the
Depression years, with Jews constituting more than one-third of party membership in the New York area. Yet, despite significant overrepresentation in
left-wing movements, allegiance to radical parties remained a minority phenomenon within the Jewish community even during the height of Depression-era activism. For all the prominent Jewish radicals and intellectuals of
the period, most Jews embraced leftist politics less as a matter of ideological
commitment or party loyalty than as part of the social fabric of Jewish existence. "Socialism was a way of life, since everyone else I knew in New York was
a Socialist, more or less," Alfred Kazin explained. "I was a Socialist as so many
Americans were 'Christians'; I had always lived in a Socialist atmosphere."[3]
During the 1930s, as in earlier decades, many more Jews sympathized with
and sporadically participated in radical campaigns than actually affiliated with
left-wing political parties. In New York's Jewish neighborhoods, politics
flourished not in the voting booth or at party headquarters, but in the streets,
as a fundamental building block of Jewish culture and social life.[4]

By the 1930s, most Jews had become accustomed to street-corner debates and occasional protests as part of the rhythm of daily life. Since the
immigrant generation, neighborhood politics had been a hallmark of Jewish
communities. During the first decade of the twentieth century, Jewish immigrants organized some of the most persistent and effective rent strikes
and consumer boycotts. The Lower East Side witnessed scores of local
protests, most of them organized by friends and neighbors dissatisfied with
the high price of meat or the rising cost of rent.[5] Jewish neighborhoods
had both a history of and a tolerance for political activism. As Irving Howe
explained, "It was different in the Jewish neighborhoods. Attitudes of tolerance, feelings that one had to put up with one's cranks, eccentrics, ide-
alists, and extremists, pervaded the Jewish community. . . . Most of the
time the Jewish neighborhood was prepared to listen to almost anyone with
its characteristic mixture of interest, skepticism, and amusement." By the
thirties, street politics had become so routine in Jewish neighborhoods that
he recalled, "You might be shouting at the top of your lungs against refor-
mism or Stalin's betrayals, but for the middle-aged garment worker taking
a stroll after a hard day at the shop you were just a bright and cocky Jewish
boy, a talkative little *pisher*."[6] Street orations and political debates were the
substance of neighborhood life, particularly in working-class Jewish districts.
When economic conditions deteriorated and Jews began struggling to pay

"Lets play Cops and Communists . . ."

22. *This cartoon, printed in the City College humor magazine, poked fun at the pervasive radicalism of Jewish neighborhoods. Courtesy of the Archives of the City College of the City University of New York.*

rent and feed their families, the foundations for neighborhood protests were already in place.

The Great Depression witnessed a resurgence of grassroots demonstrations in Jewish districts. Neighborhood Jewish activism of the 1930s began in much the same way as earlier agitation—as a response to immediate economic problems. Most working and middle-class Jews were drawn to activism by "bread and butter" issues. Protests erupted when neighbors faced eviction, food became prohibitively expensive, wages fell below subsistence levels, and existing relief measures proved inadequate. Jews were by no means unique in organizing neighborhood protests during the Great Depression. Many neighborhoods and ethnic groups participated in local protests as a means of addressing pressing economic concerns and asserting a political voice. Most notably, Harlem's black community became a hotbed of grassroots communism, and its residents initiated some of the decade's most vigorous neighborhood campaigns. But an overwhelming majority of New York's rent strikes and consumer boycotts took place in Jewish neighborhoods. The Jewish tradition of militancy and public protest as well as the long history of using strikes as a tool of economic bargaining made neighborhood demonstrations particularly common in Jewish districts.[7] Jews had employed strikes, boycotts, and activism to combat economic injustice long before the 1930s, but the Depression created an unprecedented level of fiscal distress and social unrest, heightening the frequency and tenor of protest.

Evictions provided one of the first tangible signs of economic collapse and prompted some of the earliest responses in Depression-era neighborhoods. By the early thirties, the New York housing market had plummeted into a vicious cycle in which unemployed and underemployed workers, unable to pay rent, deprived landlords of income needed to meet mortgage debts and property taxes. Although some landlords allowed nonpaying tenants to remain in their apartments, others initiated costly eviction procedures, claiming that their own livelihoods were threatened. Irving Howe recalled that in the Bronx, "Hardly a day passed but someone was moving in or out. Often you could see a family's entire belongings—furniture, pots, pans, bedding, a tricycle—piled up on the sidewalks because they had been dispossessed."[8] On the Lower East Side, Jean Margolies described similar eviction scenes: "I used to see every day furniture on the street."[9] The number of evictions rose sharply during the early thirties. In 1932, New York courts issued two to three times more dispossess orders than they had in the years before the Depression. At the same time, police-enforced evictions affected only a small percentage of tenants; less than 5 percent of dispossess notices resulted in city marshals forcefully removing families from their apartments. More often, New Yorkers left voluntarily when they could not pay the rent, moving from one neighborhood to another, finding smaller apartments, relocating in poorer districts, or doubling-up with relatives or friends. Although most Jewish families weathered the Depression without being dispossessed, they could not escape the constant moving and recurring eviction scenes invading their neighborhoods. The economic uncertainty and persistent unemployment of the early thirties, coupled with the daily reality of watching friends and neighbors forced to leave their apartments, produced anger, discontent, and sometimes utter desperation, setting the stage for popular militance.[10]

In Jewish districts, evictions brought local residents to the streets to defend their dispossessed friends and neighbors. Alfred Kazin described a typical scene in Brownsville during "those first terrible winters of the depression, when we stood around each newly evicted family to give them comfort and the young Communists raged up and down the street calling for volunteers to put the furniture back."[11] When the police arrived to evict a family, neighbors would picket, block the doors, and move the furniture back into the apartment. In neighborhoods where evictions became regular events, men and women of all ages participated in the protests and developed strategies for resistance. One Brownsville Jewish youth reported how

23. *Eviction scenes like this one in the Bronx became commonplace in Depression-era New York. City marshals would pile a family's furniture and belongings on the sidewalk, and on many occasions, local residents would replace the furniture as quickly as the marshals could remove it. Courtesy of the United States History, Local History and Genealogy Division, New York Public Library, Astor, Lenox and Tilden Foundations.*

he and his friends approached the task: "Some of us would kick ash cans and create a general ruckus; this would divert the marshal and others of us would help the families put the furniture back up. It was a war of attrition."[12] Louis Kfare explained that fighting an eviction was spontaneous rather than planned, unfolding as an immediate response rather than a calculated political action. He recalled: "We formed a squad. As soon as the sheriff left, we would take the furniture and put it back in the apartment. It was actually not organized. What would happen is someone would come in and say somebody was put out on [the] street and so we would call this one, call that one . . . and say, 'How would you like to go help these people?' We did that—boys, girls, elderly men, young men, whoever. You just called somebody and said, 'Hey, let's put the furniture back in.'"[13] By 1932, eviction resistance had become an almost routine neighborhood event in working-class districts, bringing hundreds and sometimes thousands of people to the streets in protest.

Like many participants in eviction resistance, Louis Kfare was not affiliated with the Communist Party but contributed his efforts because he believed in the justice of the cause. "I never wanted to be a member [of the party]," he insisted. "I never joined, but I took part. . . . Something had to be done. . . . Those people were entitled."[14] Although committed Communists could always be found at the center of neighborhood protests, political allegiance was not the primary factor bringing Jews to the streets. In describing their motivation to stand up for neighbors, many participants unconsciously invoked a secular interpretation of the Jewish religious principle of *tikkun olam* (repair or improvement of the world). "We wanted to make a better world," insisted one Brownsville youth educated in the Socialist Workmen's Circle schools. "My original commitment to social justice was intensified by my struggles over the dispossessed."[15] While the transmission of shared religious and cultural values can be elusive to uncover, Jews sometimes explicitly outlined their collective ideological commitments. In 1934, the director of Brooklyn's Hebrew Educational Society formulated a list of "Jewish values" that should be inculcated in club members. The list included, "devotion to Charity (*Zedakah*) and a quick sympathy with oppressed humanity" as well as "the embodiment of the principle of social justice in the world."[16] The statements of Jewish protesters indicate that they had accepted and were motivated by such secular translations of religious teachings.[17] Regardless of party affiliation, ethnic traditions of social justice and activism coupled with personal conviction and the rebirth of political radicalism brought New York Jews to the streets to fight the evictions of their neighbors.

Organized party politics did play an important role in neighborhood protests. The Communist Party was the first to capitalize on the "spontaneous discontent" building in New York neighborhoods.[18] Communism was not as popular in Jewish neighborhoods as the familiar brand of Socialist politics. As Alfred Kazin explained, the Socialists "were one big Brownsville family," but the Communists "were not cozy at all."[19] The Communist movement entered the Depression decade with only a small following, but it seized on the popular resentment and spontaneous protests building in local neighborhoods.[20] In a tactical move, party leaders recognized that the plight of the unemployed and their struggle to pay the rent provided an opportunity to recruit new members by focusing on practical issues rather than ideological platforms. Organizing unemployed councils on a neighborhood level, Jewish Communists and party leaders addressed the daily concerns of local residents. The councils' agenda reached beyond representing the unemployed. Communist agitators won popular support by mobilizing eviction resistance and rent strikes and by arguing individual cases before relief authorities. Communists failed in their attempt to recruit a cadre of committed party members, but they did provide the necessary leadership to mobilize neigh-

24. Party headquarters at Union Square provided an organizational center for the resurgence of communism during the Depression, but the movement gained much of its momentum on the neighborhood streets of New York City. The Jewish Communist newspaper, the Freiheit, maintained its offices within party headquarters. Photograph by Charles Rivers, Museum of the City of New York.

borhood activism, particularly in Jewish districts.[21] Communist organizers were catalysts for many local demonstrations, but thousands of Jews not affiliated with the party enthusiastically participated in the mass rallies that swept through working-class Jewish neighborhoods. As one historian has explained, "In neighborhoods like these, Communists' appeals to strike involved both indigenous traditions of militancy and a certain desperate practicality—since people were getting evicted anyway, why not put up a fight?"[22] Steeped in a tradition of radicalism and bearing the burden of hard times, the Jews in neighborhoods like Brownsville and the North and East Bronx were prepared to take their demands for better living conditions to the streets.

In addition to the spontaneous protests that erupted after evictions, Jewish tenants also organized some of New York City's most sustained and dramatic rent strikes. The Depression marked the first time that striking tenants were not protesting rent increases, but rather demanding reductions commensurate with lower wage rates and rising unemployment. Beginning in January 1932, as the Depression steadily worsened, New York Jews initiated the first of several prolonged rent battles. In three separate buildings in the North Bronx, almost all tenants refused to pay rent until landlords agreed to stop evictions, reduce rent by 15 percent, officially recognize tenant committees, and make necessary repairs. Landlords rejected tenant demands and responded by initiating eviction procedures against strike organizers. When New York marshals arrived to carry out the dispossess orders, however, they encountered what one local paper called a "rent riot." At 2802 Olinville Avenue, four thousand angry protesters battled to prevent police officers from evicting seventeen families. Tenants and neighbors threw sticks and rocks from their windows, engaged in fist fights with the officers, and denounced them as "Cossacks." The *Bronx Home News* reported that as the marshals tried to evict the nonpaying tenants, "fists were flying, bricks and fragments of concrete were hurling through the air and nightsticks were describing forceful arcs. Some of the 'demonstrators' gained the roof of the apartment house and hurled stones upon the policemen." The newspaper described the relentless persistence of the protesters, recounting that, "as each piece of furniture was taken to the streets, tenants in other apartments fronting on the street uttered loud boos from their windows. Off in the distance, the boos were echoed by the crowd, which had finally been pushed back."[23] The collective struggle resulted in a compromise settlement for rent reduction and the return of evicted tenants. The Olinville Avenue strike, which brought out the entire reserve force of the Bronx police, was only the first in a series of massive, often violent protests to follow in the coming months.[24]

Who were these four thousand residents who stood in solidarity with their striking neighbors? The upper Bronx neighborhood housed a small, ideologically committed Communist population along with thousands of working- and middle-class Jews who had leftist sympathies but no firm party loyalties. To be sure, the North Bronx was one of the city's most powerful Communist strongholds. The Communist-led Upper Bronx Unemployed Council coordinated the rent strike, and its members fueled the protests. Striking tenants also received support from nearby residents of the Workers Cooperative Colony, the Jewish housing project dedicated to Communist principles. Like several other Jewish housing projects, Coop residents struggled and eventually failed to maintain collective ownership of their apartment house. Although the Great Depression "sowed the seeds of the Coops' eventual destruction as a cooperative," the board of directors

25. *Thousands of protesters rallied to prevent police from evicting four families at 665 Allerton Avenue. The Communist residents of the Coops lent their support to the neighborhood demonstration. This protest, like many others in the city, became violent as police clashed with the protesters. Courtesy of UPI/Corbis—Bettmann.*

managed to avoid evicting nonpaying tenants and instead the Coops became a key source of support for neighborhood strikes. "There were times when strikes broke out against the landlords in the neighborhood," recalled Coops resident Morris Wasserman. "We, the organized tenants of the Coops, would then go on demonstrations to help out those people." Members of the Coops assumed a leading role in neighborhood protests and often housed evicted tenants from other buildings.[25] Communist leadership and participation provided a crucial foundation for the protests, but most Bronx Jews were not Communists. Neighborhood demonstrations succeeded precisely because Jews not ideologically committed to radical causes proved willing to participate. When a group of tenants initiated a rent strike, hundreds and sometimes thousands of Jewish neighbors rallied to their defense. With small pockets of leftist agitators and significant support from local residents, Jewish neighborhoods were enormously successful in staging large demonstrations.[26]

In the early years of the Depression, tenant strikes and protests swept through the city's working-class Jewish districts. Only a few days after the first rent strike protests, a similar event erupted at nearby 665 Allerton Avenue. This time the police came prepared with reserve forces to carry out the court-ordered eviction of twelve families. When the police arrived at a rent strike, author Kate Simon explained, tenants called one another to action by "banging on apartment doors," yelling, "Come! Out! Run! Leave everything, the cossacks [cops] are here!"[27] At Allerton Avenue, more than one thousand local residents mounted a formidable resistance, despite the heightened police presence. The demonstrators employed the usual tactics: shouting and fighting with police, hurling objects from the windows, and doing everything possible to stop or at least hinder the dispossession. Neighbors failed to prevent the evictions at Allerton Avenue but sustained their protest nonetheless. Even after the police had cleared the block and begun moving furniture into the street, "many residents of the house, mostly women, leaned from the windows of their apartments, hissing and jeering at the marshal and his crew."[28]

Virtually every newspaper report about neighborhood demonstrations contained some reference to women's participation in the protests. The neighborhood was Jewish women's primary political turf, and they consistently emerged at the forefront of local activism. Since the early twentieth century, Jewish women had been active participants in rent strikes and consumer boycotts, struggles that centered around their homes and families. As in earlier protest movements, Jewish women became preeminent political actors in the Depression-era campaigns that took place within their neighborhoods. Taking the lead in neighborhood activism, women were often singled out by both the Jewish and the non-Jewish press for their militancy. English-language newspapers tended to describe female activists as hysterical and irrational. The *New York Times* reported that during the Allerton Avenue strike a "swarm of women" surrounded and threatened police officers until a mounted division arrived to disperse them.[29] The Yiddish press, more sympathetic to the strike cause, expressed greater approbation for women's contributions. "The strike is organized by the men but it is led by the women," explained the *Jewish Daily Forward*. "Such is the way in all the rent strikes that are going on today in greater New York. The women are the fighters, the pickets, the agitators. A remarkable bravery and battle-cheer is displayed by the women in the rent strikes."[30] Strikers often capitalized on the emotional and strategic value of placing women on the front lines. At one demonstration, protesters implored, "We need women to come out and sock the cops."[31] Whether fighting to lower the cost of food or defending evicted tenants, women were at the heart of the political crusades brewing in Jewish neighborhoods.

Married and middle-aged women, often removed from party politics and trade unions, led the public campaigns in Jewish neighborhoods. Describing the protesters, the *Forward* pointed out that "some of them are housewives from large families, mothers with small children that in a normal time could not go out of the house for a minute, but now they stand half the day in the picket line [and] attend strike meetings."[32] Not all Jewish wives committed their energies to the cause. As Kate Simon, who grew up in the Bronx Coops, recalled, "My mother never responded [to the strikers' call to protest]. She said the women who did were '*mishigoyim*' looking for excitement, anything to get away from their sinks and kids."[33] Yet, those women who chose to participate in the strikes often maintained informal neighborhood support networks that helped care for their families during the protests. During the demonstrations, women cooperated with child care and cooked meals for each other's families. When one woman was arrested on a Friday morning, the other women in her building took over Sabbath preparations for her family. The neighborhood context of rent strikes motivated women to fight for their homes and families and provided the support networks that enabled them to do so. Jewish women's participation in rent strikes indicates not only that the neighborhood was a welcome arena for women's political activity, but also that neighborhood activism was a collective enterprise, involving Jews of all ages and both genders.[34]

Because neighborhood politics had such an intimate, communal flavor, it is easy to overlook the sophisticated political and legal maneuvering and the heated Jewish class conflict that simmered on both sides of the picket lines. A particularly interesting feature of Depression-era rent strikes was that Jewish tenants usually found themselves clashing with Jewish landlords and property owners. During the 1920s, ethnic enclaves in Brooklyn and the Bronx were fostered, in part, by a strong Jewish presence in the building trades. Jewish builders, who often remained as owners and managers of their apartments, used ethnic connections to attract Jewish tenants to their buildings. When Jews migrated from Manhattan, they settled in new ethnic neighborhoods created largely by fellow Jews. In the 1920s, "'Jewish' avenues built by Jewish developers for a Jewish clientele" promoted the mobility of second-genera-tion Jews while nurturing ethnic solidarity.[35] But during the Depression, ethnic ties could not withstand the deep class divisions between landlord and tenant. Almost every rent strike and eviction protest that erupted in Jewish neighborhoods involved Jewish tenants and Jewish landlords.

The Depression was not the first time that conflicts between Jewish landlords and tenants had surfaced. Because middle-class and affluent Jews

*26. At this Williams Avenue apartment building in Brownsville, striking tenants carried signs in Yiddish and English. Both men and women, young and old, participated in the rent strikes. Courtesy of UPI/Corbis—Bettmann.*

invested heavily in New York real estate, while working-class Jews consistently led rent strike movements, Jews had occupied opposing sides of rent battles before. Especially after World War I, when the real estate market expanded and the number of Jewish apartment houses increased, Jewish landlords and Jewish tenants found themselves in rival camps. Tenant activism quieted somewhat in the 1920s after limited improvements in New York housing laws. But the Great Depression revived the tenant movement, and this time Jews were motivated by a desperate economic situation and fortified by a resurgent radical political climate that focused attention on issues of class. When the economic crisis rekindled the conflicts between Jewish landlords and Jewish tenants, they were already familiar adversaries with a long history of battling one another in the streets, courts, and legislative arena.[36]

Following the 1932 Allerton Avenue strike, landlords mobilized to thwart tenant activism. Besieged by "the grave and alarming rent strike situation," landlords claimed that the tenants' demand for rent reduction was economically untenable. "Few if any landlords would be able to meet mortgage payments today if they acceded to the rent reduction demands of the strikers."[37] In fact, landlords suffered considerably during the Depression. Evicting tenants proved costly for landlords who not only forfeited back rent, but had to shoulder legal fees and pay city marshals to carry out the court orders. Landlords also complained about the sharp increase in "tenants who move about from place to place without paying rent," living from one dispossess notice to the next. By the early thirties, the "skipping tenant evil" had grown into a sophisticated business, aided by moving companies willing to relocate a family on short notice, after midnight, and without divulging the new address to the previous landlord.[38] Responding to their own deteriorating economic fortunes, two predominantly Jewish associations of Bronx landlords formed protective organizations to fund the cost of evictions and maintain a blacklist of tenants known for inciting agitation. Max Osinoff, a Jewish owner of the Allerton Avenue building, insisted that Communist organizers were responsible for the strikes. Other landlords agreed, declaring that "property owners everywhere must combine to combat the evil forces of mobocracy, bolshevism, communism and sovietism with all the vigor and power of their numerical strength."[39] By evicting and refusing to rent to Communist agitators, they hoped to diffuse the growing unrest in their neighborhoods. Their actions, however, often had the opposite result, fueling the fires of Jewish tenant protests.[40]

The feverish landlord-tenant disputes in Jewish neighborhoods were seldom openly addressed as intra-ethnic conflicts, but in fact, the key players on both sides of almost every struggle were Jews. Whether or not they admitted it publicly, Jewish communal leaders interpreted the battle between landlords and tenants as a Jewish issue. Concerned that the highly publicized strikes and protests might exacerbate an already dangerous anti-Semitic climate, Jewish leaders hoped to reach an amicable settlement between the warring factions. Drawing on an ethnic tradition of arbitration, a group of prominent Jews attempted to forge a compromise agreement in the 1932 Allerton Avenue strike. Arbitration had seldom been employed in rent strikes, but New York Jews had a history of settling ethnic labor disputes within a Jewish context. In the 1910s, leaders of the short-lived New York Kehillah, an organization designed to provide a comprehensive communal structure for the city's Jews, successfully mediated several strikes between Jewish employers and employees in the garment industry.[41] As the conflict between Jewish landlords and tenants grew more explosive, the city's Jewish leaders decided to try mediation. They formed an ad-hoc arbitration committee, hoping to resolve the dispute between the Osinoff Brothers (the landlords) and the striking tenants. Led by Benjamin Antin, a former state senator, the committee also included Bernard Deutsch, president of the American Jewish Congress, Rabbi Jacob Katz of the Montefiore Congregation, M. Maldwin Fertig, president of the Bronx YMHA, and other leading

Bronx Jews. Despite their best efforts, Jewish leaders were unable to negotiate an agreement between the Osinoffs and the tenants' committee. When
talks broke down, residents resumed their strike and landlords returned to
heavy-handed attempts to squelch tenant activism. (Only a week after the
failed arbitration, however, Allerton Avenue tenants agreed to a compromise
settlement that included some rent reduction, though not the full 15 percent
originally demanded.) Throughout the strikes and arbitration, none of the
tenants, landlords, nor negotiators candidly addressed the conflict as an
ethnic issue. Although the formation of a Jewish arbitration committee
suggests the desire to solve the dispute in a Jewish context, both tenants and
landlords felt no compunction to settle their differences within the community, demonstrating a clear willingness to take their battle to the courts and
streets of New York City. At the height of the Depression-era protests,
Jewish landlords and tenants viewed each other, not primarily as fellow Jews,
but as class rivals and political adversaries.[42]

Despite the refusal to view the conflict as a Jewish issue, neighborhood
activists regularly made use of communal institutions and drew on Jewish
tradition. On an informal level, local synagogues intervened in the rent
strikes, sometimes donating rent money to unemployed tenants or attempting to dissuade landlords from evictions. Community institutions also lent
support to the organized political efforts of neighborhood residents. Saul
Parker, a founder of the Washington Heights Unemployed Council, remembered that the local YMHA provided a hospitable environment for the council's regular meetings. He and his comrades organized the council by
distributing circulars throughout the neighborhood and inviting all those
with rent, relief, or employment problems to come to the Y and seek help.[43]
In addition to relying on Jewish institutions, Jewish activists also fortified
their claims by invoking Jewish values and traditions. Striking tenants, for
example, often defended their demand for rent reduction as a campaign for
social justice, maintaining that impoverished residents suffered unfairly at
the hands of wealthy landlords. Broadening the implications of their struggle, Jewish activists described the rent campaign as a means of "building a
better world," of furthering *tikkun olam*.[44] The rhetoric of Jewish protesters
contained occasional Yiddish aphorisms and frequent references to Jewish
texts and teachings, which protesters used to support the legitimacy of their
efforts. Even as Jewish radicals were eager to move their campaigns beyond
the bounds of the Jewish community, their political actions remained firmly
rooted in the shared language and culture of Jewish neighborhoods. In fact,
Jewish activists did not hesitate to employ Jewish religious symbols in their
battles. At the lengthy rent strike conducted in the Bronx Jewish neighbor-

hood of Longfellow Avenue, one strike leader roused residents to protest one morning by blowing a *shofar* through the neighborhood streets, clearly using a religious call to action to initiate a secular demonstration.[45]

The struggle between Jewish landlords and tenants, though shaped by the ethnic character of the neighborhood, was not resolved within the Jewish community. The 1932 rent strike at Longfellow Avenue precipitated a legal battle between striking Jewish tenants and a predominantly Jewish landlords' organization known as the Greater New York Taxpayers Association. The Longfellow Avenue rent strike lasted for weeks, involved five apartment buildings, and resulted in successive waves of evictions. Like its predecessors, the strike erupted in violence on several occasions. For weeks, angry protesters (ranging in number from fifteen hundred to three thousand) battled police, threw milk bottles and paper bags filled with water from windows and rooftops, and monopolized the attention of the Bronx police force. During one demonstration, the crowd recognized William Weinberg, one of the landlords, and chased him through the neighborhood streets for several blocks.[46] While such episodes suggest an intimate communal battle, the landlord-tenant conflict extended well beyond the neighborhood arena to occupy the agendas of city courts and politicians. The Greater New York Taxpayers Association, which had been struggling for a means to curb tenant activism, took its case to court. Representing Weinberg, the association successfully petitioned for a court-ordered picketing injunction at Longfellow Avenue. Declaring the suit, "a signal victory . . . in curbing the activities of those who would seek to create rent disturbances," Jewish landlords took the offensive against striking tenants.[47]

Jewish tenants did not retreat from strikes and proved willing to wage their campaign in court as well. One of the most celebrated legal battles grew out of a dramatic rent strike conducted in the Sholem Aleichem apartments, a Jewish cooperative housing project founded by Jews dedicated to preserving secular Jewish culture. Located on Giles Place just below Van Cortland Park in the Bronx, the Sholem Aleichem apartments had been established by working-class Jews who fell on hard times in the 1930s and found themselves battling a private landlord in the midst of the Depression. In late August of 1932, most of Sholem Aleichem's 212 families agreed to withhold rent until landlord Louis Klosk met their demands for rent reduction, official recognition of the tenants' committee, and other improvements.[48] Sholem Aleichem strikers, most of whom were Socialists, looked to their own party's institutions for support. In the post–World War I era, Socialists had taken the lead in tenant activism, establishing tenant associations throughout the city that at one time represented as many as 100,000 New York residents.

# TO THE TENANTS OF THE BRONX

## Organize, for rent reduction
## Organize, for decent housing

Your wages have been cut . . . Why not cut your rent?
Your families have been burned in fire traps . . . Why
don't you fight for decent homes?

**WORKERS OF THE BRONX
TENANTS OF THE BRONX**
# Unite

*Fight For Lower Rents . . . Battle Against Depressions*

Join the Bronx Tenants Emergency League
Free   Headquarters   . . .   Free   Legal   Advice

## Large Mass Meeting

*at the* Ambassador Hall, 3875 - 3rd Avenue
*Near Claremont Parkway*

### Wednesday May 11th, 1932 at 8:30 p.m.

*SPEAKERS:*

| | |
|---|---|
| Judge Jacob Panken | Aaron Levenstein |
| Samuel Orr | Henry Fruchter |
| Louis Hendin | Matthew M. Levy, *Chairman* |

*Auspices:* Bronx Tenants Emergency League
908 Prospect Avenue, Bronx

27. *Circular distributed by the Bronx Tenants Emergency*
*League. Courtesy of General Research Division, New York*
*Public Library, Astor, Lenox and Tilden Foundations.*

Although their militancy had moderated in the 1920s, tenant leagues blazed
the trail that brought residents' concerns into the legal and legislative arena.
When the rent strike movement regained momentum during the Depression, many residents, including those at the Sholem Aleichem apartments,
again looked to their Socialist-backed tenant leagues for representation.[49]

The Sholem Aleichem rent strike was conducted under the auspices of
the Bronx Tenants Emergency League. The league established a permanent
office and secured legal representation from New York attorney, Matthew
Levy. Levy shared a law practice with the prominent Socialist, Jacob Panken,

a former municipal court judge whom Irving Howe called one of "the big guns of Jewish socialism."[50] While Levy argued successive tenant cases in court, Panken contributed his oratorical skills at mass meetings and used his influence to make sure the English-language press learned about the plight of Sholem Aleichem tenants. During the strike, Panken charged that the New York Home Relief Bureau was "using relief as a club to compel 212 tenants of the apartment house . . . to desist from the rent strike." He claimed that city relief officials checked the party affiliation of applicants and discriminated against Socialists.[51] Meanwhile, as Matthew Levy appealed each eviction and clashed repeatedly with New York judges, Sholem Aleichem tenants moved their picket lines from the neighborhood to the courthouse. During one court session in which forty-eight tenants faced eviction, twenty-five truckloads of protesters arrived outside the Bronx Municipal Court to voice their opposition.[52]

The Sholem Aleichem rent strike, like most in the city, concluded with a compromise settlement. Landlord Louis Klosk agreed to a rent reduction, the establishment of an official tenants' committee, and the reinstatement of some evicted tenants. Residents also secured a one-month grace period for rent, an additional reduction for use in unemployment relief, as well as other concessions. In return, tenants promised to pay the rent owed to Klosk in installments. Matthew Levy declared the settlement a "complete victory for the tenants" and insisted that the tenants league would continue its campaign to organize area residents.[53] The Sholem Aleichem strike demonstrated not only the organizational strength of the tenants, but also the political sophistication of their efforts. Jewish tenant activism was rooted in, but not confined to, the ethnic neighborhood. During the Depression, local residents took their demands from neighborhood streets to municipal courts and finally to state and federal authorities.

Legal maneuvers ultimately proved more successful for landlords than for tenants, but not due to lack of effort on the part of unemployed councils and tenants leagues. Even after the settlement of the Sholem Aleichem strike, the Bronx Tenants League remained a vigilant advocate of tenant rights. Representing the league, Matthew Levy petitioned the legislature to enact liberal changes in New York housing policy. The list of demands included extending the time to execute eviction warrants from five days to six months, requiring that landlords have prospective tenants before evicting current ones, and allocating additional funds for rent relief.[54] Not surprisingly, landlords lobbied forcefully against such legislation, denouncing it as nothing more than a Communist ploy to "[make] it mandatory upon apartment owners to run free lodging houses for unemployed tenants."[55]

Jewish property owners, like their non-Jewish counterparts, were truly fearful that further tenant agitation would mean financial ruin. By 1933, eviction resistance and rent strikes had reached epidemic proportions throughout the city, particularly in Jewish neighborhoods. Many landlords had already conceded rent reductions which, according to the Greater New York Taxpayers Association, resulted in 40 percent of Bronx property owners falling behind in tax payments by the close of 1932. New York's overextended relief system also placed serious strains on landlords. In the early years of the Depression, the city's Home Relief Bureau gave relief recipients rent vouchers, but landlords often encountered delays and even nonpayment when they attempted to redeem them. Moreover, welfare policy required that tenants be evicted before becoming eligible for rent relief, so that landlords had to incur eviction expenses and loss of income before receiving even the promise of rent payment.[56]

Given their perception that New York government had already made them bear an unfair portion of the relief burden, property owners felt doubly beleaguered by the rent strike movement. Landlords attempted to suppress tenant activism by closely monitoring so-called dangerous tenants. Through their tenant checking bureaus, property owners investigated the backgrounds of prospective tenants and tried to prevent "rent-strikers and their ilk from obtaining apartments."[57] At the same time, landlords launched an offensive campaign to make rent strikes illegal. "While peaceful picketing may be sanctioned by the law in its application to labor strikes," declared property owners, "it should never be tolerated against housing." In March 1933, New York Corporation Counsel Arthur Hilly supported the landlords' position, informing the city police commissioner that "there is no such thing known to the law as a 'Rent Strike'"[58] The prohibition against rent strikes dealt a serious blow to tenant activism. Occasional prosecution of individual demonstrators combined with the blacklisting of strike organizers diminished the spark of the rent strike movement. Matthew Levy and others like him continued to represent tenant interests and to argue the legality of rent strikes, but landlords appeared to have gained the upper hand in the legislative arena. Although sporadic protests erupted throughout the 1930s, eviction resistance and rent strikes never again reached the feverish pitch of 1932 and 1933.[59]

The implementation of New Deal programs coincided with the decline of the rent strike movement. With the federal government coming to the aid of unemployed workers and providing financial assistance for food and rent, the terms and targets of neighborhood politics gradually began to change. During the Depression, New York Jews, like other Americans, began to look to the federal government for help. At the height of their rent disputes, Jewish landlords and tenants agreed on one issue—that New York City's inadequate relief system was to blame for much of their troubles. Just as landlords attacked ill-conceived welfare policies for increasing their costs, tenants insisted that better relief provisions would prevent evictions and strikes by enabling residents to pay their rent. None of this was exclusive to the Jewish community. Government welfare, like so many New Deal programs, transformed the relationship between individuals and the state and encouraged Americans to make demands of their government. Although Jews were hardly alone in experiencing the sweeping social and political changes of the Depression, the new role of government did alter the tactics and ultimate outcomes of Jewish neighborhood activism. In the thirties, ethnic neighborhood politics retained its grassroots strength, cultural traditions, and concern with immediate economic problems, but with the emergence of state relief and the New Deal, neighborhood efforts extended beyond strictly local concerns, often succeeding by mediating between the neighborhood and the government. Jewish activists demanded not only solutions to existing problems but also intervention and lasting change from local and federal authorities. Depression-era Jewish activism remained rooted in the neighborhood, while at the same time providing a bridge that led to a changing American political arena.

As New Deal programs brought greater respectability, increased funding, and improved organization to the welfare system, the Home Relief Bureau became the prime target of protests throughout the city. In their neighborhoods, Jewish activists insisted that the government take responsibility for providing adequate rent allocations so that evictions and rent strikes would be unnecessary. Although they directed their demands at the government, Jewish protesters continued to rely on neighborhood-centered events and familiar militant tactics. At neighborhood relief bureaus, which were often housed in local schools, activists picketed, made speeches, barricaded the doors, and staged sit-ins.[60] Protesters "pounded and kicked" on the locked doors of one relief bureau until police dragged them away. In Brownsville, "bottles were thrown and fists flew" outside the local relief station as nine Jewish protesters fought with police attempting to quell their demonstration. Violence and arrests became regular events outside New York's home relief bureaus, and as had been the case in rent strikes, Jews were disproportionately represented among those arrested throughout the city and Jewish women remained at the forefront of the protests.[61]

As the New Deal gained momentum, the radical movements that had galvanized neighborhood strikes also turned their attention to the public welfare system. In fact, leftist agitators performed some of their most important work as advocates for relief applicants. Unemployed councils consistently pressured relief bureau officials to serve the needs of neighborhood residents. Taking even the smallest case before relief authorities, the councils responded to "individual grievances on [an] incredibly primitive level."[62] Saul Parker described one incident in which residents informed the Washington Heights Unemployed Council that they had received spoiled surplus potatoes from the relief bureau; the council brought the potatoes back to City Hall and put an end to their distribution. On another occasion, when council representatives learned that local WPA workers had not received Friday paychecks, they arranged for a special relief payment that same day. Relief stations were located in local neighborhoods where activists could respond to individual needs, often by mounting platforms and informing the entire neighborhood when any relief applicant had not been treated fairly. Because of their successful efforts, unemployed councils received unofficial recognition as bargaining agents for relief recipients. Anna Taffler, a Depression-era Jewish activist, remembered that council members met weekly with relief authorities and struggled to secure better provisions on a case-by-case basis. Neighborhood activists succeeded, just as they had during the height of eviction resistance, by representing the immediate and basic needs of local residents. Moreover, as the welfare system improved, government officials responded more favorably to activist demands. In 1933, New York Mayor O'Brien ordered city marshals to notify relief bureaus whenever a family had been dispossessed so that rent consultants would be able to provide assistance and prevent the eviction. In Jewish and non-Jewish neighborhoods alike, radical organizations succeeded in meeting the needs of local residents by forging a working relationship with the government.[63]

The demands made on the government welfare system represented both the strength and ultimate weakness of leftist agitation in Jewish neighborhoods. Committed Jewish radicals, like Communists and Socialists throughout the city, were a forceful lobby for improving government welfare policy. Arguing for cash relief instead of food and rent tickets, local activists rallied broad communal support by defending the dignity of the unemployed and insisting on better relief provisions. They pressured local and federal officials to increase work relief programs, regarded as a far more respectable alternative to the "dole."[64] Yet, as the government responded to activist pressure, provided more services for the unemployed, and enacted sweeping national insurance programs, radical leaders lost much of their popular support. The Roosevelt Administration's far-reaching work relief programs along with passage of the Wagner Act and Social Security Bill clearly reduced the momentum of the leftist movement. New Deal programs relieved the acute financial distress that had attracted average Jews to radical campaigns. Although local Jews did not completely retreat from activism, the epidemic quality of mass neighborhood protests diminished with improved relief provisions. Most Jews had never had a true ideological stake in the political agendas advanced by the Socialists and Communists; they joined radical campaigns that appealed to their ethnic activist tradition and, more important, addressed their immediate economic problems. The reformist accomplishments of the New Deal undermined the activist spark by meeting radical demands for federal jobs programs and unemployment assistance. Although radical organizers had not intended to do so, they ultimately had greater success in mobilizing Jews within the community to make demands of the existing government than in building support for radical alternatives.[65]

At the same time, New Deal programs by no means brought an end to Jewish neighborhood movements organized around basic subsistence issues. Throughout the Depression, Jewish activists, particularly Jewish women, conducted bread and meat strikes whenever prices became too inflated for the budgets of working families. Jewish women had led such campaigns for years, but by the mid-thirties, spontaneous local movements began to assume a broader, more sophisticated political character, extending beyond the confines of individual neighborhoods. For example, in May 1935, Jewish women initiated a citywide meat boycott, calling for a reduction in prices of ten cents per pound.[66] The high price of kosher meat had plagued Jewish consumers for years, precipitating sporadic consumer boycotts for more than three decades. By the 1930s, Jewish women had gained a generation of experience in leading consumer protests and brought their seasoned talents to the 1935 campaign.[67] Violence erupted on several occasions as strikers assaulted "scabbers," people seen purchasing meat during the boycott.[68] Willing to face arrest for their cause, women waged the strike as a means to fulfill their economic responsibilities within the home. The high price of kosher meat was particularly devastating to household economies during the Depression. As the *Forward* explained, "With the small wages that workers bring home today, it is absolutely impossible for their wives to buy what is needed at home."[69] As household managers, Jewish women viewed inflated meat prices as a threat to their vital economic role and fought on behalf of their families' survival. But this campaign was neither a limited action on the part of housewives nor an effort confined solely to the Jewish community. Clara Lemlich Shavelson and Rose Nelson, two leading Jewish radicals and veterans of women's consumer movements, organized the protests through the United Council of Working Class Women (UCWW), a group that included women from across the United States and from different ethnic and racial backgrounds. Jewish women, who predominated in the organization, initiated the national campaign in their own neighborhoods, areas where the tradition of militancy and protest had been firmly established and where local consumer actions invariably met with enormous popular support. Conducted under the banner of the City Action Committee Against the High Cost of Living, the protests began in the Jewish neighborhoods of Brighton Beach and Coney Island and quickly spread throughout the city. Like other grassroots protests of the 1930s, the kosher meat boycott was a locally based effort that centered around the home and family, but its reach extended well beyond the neighborhood arena.

The boycott that began in kosher butcher shops rapidly expanded to nonkosher shops as well. The strike gained support in New York's other ethnic neighborhoods, particularly in Harlem, and ultimately took hold in cities across the United States, as working women united to combat a shared consumer problem. Jewish women initiated and predominated in the campaign, but the UCWW was an umbrella organization that included women's groups from the Black community, Communist and Socialist associations, as well as settlement houses and mutual benefit societies. In transcending ethnic boundaries and linking the grassroots efforts of several neighborhoods, the 1935 boycott exhibited a breadth of organization not evident in earlier protests. The campaign also reflected a sophisticated political understanding on the part of Jewish women. Women referred to themselves as "consumers" and scheduled meetings with city officials, including the Commissioner of Markets. They demonstrated a clear grasp of market economy, emphasizing that retailers also suffered from high prices because housewives purchased less meat. Jewish women targeted wholesalers, known as the Meat Trust, for artificially inflating the price of meat. Pearl Kaufman, leader of the North Bronx section of the boycott, quoted Department of Agriculture statistics on meat production to support the strikers' contention that wholesalers were hoarding large quantities of meat in order to drive prices higher. Clara Shavelson, along with her colleagues in the working women's movement, ultimately took their case to Washington to lobby for federal intervention and the implementation of permanent price-control measures.[70]

The 1935 meat boycott ultimately achieved limited success. After being closed for a week, retail butcher shops gradually began reopening despite the ongoing protests. Some shops reduced poultry prices by as much as nine cents a pound, but the Meat Trust remained a powerful force. Two years later, meat retailers themselves declared a strike against wholesalers for setting inflated prices. Not until government regulators did what women had demanded and began to apply strict guidelines to the meat industry did price gouging become a less pressing consumer problem. Nevertheless, the meat boycott demonstrated women's evolving political role as local organizers. Jewish women understood the importance of securing government intervention in the food industry and during the New Deal era began directing their protests to government authorities. In the 1930s, women's activism remained rooted in the neighborhood, but local campaigns reached beyond neighborhood and even ethnic boundaries. Jewish women cooperated with other women's groups and made demands of government officials, demonstrating heightened political consciousness and a new level of organizational sophistication. Like the rent strike movement and campaign for relief, the meat boycott testified not only to women's political prowess, but also to the expanding political sphere of neighborhood Jewish activism in the thirties.[71]

The dispute over kosher meat prices, much as the conflict between Jewish landlords and Jewish tenants, emerged but was not resolved within an ethnic setting. Throughout the Depression, New York Jews continued to draw on the tradition of neighborhood activism, but their collective action increasingly reached beyond the neighborhood to the federal government. Whether arguing for better relief provisions or fighting for price controls, Jewish activists, like other Americans of the Depression era, came to expect their government to take a more active role in securing their economic welfare. The Depression crisis and the creation of New Deal programs encouraged people of all ethnic backgrounds to demand federal solutions to the problems of daily subsistence. "It is very possible," observed historian Lizabeth Cohen, "that the New Deal's impact should be measured less by the lasting accomplishments of its reforms and more by the attitudinal changes it produced in a generation of working-class Americans who now looked to Washington to deliver the American dream."[72] The federal government, once a distant and elusive entity in the eyes of immigrants and their children, seemed closer and more receptive to its Jewish citizens as the Depression wore on. Yet, even as the New Deal altered the political perceptions and loyalties of New York Jews, Jewish political culture retained its ethnic center and neighborhood foundation. Using local organizing strategies and articulating support for the new Democratic agenda as a fulfillment of Jewish political ideals, Jews extended their ethnic territory to the emerging political landscape of New Deal America.

Long before the national Jewish-Democratic coalition took shape under Franklin Roosevelt, New York politics revolved around the city's many ethnic subcultures. Prior to the Great Depression, Jews proved to be an elusive group for political candidates. New York Jews spread their votes across the party spectrum, supporting candidates on an individual basis and evaluating their particular positions, rather than demonstrating loyalty to any single party. Jews voted for Socialists, Democrats, and Republicans and, in several elections, backed Gentile candidates over Jewish politicians. The Jewish vote was neither ethnocentric nor party oriented; it coalesced around a liberal and leftist core of values that included a strong universalist strain, a concern with urban issues, and an emphasis on social reform and minority rights. As many historical accounts have documented, Roosevelt's New Deal succeeded in capturing Jewish allegiance by appealing to Jewish ideological commitments and responding to the economic and social demands of urban Jews who looked to the government to come to their aid in the Great Depression. But Jewish devotion to the Democratic Party was not formed through an abstract consolidation of ideological beliefs. Jewish behavior in national electoral politics took shape within the context of ethnic urban neighborhoods. New York Jews formulated what became an overwhelming national political profile through the familiar channels of local political networks, gradually linking their ethnic agendas with the platforms of Roosevelt and the Democratic Party.[73]

The Jewish voting behavior evident in national elections was shaped in the daily interactions and associational networks of the neighborhood. Grassroots activism was only one of many paths that Jews used to exercise their political voice. Radical protests generally erupted in working-class Jewish neighborhoods, but local political clubs could be found in virtually every Jewish neighborhood, providing Jews across the class spectrum with an ethnic setting in which to participate in the political process. Political clubs formed the backbone of ethnic politics in New York City, combining the recreation and friendship of social organizations with the tools of political leverage and representation. New York political clubs reflected the city's diverse class and ethnic composition and often facilitated the ability of ethnic groups to influence and benefit from the political system. Within the Jewish community, political clubs could be found from the upper-middle-class enclaves of Eastern Parkway to the tenements of Brownsville. Democratic, Socialist, and even Communist political clubs dotted Jewish neighborhoods, with radical clubhouses predominating in working-class districts. New York's clubs blended political polemics with social activities. Political scientist Roy Peel, who evaluated the city's political clubs in the thirties, noted the ethnic tone that distinguished the social climate of each clubhouse. "The Italian clubs in Queens and Brooklyn give '[card] parties' frequently," Peel reported. "The Jews are great lovers of pinochle, and wherever a club has a large Jewish following, small groups of men may be found enjoying their favorite pastime."[74] In the informal atmosphere of their neighborhood political clubs, Jews became a part of New York politics. Like other Jewish political expressions of the decade, political clubs served as an ethnic vehicle that eased the path of Jewish political integration in the Depression era.

Within New York's ethnic political structure, the neighborhood Jewish political club functioned as a means for promoting individual Jews to public office and for securing the "Jewish vote." Although New York Jews unequivocally maintained that "elections should be determined exclusively on an American basis rather than on the basis of the alleged separate interests of any religious or racial group," they did not hesitate to voice their collective concerns in the political arena.[75] During the Depression, New York's Jewish political clubs represented a wide range of Jewish interests, including formally protesting instances of job discrimination. Several Jewish assemblyman and Democratic Party leaders began their political careers in local clubhouses, garnering communal support and voicing ethnic interests in the party. For example, Judge Nathan Sobel, who began his career in an Eastern Parkway Jewish political club, worked diligently to increase Jewish representation in Brooklyn's Democratic organization during the 1930s. In addition to providing a start for Jewish political leaders, local political clubs helped many New York Jews secure government jobs. Lillian Gorenstein recalled that her husband, Saul, found a WPA position after befriending a captain in the local Democratic club. "Saul began to hang around the Democratic Club all the time, leaving in the morning with [the captain] and returning in the late evening after having eaten a supper of frankfurters on rolls free of charge. Eventually he got a job as a time-keeper for a group of WPA workers in Bronx Park."[76] Within the social, grassroots atmosphere of the local clubhouse, New York Jews secured their share of political favors, power, and representation.

The drive for ethnic representation had its unsavory moments. In 1930, Maurice Biederman, founder of the Judea Democratic Club of Brooklyn, formally brought to New York Mayor Walker's attention the plight of Jews who "are denied this opportunity [to work] simply because they are Jews." But Biederman's efforts were not entirely altruistic. He had founded the club in order to facilitate his own political advancement and was ultimately pressured by Jewish leaders to eliminate the title "Judea" from the club's name and remove the implication of any formal association with the Jewish community. The articulation of ethnic influence and political power was often a tenuous affair, but neighborhood organizations and local representatives enabled Jews to negotiate their position within the political machinery of New York City.[77]

Jews avoided presenting themselves as a segregated or parochial political constituency, but on a fundamental level, New York politics functioned by courting ethnic groups. During the worst years of the Depression, Irish and Italian, as well as Jewish, political clubs funded the distribution of thousands of Passover packages to needy Jewish families in an effort to win the loyalty of the Jewish community. The Thomas Farley Club, for example, provided Jewish residents of its Fourteenth Assembly District with Passover provisions, "explaining to Italian and Irish householders that those of Jewish faith were first in line for the matzoths and other groceries." Political clubs made similar overtures to the non-Jewish population during Christmas and other holidays. Through acts of charity, political club leaders attempted to secure the allegiance of each ethnic group by maintaining "at small cost their reputations for generosity."[78] During the 1930s, neighborhood constituencies remained the basic building blocks of New York politics, enabling Jews to enter the political process through local associational networks. For Jews of all economic classes, neighborhood-centered political activity paved the road that led from their ethnic residential enclaves to the larger political arena.

As their political voice strengthened in the Depression years, New York Jews walked a fine line between ethnic representation and the perception of undue Jewish influence. By the 1930s, Jews were more willing to assert their right to participate in government. When Samuel Levy became Manhattan Borough president, *The Day*'s editors openly proclaimed that "there are close to two million Jews in New York City who are entitled . . . [to] their share in the government of the city."[79] But at the same time, in the mounting anti-Semitic climate of the Depression, many Jews worried about the potential backlash of Jewish prominence in government. With Herbert Lehman serving successive terms as governor of New York and several Jews winning positions in state and city government, Jewish politicians and newspapers frequently articulated fears about the dangers of any appearance of Jewish overrepresentation. The appointment of Jews to positions in the Roosevelt administration only exacerbated those fears. In 1938, already coping with accusations that the New Deal was a "Jew Deal," a group of prominent Jews, including Secretary of the Treasury Henry Morgenthau, Jr. and *New York Times* publisher, Arthur Hays Sulzberger, urged Roosevelt not to appoint Felix Frankfurter to the Supreme Court. They believed that with Louis Brandeis already serving as a justice, "putting a second Jew on the Court would only play into the hands of anti-Semites at home and abroad."[80] The

*"WHAT EVERY CONGRESSMAN SHOULD KNOW"*

28. *Charges of undue Jewish influence plagued American Jews in the 1930s. Anti-Semitic groups regularly claimed that Jews controlled government, frequently labeling the "New Deal" a "Jew Deal." Courtesy of the American Jewish Historical Society, Waltham, Massachusetts.*

position of Jews in government remained a tense and highly contested source of debate within the Jewish community throughout the Depression. Although some Jews feared the anti-Semitic repercussions of Jewish visibility in politics, others believed that Jews in positions of high office provided the best defense against the claims of anti-Semites. During Lehman's 1932 gubernatorial campaign, the editors of *The Day* reminded readers "to consider the effect of the election of a Jewish governor of the State of New York on the status of Jews throughout Europe," insisting that a Lehman victory would signal that American citizens refused to embrace the anti-Semitic prejudice sweeping through Europe.[81]

No matter what position they held about the consequences of Jewish office-holding, Jews consistently maintained that religious or ethnic affiliation was never a reason to support or reject any candidate. Even as Jews began asserting influence in the political arena, they continued to deny the existence of a segregated Jewish vote, contending instead that Jews were integrated constituents in the American political system. As the Depression wore on, a Jewish voting bloc did indeed take shape, but it remained a coalition based on shared political values rather than ethnic parochialism. At the same time, the landscape of American politics was changing and providing more room for Jewish interests to be articulated within mainstream political dialogue. As Jews staked out a place in Depression-era politics, the terms of ethnic political expression shifted and took new forms.

The formation of an unwavering Jewish loyalty to the Democratic Party constituted the most remarkable political transition for Jews in the Great Depression. Jewish devotion to the Democratic Party, cemented nationally under Franklin Roosevelt's New Deal, began to take shape even earlier for Jews in New York City. It was during the 1920s that New York Jews began to drift toward the Democratic Party. Al Smith, who served as the governor of New York from 1922 until 1928, won the allegiance of Jews by supporting organized labor, opposing anti-Semitism, appointing Jews to positions in government, and endorsing liberal immigration policies. Smith represented the ideological political commitments of New York Jews and demonstrated an ability to speak "in the accents of the urban masses." Although he was not Jewish, Smith addressed the concerns of urban Jews and knew the language of the Jewish streets well enough to pepper his speech with occasional Yiddish sayings. Smith's personality and policies turned many New York Jews into Democrats for the first time. When he ran for president in 1928, Smith garnered almost three-quarters of the city's Jewish vote. The Democratic coalition that formed around Al Smith in the 1920s further consolidated during the Depression. Herbert Lehman served as the governor of New York for most of the Great Depression and he, too, fulfilled the requirements of the city's Jewish voters. A banker of German descent who actively supported organized labor and progressive reform movements, Lehman attracted both affluent Jews who had once backed Republican candidates as well as working-class Jews who had previously voted the Socialist ticket. Smith and Lehman, along with other prominent Democratic elected officials, including New York Senator Robert F. Wagner, Sr., succeeded in drawing Jews to the party by appealing to the political sentiments and ideological tenets that drove grassroots Jewish politics. As New York's Democratic politicians came to support social reform and organized labor, fought against immigration restriction, and vocally opposed anti-Semitism at home and abroad, the political agendas of the Jewish community and the Democratic Party began to merge.[82]

If Lehman, Smith, and other leading New York politicians made Jews feel at home in the Democratic Party, Franklin Roosevelt cemented an unbreakable Jewish-Democratic bond. New York Jews had begun voting Democratic in the 1920s, but not until Roosevelt and the New Deal did they demonstrate an unshakable commitment to the Democrats. In 1932, almost three-quarters of New York Jews voted for Roosevelt, and by 1940, that number had grown to almost 90 percent, far surpassing the Democratic presidential vote of any other ethnic group.[83] What motivated the overwhelming Jewish support for Roosevelt? Leftist Jewish politics had long emphasized the government's responsibility to care for its citizens, making Jews particularly receptive to the New Deal agenda. Some scholars have argued that the Jewish value of *tzedakah* (righteousness or charity) along with other religious precepts translated into political support for Roosevelt's welfare programs.[84] Religio-cultural values undoubtedly shaped Jewish political culture, but the secular Jewish agenda, with its emphasis on social justice, reform efforts, organized labor, and public welfare responsibility, more directly influenced Jewish political sentiments. Social insurance and public welfare programs had long been central tenets of Jewish socialism and Jewish labor unions. Jewish political convictions merged easily with the New Deal platform. As Roosevelt and the Democrats promoted sweeping social reforms, New York Jews discovered that their ideological commitments could be represented by a leading American political party. Roosevelt also appointed hundreds of Jews to civil service positions and elevated prominent Jewish individuals, including Bernard Baruch, Henry Morgenthau, Jr., and Felix Frankfurter, to senior positions in his administration. The combination of Roosevelt's social legislation, welfare policy, and support for labor along with his willingness to include Jews at the highest level of government convinced New York Jews that the Democratic Party represented their ethnic commitments and interests. Although Jews criticized many elements of the New Deal and constantly pressured Roosevelt to act more forcefully to liberalize immigration quotas and combat the Nazi threat, Jews remained the most ardent Roosevelt supporters and most loyal ethnic constituency within the Democratic Party.

The radical movements that had shaped so many grassroots Jewish political efforts lost most of their popular support to the new Democratic coalition by the mid-1930s. The road from Jewish radicalism to the Democratic Party, like so many other Jewish political developments of the decade, was paved with an ethnic political effort. The American Labor Party (ALP), created in New York City in 1936, facilitated Jewish entrance into the new Democratic coalition. Founded by leading Jewish labor leaders, including David Dubinsky and Sidney Hillman, the ALP provided Socialists with a means to vote for Roosevelt without supporting the "capitalist" Democratic Party. The ALP endorsed Roosevelt's national election while running its own candidates locally. In effect, the ALP signaled the demise of Jewish socialism by providing an intermediate political alternative that eventually led Jewish leftists and radicals into the Democratic Party. "Remaining outside the Democratic party, the ALP functioned in some ways as if it were a tendency within it—which, in time, it became." As Irving Howe explained, "All this was merely the organizational reflex of a massive enthusiasm for Roosevelt within the Jewish community: the whole of it, from working-class to bourgeois, from east European to German, from right to left. To the garment workers, Roosevelt's proposals for social security, unemployment insurance, and legislation enabling union organization seemed like a partial realization of their old socialist program—even if capitalism remained."[85] In 1936, the Socialist *Jewish Daily Forward* endorsed Roosevelt's reelection campaign. Defending the decision to support a Democratic rather than a Socialist candidate, *Forward* editors insisted that their position reflected the overwhelming sentiment of "intelligent workers [and] Socialists" throughout the Jewish community. "In the Jewish world," the editors candidly asserted, "the feeling for Roosevelt burns and blazes."[86]

The New Deal and the Democratic Party created a genuine coalition within the Jewish community, appealing to a broad cross section of New York Jews. Not only working-class but also affluent Jews rallied behind Roosevelt. On Manhattan's West Side, the city's most prosperous Jewish neighborhood, Democrats outnumbered Republicans by a margin of more than two to one. Even after attaining upper-class status, New York's wealthiest Jews retained liberal political loyalties, continuing to vote their ideological commitments rather than their pocketbooks.[87] Roosevelt's social programs commanded the allegiance of virtually all sectors of the Jewish community, creating a Jewish-Democratic bond that endured for decades. From the garment workers and street-corner Socialists of Brownsville to the middle-class Jews of Flatbush and Eastern Parkway to the Jewish community's elite on the Upper West Side, Jewish politics had become inexorably linked to the Democratic Party.

During the course of the Great Depression, New York Jews traveled a political road that led from their ethnic neighborhoods to the national

Democratic coalition. Although the 1930s marked the first time that Jewish political allegiance rested firmly with a leading American party, Jewish neighborhoods retained a distinct political character. Despite overwhelming support for Roosevelt and the Democratic Party, Jewish political culture continued to be driven by an ethnic ideological liberalism and "given shape and tone by a vital minority of left-oriented street speakers and activists."[88] Local Jewish politics remained rooted in the neighborhood, predicated on a commitment to social justice, and indebted to an activist tradition. The political campaigns conducted within New York's Jewish neighborhoods, whether by political clubs, radical activists, or organized parties, reflected the evolving dynamic of ethnic politics in the Depression era. New Deal reforms translated many Jewish social and political values into public policy, cementing Jewish support for the Democratic Party while lending ethnic flavor to Jewish political assimilation. By the time the Depression ended, the Democratic and Jewish political agendas had become so thoroughly intertwined that for Jews, voting Democratic had become an expression of ethnic political ideals.

For New York Jews, the emerging welfare state constituted a national affirmation of their ethnic political commitments and marked their coming of age as legitimate participants in mainstream American political culture. But although individual Jews reconciled their ethnic ideals with the New Deal's social agenda, Jewish charities and philanthropic institutions grappled with the consequences of public welfare. Government welfare threatened to render private Jewish relief agencies obsolete. As Depression-era Jews began to look beyond their ethnic communities and toward the federal government for material assistance, Jewish institutions were forced to reformulate their communal role under the new conditions of the welfare state.

# 6

# Private Jewish Philanthropy in the Welfare State

*What is true of New York Jews is true of their coreligionists everywhere. The Jew has always cared for his own poor.*
—Lee K. Frankel, "Philanthropy—New York" (1905)

*That proud proverb, "The Jews take care of their own" could not withstand the stress of the times.*
—*Inside Information from the Jewish Social Service Association* (1934)

By the time the Great Depression struck, philanthropy had become a mainstay of Jewish communal life in America. Required to care for their own poor as a condition of admission to Colonial America, Jews had transformed their charitable obligation into a source of communal pride. The long tradition of Jewish mutual responsibility, combined with the desire to deflect possible anti-Semitism by projecting only the most positive image of the Jews, reinforced the Jewish commitment to philanthropy and spurred the development of a far-reaching system of Jewish benevolence. The sophisticated charitable endeavors of the Jewish community consistently earned the praise of non-Jewish observers who extolled Jews as an "example of a people that cares wholly for its own sick and poor."[1] American Jews derived great satisfaction from their reputation for self-sufficiency and communal responsibility. "The task which was at one time assumed of necessity," explained one turn-of-the-century Jewish historian, "has to-day become a proud duty."[2] Moreover, philanthropy emerged as a vehicle of Jewish communal solidarity, providing a point of unity for Jews of different religious, ethnic, and political identities. By the twentieth century, Jewish charity was firmly entrenched as a staple of American Jewish life, complete with a network of communal institutions and a cadre of professionally trained social workers. The Great Depression undermined the financial stability and social viability of private Jewish philanthropy, shaking one of the cornerstones of Jewish identity in America.

The Great Depression presented the first serious challenge to the Jewish communal ideal of self-sufficiency. Like other private charities, Jewish organizations faced a dual challenge in the Depression era; they were overwhelmed by unprecedented relief demands during the early 1930s and then forced to reinvent themselves under the new conditions of the New Deal and the welfare state. The Great Depression was a time when Americans of all ethnic groups came to look beyond their ethnic communities for assistance and toward an interventionist federal government. Some scholars have identified the Great Depression as an event that accelerated the demise of ethnic social institutions, particularly private charitable and relief organizations.[3] A closer examination of Jewish philanthropy in the Depression years, however, reveals a more complex process at work within the Jewish community. Government welfare brought serious challenges to private Jewish relief organizations but did not lead to their demise. Rather than destroying private Jewish philanthropy, public welfare forced Jewish agencies to clarify their ethnic mission. In the wake of the Great Depression and the New Deal, Jewish social workers and communal leaders carved out a place for ethnic philanthropy within the new welfare state, formulating a program that demonstrated wholehearted support for public welfare while also defining a distinct role for private Jewish organizations.

Jewish social service agencies had never before faced a crisis of the magnitude of the Great Depression. At the turn of the century, Jewish charities tackled the formidable task of resettling thousands of new immigrants. The massive influx of Jewish immigrants challenged the existing structure of Jewish philanthropy, but Jewish organizations responded by increasing their budgets, programs, and professional staffs. By the 1920s, the prospects for Jewish philanthropy looked bright; immigration quotas had lessened the demands for immigrant aid and Jewish institutions were left to reap the benefits of the postwar economic boom. Jewish federations and social service agencies enjoyed their most expansive and prosperous years during the 1920s. When the Depression struck, Jewish organizations were utterly unprepared to cope with the sudden avalanche of relief cases and the severe budget shortfalls. As early as 1930, both the New York and Brooklyn Jewish Federations reported mounting deficits and began reducing allocations to the agencies that they supported. Faced with shrinking financial resources and a sharp rise in relief applications, many Jewish social workers became convinced that the relief burden could no longer be shouldered by private agencies alone. They argued that Jews, like other Americans, would have to rely upon state and municipal funds. The notion that Jews "take care of their own" had long been a cherished Jewish ideal as well as an accepted doctrine of proper Jewish behavior in America. The harsh realities of the Depression forced Jews to take stock, reevaluate institutional priorities, and confront deeply ingrained myths that had defined the American Jewish community for more than two centuries.[4]

During the first years of the Depression, Jewish communal leaders grappled with the consequences of accepting public welfare. Given the state of the economy, the debate over public relief was extremely short-lived and had essentially been resolved by the time Roosevelt initiated New Deal programs in 1933. New York's Jewish community came to terms with public welfare in the early years of the Depression, since state relief began in New York in 1931 under Governor Franklin Roosevelt. Although the question of public relief quickly became moot as the nation plummeted into economic crisis, the brief interval in which private Jewish agencies redefined themselves within the welfare state is particularly instructive. As they reconfigured Jewish philanthropy in the 1930s, Depression-era Jews balanced the effort to integrate fully within American society and to participate actively in the construction of New Deal America with the desire to maintain the integrity and the distinctiveness of the ethnic community.

The suggestion that Jews might allow their poor to become public charges provoked an emotional debate about the Jewish community's obligation to care for its own members. A minority of Americans and an even smaller percentage of Jews actually required government assistance during the Depression.[5] The difficult issues confronting the Jewish community went beyond the numbers of relief applications. Jewish professionals worried that removing charity from private Jewish auspices might erode communal solidarity and tarnish the Jewish image in the United States.

Public welfare challenged the boundaries of ethnic responsibility and forced Jews to evaluate their position within American society. As they came to terms with public welfare, Jews refined the contours of Jewish community in America.

The ideal of collective responsibility had roots in Jewish religious teachings and European historical experience. Talmudic precepts of *tzedakah* taught that "all Israel is responsible for one another." Europe's autonomous Jewish communities gave concrete expression to those religious values through a network of independent charitable associations. Immigrant Jews arrived in America with considerable experience in ministering to their own needy population.[6] Moreover, the terms of Jewish settlement in America required Jews to "take care of their own." In 1654, when the first Jews arrived in New Amsterdam, Governor Peter Stuyvesant petitioned his superiors at the Dutch West India Company to forbid their settlement. The company, however, admitted Jews to the colony on the condition that "the poor among them shall not become a burden to the company or to the community, but be supported by their own nation."[7] Successive generations of Jews fulfilled the pledge to Peter Stuyvesant by building Jewish philanthropic organizations and consistently opposing government intervention in private charities.[8]

Until the Great Depression, the so-called Stuyvesant Promise stood as a fundamental principle of Jewish communal philosophy. Jewish charity had by no means remained stagnant since the seventeenth century. Small charitable organizations evolved into sophisticated philanthropic endeavors, culminating in the federation movement. Jewish federations represented no single religious or ideological position within the community but rather served as umbrella organizations for diverse Jewish groups. As one Jewish social worker explained in 1938, "Federations became communal agencies whose function it is not only to provide financial support for their constituent societies but to plan for the community needs along constructive lines. . . . The federations aim to support, coordinate, and control the needed social service agencies and activities in their respective communities."[9] Instituting centralized fund-raising while allowing constituent societies to maintain their autonomy, the New York Federation created a basis for Jewish communal cooperation.[10] At the same time, federations emerged as thoroughly American institutions that mirrored the pattern of American voluntary organization. Avoiding a specific ideological platform, they emulated the American model of nonsectarian philanthropy popularized by Andrew Carnegie's Gospel of Wealth. The New York Federation consistently contributed to nonsectarian causes and emphasized that its institutions served both Jew and Gentile. Although Federation leaders boasted that their commitment extended to "people of all races, creeds and colors," they never questioned that Jews should be cared for exclusively by Jewish organizations. American Jews not only accepted but took pride in the "Stuyvesant Promise." Fifteen years before the Wall Street Crash, the prominent Jewish philanthropist Jacob Schiff remarked that "a Jew would rather cut his hand off than apply for relief from non-Jewish sources."[11]

For more than a year after the Crash, Jewish agencies weathered the economic crisis without severe setbacks. In 1930, Jewish institutions actually fared better than other family welfare societies, recording a less dramatic increase in caseloads and requests for relief. "However," the Bureau of Jewish Social Research reported, "in the first three months of 1931 the trend of Jewish agencies was approaching more closely the general trend." Between 1930 and 1931, the number of Jewish families receiving aid increased by more than 40 percent. Before the close of 1930, New York's Jewish Social Service Association had exhausted its resources, forcing the directors to request additional funds from the Federation to meet growing relief demands. By the first year of the Depression, the fiscal reserves of the Jewish community had been virtually consumed.[12]

Already facing a budget deficit, the Federation launched an emergency fund-raising drive. Paul Block, chairman of the 1931 deficit campaign, approached the crisis as a temporary economic downturn that would motivate Jews to contribute generously. The Depression, he claimed, "has had the effect of awakening the community to the pressing needs of our less fortunate fellows. There is more friendliness and more real charity today than there has ever been before."[13] The Federation's executive director echoed his sentiments, explaining that "if the situation does not become progressively worse . . . we can look forward with hopefulness to a continuation of our income approximating the old basis." To the disappointment of Federation leaders, voluntary contributions did not begin to meet the Jewish community's fiscal needs. The Depression grew more severe, debts mounted, and the Federation simply could not support its relief agencies alone. Despite reducing budgets and salaries as well as mortgaging its own building, the Federation was forced to seek assistance from outside sources.[14] The Jewish Social Service Association reluctantly admitted, "That proud proverb, 'The Jews take care of their own' could not withstand the stress of the times."[15]

The Depression forced a reassessment of Jewish charity. Less than a year after the Crash, Jewish social workers began to weigh the merits of public welfare. One WPA worker recalled, "The reluctance of the Jewish community to accept the idea of public responsibility for Jewish relief weakened under the pressure of realities."[16] In June 1930, the National Conference of Jewish Social Service scheduled a panel discussion entitled, "What Do We Owe to Peter Stuyvesant?" The prominent social worker, Isaac Rubinow, known for his support of organized labor and Socialist ideas, opened the session by questioning Jewish allegiance to the Stuyvesant Promise. He insisted: "The promise itself may have been not only diplomatic but fair and just in its own day and generation. . . . Perhaps the shrewd business people who signed that blank check 250 years ago had good reasons to believe that the amount to be written in need would never become a very heavy burden. But conditions have changed. Very much so! . . . Why, then, under these conditions do we have this somewhat naive, antiquated emphasis upon isolation in philanthropic work?"[17] Rubinow demanded that Jewish agencies relinquish outdated notions of communal isolation. He defended the legitimate and important role played by private Jewish social work, asking only that Jews redefine "the lines of demarcation [sic] as to what is properly a State responsibility and to what is equally properly a group responsibility." A foresighted proponent of public welfare, Rubinow encouraged his colleagues to abandon the ideal of Jewish self-sufficiency as a parochial relic of a former age.[18]

Before the Great Depression, Jewish social workers rarely discussed the Stuyvesant Promise at their annual conferences or within the pages of their professional journals. The Stuyvesant Promise became a subject of heated debate during the Depression, precisely at the moment when Jewish leaders were confronting and reinventing their shared communal mythology. For Jewish communal workers, the Stuyvesant Promise had ceased to be a condition of Jewish admission to America and had become instead a source of pride and a legitimating ideal of Jewish philanthropy and social work. The Depression forced the Jewish community to examine its collective ideals and organization. Most participants at the 1930 Jewish social service conference agreed that the Stuyvesant Promise was little more than "a beautiful myth." "If Jews have thought that they were taking care of their own," remarked one respondent to Rubinow's paper, "then they have been laboring under a delusion and the myth of Peter Stuyvesant has been much more insidious in its implications than we can offhand estimate."[19] Forced to alter Jewish social service in the face of the Depression, most Jewish professionals began to challenge the Stuyvesant Promise as a myth that had never provided an adequate rationale for Jewish philanthropy. "I have very little sympathy with Jewish social service merely on the basis of the 'Stuyvesant-promise' tradition," confessed one Jewish worker in the course of the debate.[20] The welfare state undermined an age-old communal ideal but also provided the opportunity for Jews to create a new ideological foundation for Jewish charity, one more compatible with the social milieu of New Deal America. Assessing the impact of the Depression on the organized Jewish community, Federation leader Maurice Taylor proclaimed, "the ghost of Peter Stuyvesant has been permanently laid."[21]

Yet, not all Jewish social workers immediately rallied behind the public welfare platform. Maurice Karpf, president of New York's Graduate School for Jewish Social Work and more conservative in his views toward government welfare and Jewish philanthropy, admitted that there was nothing "inherently wrong or undesirable in Jewish communities seeking their due share of public funds." However, he added forcefully, "It has been a source of pride of Jewish communities and of Jewish social workers that we do not have a pauper population. . . . Shall we abandon our clients, give up our ideals and ambitions for complete and effective community organization, forego standards which it has taken decades to develop, and see our prestige and that of our communities go crumbling, because of a temporary depression[?]"[22] American Jews had created a sophisticated network of Jewish organizations and professionals charged with dispensing charity according to the precepts of both Jewish tradition and American philanthropy. Public welfare not only challenged deep-seated values of caring for needy Jews within the community but also threatened to unsettle the very foundation of Jewish communal organization.

Throughout America, Jews as well as non-Jews expressed concern about the deleterious effects of public relief on private philanthropy. In fact, Rubinow's call for public welfare caused considerable apprehension both inside and outside the Jewish world. In 1928, the editors of *Survey*, a leading social service journal, refused to publish a paper submitted by Rubinow which predicted that private philanthropy would be unable to cope with severe economic crisis. Rubinow was known to support Socialist programs and *Survey*'s editors found his argument too controversial, challenging fundamental principles of American voluntarism and private charity. Especially before the Depression era, public welfare appeared as antithetical to American values as it did to Jewish tradition. Most Americans, including progressive social workers, believed that "mutual self-help through voluntary giving" represented the best response to poverty and unemployment.[23] At the onset of the Depression, the Welfare Council of New York City, a voluntary organization representing the city's private charities, instituted emergency relief measures to meet the crisis. In marshaling the collective resources of private charities, the Welfare Council demonstrated its deep commitment to serving the needy through voluntarism and private charitable efforts. But before the close of 1930, council leaders confessed that "it seemed unlikely that all the [city's] resources combined would be able completely to prevent distress and destitution." New York's social workers reluctantly admitted that private efforts could not keep pace with the unprecedented economic need created by the Depression. In 1931, at the urging of reformers and social workers, Governor Franklin Roosevelt initiated a state program of public welfare.[24]

Before the city's welfare efforts were well coordinated, independent Jewish charitable endeavors sprung up outside of both government and Federation auspices. Some Yiddish newspapers sponsored their own relief campaigns. The *Forward*'s Fund for the Unemployed collected money and other supplies for needy families and *The Day* ran a regular column that described the background and qualifications of an unemployed man with the headline, "Do You Have a Job for Him?"[25] Several New York Jews established free kitchens and breadlines for the Jewish poor. A group of prominent Jewish business and communal leaders, including attorney Jonah Goldstein and former Deputy Attorney General Nathan Padgug, sponsored a free kosher kitchen on the Lower East Side that served seven hundred people a day.[26] By the winter of 1931, there were at least two kosher breadlines serving New York's Jewish poor as well as other kitchens operated under Jewish auspices. Some breadlines represented genuine attempts to serve the needy, but many suffered from corruption, poor management, and political opportunism. Political clubs and elected officials often sponsored breadlines in order to win communal support; some mismanaged and even occasionally embezzled donated funds.[27] A worker at the Henry Street Settlement described the East Side kosher kitchen as "a very dirty and poorly managed place."[28] Jewish and non-Jewish social workers denounced breadlines as an inefficient and undesirable response to poverty and unemployment. Solomon Lowenstein, executive director of the New York Jewish Federation and chairman of the Welfare Council's Coordinating Committee on Unemployment, insisted that "there was no need for feeding children and families in public."[29] Independent breadlines were an initial response to the Depression that faded with the onset of state welfare and New Deal programs. In the Jewish community, Jewish social workers led the campaign to close the kosher kitchens and breadlines. By the spring of 1931, small-scale charitable efforts could not withstand the tremendous economic demands of serving the Jewish poor. Social workers succeeded in eliminating most free kitchens and breadlines, attempting to enforce a "scientific" approach to relief.[30] Individual Jews and small Jewish organizations continued to sponsor their own limited charitable campaigns, but the work of welfare fell primarily to the government, with even large private philanthropies struggling to meet the challenges of the Great Depression.

Jewish social workers, like their non-Jewish colleagues, accepted public welfare as an absolute necessity but worried about its effects upon the Jewish community. For Jews as well as other Americans, government welfare was a radical change that required a new ideological basis for social planning and communal organization. Jewish charity had always been a means of inspiring communal loyalty and involvement. As one observer remarked, "Private group philanthropy forms a part of Jewish ideology."[31] Philanthropy united diverse groups within the community, joining affluent German Jews and newer East European immigrants in a shared communal endeavor. Cooperation between German and East European Jews had reached new heights during the 1920s. Maurice Karpf, a sharp critic of the policy of "abandoning Jewish poor to the public-welfare departments," feared that East European immigrants would resent Jewish participation in public welfare. Karpf claimed that public relief threatened to "split the Jewish communities and undo what has been accomplished in the last decade in cementing them." He also believed that Jewish social workers would be the prime targets of immigrant hostility. Karpf explained: "The derisive attitudes toward the Jewish social worker current during the latter part of the last century and the first part of the present will reappear. The Yiddish press, all-too-eager for controversial issues and none-too-friendly to the Jewish social worker, will not pass up this opportunity to raise a hue and cry that will resound from one end of the country to the other. We shall lose the prestige, recognition, and good will of that part of the community."[32]

But Karpf may have overestimated the Jewish community's opposition to public welfare. Rather than criticizing Jewish agencies for participating, the Yiddish press often championed the campaign for government welfare. The Socialist newspaper, the Jewish Daily Forward, interpreted the diminishing role of private charity as a sign of progress. As long-standing advocates of the government's responsibility to care for the needs of all citizens, Socialist Jews welcomed the institution of public welfare programs. When private charities announced that public relief was the only solution to the crisis, Forward editors replied, "The socialists have been saying this for a long time." Even the non-Socialist, more conservative Jewish Morning Journal declared, "The recognition that [unemployment relief] is a job for the government and Washington is a step forward."[33] To be sure, derisive attitudes toward Jewish social workers and organizations run by upper-class Jews were prevalent in the community, as they had been long before the Depression. The Yiddish press faithfully covered the Federation's fund-raising campaigns, however, and reported the important work accomplished by Jewish agencies during the difficult years of the Depression.[34]

Most Jews welcomed government welfare as a matter of public policy, but they viewed both public and private assistance as a last resort, preferring to rely on their own support systems whenever possible. By the 1930s, New York Jews had established scores of ethnic loan and mutual benefit societies. These institutions were usually the first place that Jews turned once their family resources had been expended. Even during the worst years of the Depression, New York's Hebrew Free Loan Society provided approximately one million dollars per year to struggling business owners and families that needed help with living expenses. The sharp increase in requests for funds combined with a dwindling pool of resources devastated many Jewish loan societies during the Depression. But despite reducing the amount of the average loan by about 20 percent, New York's Hebrew Free Loan Society remained a viable economic safety net for those Jews who needed financial assistance but were not desperate enough to turn to charitable or relief organizations.[35]

Most ethnic associations did not fare as well as the Hebrew Free Loan Society during the Great Depression. Mutual aid societies, particularly those sponsored by *landsmanshaftn* (hometown societies), were the backbone of the immigrant Jewish community. These grassroots associations, organized according to immigrants' European towns of origin, provided a wide variety of religious, social, and cultural activities along with a range of relief services, financial assistance, and sick benefits. In their heyday, landsmanshaftn offered their members a source of community on American soil and an economic cushion during hard times. Landsmanshaft organizations had deep roots within the Jewish community. In 1938, three thousand landsmanshaftn existed in New York, with more than half a million total members; approximately one out of every four Jews in the city was a member.[36] Despite their numerical strength, landsmanshaftn and mutual aid societies could not meet the increasing relief demands of their memberships during the Great Depression. Although they had traditionally provided aid to members during periods of illness and unemployment, most societies reduced or even eliminated benefit payments during the 1930s. For example, both the Progress Mutual Society and Strelisker Young Men's Benevolent Association dispensed sick benefits regularly until the early 1930s, fulfilling as many as three requests per week. But by the close of the decade, the societies rarely approved even a single sick payment. Requests for loans, sick benefits, and unemployment relief increased dramatically with the onset of the Depression, but landsmanshaftn and mutual benefit societies simply lacked the financial resources to help their members.[37] Joblessness was so common in these societies that unemployment benefits ceased entirely. In the late thirties, the composition of Jewish societies was overwhelmingly working-class, with approximately 75 percent of members categorized as laborers, 15 percent as small business owners, and only 10 percent as professionals.[38]

Although landsmanshaftn and mutual benefit societies survived the Depression, they ceased to fulfill the social and economic needs of New York Jews. Even before they faced the setbacks of the economic crisis, landsmanshaftn remained predominantly immigrant organizations, failing to attract the new generation of American-born Jews. By the late 1930s, second-generation Jews constituted only 15 percent of the membership of New York landsmanshaftn.[39] As late as 1938, three-quarters of New York landsmanshaftn recorded their minutes in Yiddish rather than in English. Doubly beleaguered by financial woes and the inability to appeal to the younger generation, landsmanshaftn and mutual benefit societies could not cope with the vicissitudes of the Depression era. "Charities such as the Federation of Jewish Philanthropies," explained one historian of landsmanshaftn, "were much better equipped, both financially and organizationally, to deal with problems of poverty and unemployment."[40]

The Federation had more extensive resources, but many New York Jews, particularly in the working-class community, were not inclined to turn to Federation agencies, which were funded by more affluent sectors of the Jewish community and run by middle-class professionals. As the Depression wore on, communal leaders came to recognize that most Jews did not resent the Federation's acceptance of public welfare, but rather felt nothing but indifference for the Federation and its programs. A 1934 Jewish social service report concluded that the "Federation is too far removed from the Jewish masses, the community whose wishes it presumably represents and whose needs it is designed to serve."[41] During the Depression, in response to a combination of new conditions created by the economic crisis, the Federation set out to build a broader base of communal support. The effort to reach a more representative Jewish constituency was, in part, a response to public welfare. Many communal leaders expressed great concern that once charity was removed from Jewish auspices, Jewish organizations, lacking the emotional appeal of relief for the poor, would be unable to elicit voluntary contributions. "Eliminate the care of dependents from your community responsibility," warned Karpf, "and you will find it exceedingly difficult to raise funds for the other needs."[42] The Federation had never been a broadly based organization; instead it depended on large contributions from a select group of wealthy and middle-class donors. During the Depression years, large donations decreased substantially, exposing the weakness of the Federation's elite membership. As contributions from upper and middle-class Jews declined during the 1930s, Federation leaders recognized the importance of securing modest contributions from the larger community. The fiscal distress of Federation agencies coupled with a desire to maintain and extend Jewish communal allegiance in the wake of public welfare motivated community leaders to address the lack of popular support for the Jewish Federation.[43]

The Federation claimed to be New York's representative Jewish communal institution, but it had not captured the mass support or numerical strength of the city's small grassroots Jewish organizations. Landsmanshaftn may have lacked the resources to combat the Depression, but they possessed the broad communal base that the Federation hoped to attain. During the Depression years, landsmanshaftn retained a collective membership larger than any other single Jewish organization. As late as 1942, the New York Federation could claim only half as many contributors.[44] In 1935, the Federation initiated a program designed to create a more comprehensive foundation of communal support and to ease the financial burdens brought on by the economic crisis. The Council of Fraternal and Benevolent Organizations, heralded as "a new instrument for community understanding," brought together hundreds of small Jewish landsmanshaftn and mutual aid societies. Reflecting the collective spirit of the New Deal, the council enabled the Federation to solicit members through their group affiliations rather than campaigning for individual contributions.[45] In the 1920s, Federation fund-raising had targeted individual Jews in their places of business. The council both rejected the individualistic approach of the previous decade and emphasized the Federation's desire to "bind more closely together . . . the great historic Jewish community institutions of New York and the rank-and-file of Jewish life."[46] At a time when the Federation faced severe financial hardships and feared that public welfare would mean a loss of communal support, the council extended the Federation's reach to the immigrant community while also providing a new source for fund-raising.[47] The council did not suddenly transform the Federation into an institution that inspired grassroots loyalty from the Jewish community; throughout the 1930s, the Federation retained its reputation as an elitist organization. Yet, the creation of the council testified to the Federation's recognition that survival in the Depression years required a stronger foundation for communal solidarity.

The rhetoric surrounding the Council of Fraternal and Benevolent Organizations reflected the reformulation of Jewish communal priorities sparked by the Depression and the welfare state. Financial hardships forced the Federation to develop new fund-raising tactics, but Federation leaders understood that more than fiscal solvency was at stake. Samson Benderly, director of the Bureau of Jewish Education, insisted that the economic threat paled in comparison to the challenge posed to Jewish communal survival. Benderly expressed confidence that "the money would be raised and that it would be forthcoming, probably in small donations from the poor and the middle class." But he was more concerned about "the inability of the Jews of New York to recognize the necessity of serving and saving Federation."[48] As president of the Council of Fraternal and Benevolent Organizations, Edwin Goldwasser succinctly explained that the council was essential, not only for raising funds and promoting grassroots support, but also for "strengthening New York Jewish life and safeguarding our communal future." As welfare became largely the province of the state and federal governments, appeals to the Jewish community increasingly emphasized the Jewish duty to support ethnic philanthropy. In creating the council, Federation leaders stressed that the members of landsmanshaftn and mutual aid societies "know in a deep sense what the Jewish charitable tradition means."[49] The advent of government welfare directly challenged the Jewish tradition of communal charity and self-sufficiency, requiring a reformulation of the ethnic community in the welfare state.

As Jews reassessed the ethnic tradition of private charity within New Deal America, they defended the legitimate coexistence of public welfare and sectarian philanthropy. The redefinition of private Jewish philanthropy involved several ideological constructs. From virtually all sectors of the community, Jews argued that the new welfare state reflected the basic tenets of Jewish tradition, drawing a correlation between Jewish teachings and the fundamental character of New Deal programs. At the same time, Jewish social workers insisted that government welfare offered Jews the opportunity to integrate more fully within American culture, as both contributors to and beneficiaries of New Deal society. By promoting the communal realignments of the Depression era as consistent with both Jewish and American ideals, Jewish leaders set out to preserve the integrity of ethnic philanthropy while also emphasizing Jewish commitment to the national recovery effort. By the time the New Deal reached its stride, support for public welfare stood alongside private Jewish philanthropy as one of the most cherished Jewish communal ideals.

Jewish professionals sought to interpret public welfare as a means to fortify the Jewish community. Rather than lamenting its consequences, a growing number of Jewish social workers championed the benefits of government welfare. Reliance on public funds "does not represent a breakdown in private philanthropy," explained one Jewish leader. "In a time of great disaster, no community is self-sufficient."[50] Jewish communal leaders insisted that since Jews shared the burdens of the Depression with other Americans, they ought to contribute to the national recovery. Moreover, they argued that by participating in a burgeoning public welfare system, Jews might actually strengthen their position in American society. Samuel Goldsmith, an American-born Jewish leader, maintained that it would be detrimental for American Jews *not* to support public relief programs. "It is stupid to assume that the Jewish family agency must or can carry the full Jewish load," he insisted. "It is more than stupid to assume this. It is actually vicious and detrimental to the best interests of the Jewish community and the Jewish clients." Goldsmith argued that "to exempt the Jews from the benefits of governmental action to make them not only a separate religious, and to some extent, social community, but to actually endeavor to make them a separate economic community, would be to add to whatever social and mental ghetto might exist a physical, economic ghetto from which the Jewish community would find great difficulty in ever escaping."[51]

Public welfare, then, served as a vehicle for Jewish integration, an opportunity for Jews to become fully American. Rather than eroding communal solidarity, support for government welfare offered Jews a more secure future in America. Conversely, failure to participate in public projects might endanger Jewish status. Harry Lurie, director of the Bureau of Jewish Social Research, claimed that Jews had a "distinct obligation" to take part in the country's relief efforts. "As part of the general body politic," he argued, Jews had a duty to contribute to and a right to benefit from government programs. "The Jewish social service community has a legitimate place in its relationship to a developing system of public welfare services," declared Lurie.[52] Samuel Kohs of the Graduate School for Jewish Social Work, agreed, insisting that "we should, as Jews and as Jewish social workers, make it our primary obligation to help develop public social work."[53] By 1933, the leading Jewish social service publication announced: "Jewish social workers and community leaders are becoming more and more concerned about movements for social legislation and economic planning in which they take their place not as Jews but as citizens, working along-side their non-Jewish colleagues as one unit for all." By seeking their "legitimate place" in the emerging system of public welfare, Jews declared themselves full members of the American community.[54]

Solomon Lowenstein, executive director of the New York Jewish Federation, was particularly sensitive to the need for Jews to demonstrate wholehearted commitment to public welfare. Even before government programs were created, Lowenstein actively participated in the New York Welfare Council, chairing its Coordinating Committee on Unemployment which sometimes met at the Federation office.[55] In Federation board meetings, Lowenstein emphasized the importance of a strong Jewish commitment to New York fund-raising campaigns, warning of the "unpleasant discussion" that might arise if Jews failed to do their share. The Jewish community also benefited materially from nonsectarian and government-sponsored relief programs. Federation board members conceded that without subsidy from the city's emergency committees, they would have been unable to support their own agencies. In 1931 alone, the Jewish Social Service Association accepted more than $700,000 from the Gibson Committee, a private, nonsectarian organization funding New York charities. That same year more than six thousand Passover food packages were distributed to needy Jewish families by the Mayor's Committee on Unemployment. New York's Jewish leaders discovered that participation in relief efforts enhanced Jewish prestige while producing tangible benefits for the community. By the time Roosevelt initiated New Deal programs, the Federation's board of trustees had already endorsed the campaign for federal welfare.[56]

During the Depression years, the Federation debated whether it should formally declare its political support for social legislation. Solomon Lowenstein reminded the board of trustees that "Federation is considered in the community the representative of the Jewish people" and its stand on social issues was important for New York Jewry. Asked to deliver an opinion about the board's right to endorse social legislation, the Federation's Law Committee concluded that, "Unquestionably, Federation has the right to favor or oppose legislation specifically affecting the Jews of New York City."[57] Federation leaders also insisted that, as a representative Jewish organization, the Federation had a duty to support any political efforts that would benefit American citizens, both Jewish and non-Jewish. In its decision to endorse state and federal social programs, the Federation emphasized that the welfare of the Jewish community was inextricably intertwined with the rest of the nation.

As they underlined their commitment to American public programs, Jewish leaders also promoted government welfare and social legislation as an expression of Jewish ideals. Jews had long celebrated Jewish tradition as "ethically sensitive, equalitarian and democratic." In the New Deal era, they emphasized the relevance and contributions of that tradition in the national recovery effort. Rabbi Ben Zion Bokser insisted that "the Jewish past . . . is rich in social values and moral ideals . . . which have a functional significance for our social needs today." Bokser reminded participants at the National Conference of Jewish Social Welfare that Jewish teachings required that an individual who "suffered impoverishment and was in need . . . had the right to expect society to maintain him." In a decade of enormous social change, Jewish leaders advertised the correlation between Judaism and progressive social movements. "Judaism asserts the faith that man will gradually rise above his imperfections and build the more perfect society."[58] In 1933, Rabbi Israel Levinthal of the Brooklyn Jewish Center claimed that the National Recovery Administration fulfilled Jewish precepts of communal obligation. In a reformulation of Jewish tradition, he declared: "The N.R.A. teaches the lesson that we are all one people, all responsible for each other." Levinthal further maintained, "The N.R.A. speaks to us in the spirit of the words which Moses spoke to the Israelites."[59] Roosevelt's political program merged easily with Jewish principles of social justice; many Jews considered Roosevelt "the next thing to Moses."[60] By translating Jewish values into the language of American politics, Depression-era Jews emerged as enthusiastic advocates of social legislation while forging a new framework for ethnic expression. As one communal leader insisted, "Jewish communal organization must be progressive, if it is to be truly Jewish, and must cooperate with all forward-looking American forces."[61] Such rhetoric was pervasive within the Jewish community during the Depression years, as Jews molded their ethnic convictions and communal organizations to fit the conditions of New Deal America.

Yet, although Jews accepted and even championed government welfare by the early thirties, Jewish agencies remained less inclined to accept public funds than other American groups. A 1934 study revealed that the percentage of public subsidies to Jewish institutions rose steadily during each year of the Depression, but never reached the level of public funds accepted by other sectarian and nonsectarian agencies. Statistics seemed to support the claims of those Jewish professionals who maintained that the "idea of taking care of one's own is a part of Jewish thinking . . . so that the whole concept of public agency responsibility is foreign to them."[62] But more important than their reluctance to accept government subsidy was the relative success of their fund-raising efforts; Jewish institutions simply required fewer public funds. Although all private charities experienced decreases in voluntary contributions during the Depression, Jewish agencies reported a proportionately smaller decline in voluntary giving. The relative health of Jewish institutions reflected a combination of well-organized fund-raising drives, Jewish willingness to support community programs, and levels of economic security that permitted charitable contributions.[63] Yet, despite their comparatively advantageous position, Jewish welfare societies certainly did not have the resources to shoulder the relief burden alone. Like other private institutions, Jewish agencies relinquished the bulk of relief work to the government. By 1934, an estimated 70 to 90 percent of American Jews receiving relief were cared for by public welfare departments.[64]

Private agencies sent most of their clients to government offices, but both Jewish and non-Jewish social workers expressed great concern about the quality of service offered by state relief bureaus. Despite the efforts of local officials, standards of public relief had not kept pace with the rush to build government assistance programs. A 1935 New York report described relief bureaus as having "inadequate heating, poor light, poor ventilation, no privacy for interviews, and grossly inadequate toilet facilities."[65] Relief applicants encountered long delays, discriminatory practices, and poorly trained, inexperienced caseworkers. The average government worker (often recruited from the relief rolls) handled three times as many cases as most private social workers. Not only the methods but the provisions of relief were inadequate. Work relief was available to very few clients, particularly in the early years of the Depression. Home relief remained the most common form of assistance and provided only relief in kind. Clients received food tickets and rent vouchers, which not only met with considerable resistance from merchants and landlords, but also compounded the stigma associated with relief. Speaking on behalf of the Welfare Council, Solomon Lowenstein called the city's relief practices "indefensible" and "shocking to the humane instincts of this community." New York reformers of all denominations agreed that the public welfare system functioned poorly, failing to meet basic material needs and destroying self-respect.[66]

Because of its many shortcomings, Jewish social workers demonstrated some reticence in sending clients to the state relief bureau. A 1935 study concluded that "workers in Jewish agencies are generally reluctant to transfer cases completely to the public agency, because of the inadequacy and uncertainty of public relief, the circumstances under which public aid is granted and their effect upon family morale, the furnishing of much of the relief in kind, and the unsuitability of commissary relief for Jewish dietary needs."[67] Beginning in 1933, New York upgraded relief practices somewhat, instituting a system of cash relief designed to "preserve the dignity and morale of the family." Nevertheless, private agencies continued to offer their clients greater attention and higher budgetary allowances. In 1935, for example, a family of five with no regular income received twelve dollars per week from the Home

Relief Bureau but more than twenty dollars from the average private agency. Jewish welfare societies not only made provisions for kosher food within relief budgets but also added allowances for carfare and occasional recreation. Like other private institutions, Jewish agencies were able to maintain higher standards only because they transferred the vast majority of relief cases to the state. Most Jewish relief clients applied directly to the Home Relief Bureau, never having any contact whatsoever with Jewish agencies.[68]

Working in concert with the public welfare department, Jewish social workers attempted to raise the standards of state relief and to integrate Jewish efforts within New York's welfare system. Jewish agencies continued to serve clients of their own, sometimes supplementing government relief with additional funds or, more commonly, by providing public relief recipients with personal and vocational counseling. Yet, at the same time, Jewish institutions also released some staff members to the public welfare department, which placed them in the relief bureaus serving predominantly Jewish neighborhoods. By working with members of their own ethnic group, Jewish social workers helped the government better serve the needs of Jewish clients.[69] For example, government distribution of groceries often failed to consider religious dietary laws and ethnic food preferences. One observer noted that although federal grocery provisions were "theoretically adapted to families of different nationalities, [they] contained much that the families did not know how to cook or did not like; for instance, the Negroes did not like what the Italians liked, and the Jews would not eat the things given to them, yet the things were common to all boxes."[70] Jewish social workers who worked in the welfare department informed government officials about Jewish dietary needs and helped them plan low-cost menus that accounted for those who kept kosher. New York's welfare department recognized the need to reach the city's many ethnic groups. The Emergency Relief Bureau regularly reported important welfare information on New York radio, issuing broadcasts in several languages, including Yiddish.[71]

While Jewish social workers attempted to improve the welfare system from within, more radical members of the New York Jewish community voiced their concerns by staging protests at the city's Home Relief Bureaus. Picketing, giving speeches, and clashing with police, Jewish demonstrators demanded better government service. Outside one relief bureau, Jews carried signs with slogans like "Down with Charity!" and "Give the Bankers Home Relief—We Want Jobs." The demonstrators, many but not all of them Communists, regularly protested the policy of relief in kind and the shortage of available work relief. Interestingly, Jewish protesters and social workers advocated many of the same ideas about how the government should serve its unemployed citizens. Social workers forcefully pressured the state to replace relief in kind with cash payments and mounted an "increasingly insistent clamor for the expansion of work relief." Liberal social workers joined Socialist publications like the *Forward* in championing work relief instead of the "dole" and urging greater government action on behalf of the unemployed. Although the two groups hardly regarded each other as allies, radical Jews and more moderate reformers shared common ground in matters of welfare reform.[72]

During the Depression era, the ideological lines dividing Jewish social workers from the labor movement and radical politics grew less distinct. Harry Lurie, director of the New York Bureau of Jewish Social Research and a voice of leftist politics within the social work community, was a sharp critic of capitalism and its failure to provide secure employment for workers. Echoing Socialist teachings about the value of labor, Lurie supported work relief on the grounds that "only by participating in the work of the world can [laborers] achieve real economic security or feel the sense of importance which comes from belonging in the ranks of persons who really matter because they are productive."[73] Prominent Jewish social workers like Isaac Rubinow and Abraham Epstein maintained strong ties to organized labor and played leading roles in social service reform and New Deal politics. Their programs for social insurance and unemployment compensation derived in large part from Socialist principles. Jewish Socialists joined social workers in supporting Roosevelt and the New Deal, although both groups remained quick to point out the shortcomings of New Deal programs.[74] But even before Roosevelt's election, Jewish social workers outlined a program of government responsibility that reflected Socialist influence. As early as 1931, the National Conference of Jewish Social Service issued a resolution calling on the president and the Congress to, "take such steps in the form of federal emergency relief on a large enough scale to alleviate existing and future suffering," endorsing "the construction of public works to stimulate and revive industry; the formulation of a comprehensive program of social insurance; and the creation of such commissions as will assure social administration of these and other necessary measures."[75]

The public programs initiated during the crisis reflected a new vision of social responsibility within American government and society. Jewish social workers, like their non-Jewish colleagues, had become enthusiastic advocates of social programs long before the New Deal. By the mid-1930s, a new rank-and-file movement had significantly altered the social work profession. Many Jewish social workers were the college-educated children of immigrants who brought to their work a new emphasis on activism and social change, even organizing themselves into a trade union.[76] So pervasive was the radical sentiment among students at the Graduate School for Jewish Social Work that President Maurice Karpf described some student activities and publications as a "Communist uprising."[77] Although class and ideological differences remained, committed Jewish Socialists, labor activists, and social workers discovered a basis for cooperation in the campaign for social legislation. Rooted in the tradition of social justice, support for government programs cemented bonds among different sectors of the Jewish population. Widely shared Jewish values of communal responsibility translated easily into the new language of American politics. As public welfare and social legislation gradually became respectable American politics, Jews discovered a new, thoroughly American, foundation for ethnic solidarity beyond the realm of private philanthropy.

The emerging public welfare system required private Jewish philanthropy to redefine its purpose in order to justify its continued existence. "The rapid journey toward responsibility under public auspices . . . has necessitated a redefining of agency function and agency scope," declared one Jewish social service publication.[78] By actively supporting public welfare, Jewish social workers had placed their own agencies in a precarious position. The "recent development of public relief," admitted one Jewish social worker, "has taken away many of the functions of the private agency, and given rise to the fear that this organization will be eliminated." Jewish social workers anticipated that economically strained members of the Jewish community would ask: "Why continue private charities? Why not turn all the needy over to the Home Relief Bureau and close your doors?" Even Isaac Rubinow, an unwavering advocate of public welfare, conceded that "private social agencies are fighting virtually with their backs to the wall, fighting for a place in the sun, for a right and justification of their existence." In view of their diminishing responsibility for relief, Jewish welfare societies were forced to legitimate and reformulate their role within the Jewish community.[79]

During the Depression years, Jewish leaders carved out a place for sectarian relief work within the welfare state. "Where public social work and the protective devices of social legislation are in operation," declared one Jewish social service report, "Jews will participate as citizens in the general community." That same report firmly maintained, however, that "Jews will retain and foster services to help fellow Jews."[80] The ideal of ethnic philanthropy as a cornerstone of Jewish values continued to exert enormous power within the Jewish community, even after the government assumed responsibility for the Jewish poor. Communal leaders reminded their constituents that in the welfare state, "Jews will shoulder the full and sole responsibility for distinctly Jewish community work," insisting that "the fulfillment of duties which Jews owe their kind will not be shirked."[81] Defining precisely what "duties" legitimately fell within the purview of private Jewish organizations remained the primary task and constant preoccupation of Jewish communal leaders in the Depression era.

With government welfare providing the bulk of relief work, Jewish social workers outlined a program that expanded their communal role while contracting their material relief efforts. Jewish agencies did not completely abandon welfare activities and continued to offer services ranging from financial assistance to medical care to home economics training.[82] Yet, as one agency publication explained, "Though we must still give relief to a large proportion of the families under our care, the Jewish Social Service Association, like other family welfare agencies, refers to the Home Relief Bureau clients whose needs can be met by relief alone." In 1935, the Jewish Social Service Association cooperated with the Home Relief Bureau in more than one thousand cases; public funds provided the material relief, and any clients who required additional counseling or assistance were sent to the private agency.[83] Relief remained a regular feature within Jewish agencies, but Jewish social workers no longer considered material aid their primary responsibility.

As the Depression grew more severe, Jewish social workers claimed that working with Jewish families in crisis remained the responsibility of private Jewish agencies. In the wake of public welfare programs, Jewish leaders argued that family welfare agencies "have to do with the preservation of family life and not with the giving of relief."[84] As the Depression created discord and disruption within Jewish families, Jewish professionals claimed that their familiarity with ethnic family patterns, religious traditions, and community issues made them uniquely qualified to serve the particular needs of Jewish clients. "Only a Jewish worker," they argued, was fully "aware of the customs, traditions and living standards of Jewish families."[85] Like other social workers of the 1930s, Jewish caseworkers emphasized the importance of psychological counseling, directing their efforts to "the prevention and cure of frustrations and maladjustments of individual Jews, Jewish families and Jewish groups."[86] They committed their energies to helping those Jews "whose courage has crumbled under the prolonged strains of unemployment."[87] As the yearbook of Jewish social work declared in 1933, "The full battery of case work services are to be employed to strengthen and preserve Jewish family life."[88] To make the community aware of its new emphasis on family counseling, Jewish agencies published fictionalized case histories in which troubled clients were helped by "sympathetic and understanding" social workers.[89] Jewish agencies sought to remind fellow Jews of the important services still provided by the Federation and to underscore the ongoing need for private philanthropy. While fully supporting the development of public welfare, private Jewish agencies defended their unique ability to serve Jewish families and to address particular Jewish concerns.[90]

According to Jewish leaders, the needs of Depression-era Jews included, not only personal counseling, but also vocational service and employment assistance. The Federation Employment Service (FES), established in 1934 and directed by Irwin Rosen, was created precisely because Jewish communal leaders considered Jewish employment and job placement a paramount communal responsibility. Harnessing all the resources of Jewish agencies to assist Jewish jobseekers, the Federation interpreted employment services as part of the mission of ethnic philanthropy. Jewish social workers claimed that due to job discrimination and Jewish occupational tendencies, Jews faced "special economic problems . . . over and above the hazards of insecurity to which all Americans are subjected in our present economy." Therefore, they insisted that offering vocational training and job placement to Jews was "the charge laid upon the Jewish agency of the future."[91] Facilitating Jewish employment addressed the immediate concerns of the Depression-era Jewish public, bolstering Jewish agencies' claim to represent communal interests and helping to secure their survival in the welfare state.

The challenge presented to the FES and other Jewish employment bureaus was to serve the particular needs of Jewish clients without appearing "clannish." While Federation leaders and Jewish social workers enthusiastically supported the FES, they also recognized that separate Jewish employment bureaus might fuel anti-Jewish sentiment. In 1932, Isaac Rubinow expressed his reservations about initiating a large-scale Jewish employment effort. "I must confess that I cannot get very enthusiastic about the plan of organizing special Jewish employment offices, particularly under the auspices of Jewish social service agencies. . . . In the long run a special Jewish employment office may only facilitate anti-Jewish discrimination."[92] Despite such concerns, Federation leaders believed that Jewish economic needs required a far-reaching job placement program sponsored by the organized Jewish community. "The exclusion of Jews from participation on an equal footing with the Gentiles in the economic and social life of the nation, makes it imperative for Jews to interest themselves in one another's welfare."[93] Jewish leaders generally endorsed the mission of the FES and defended the maintenance of separate Jewish employment agencies, but at the same time, they carefully and consciously reiterated their commitment to the broader American community and cooperated in several citywide employment efforts. As one FES report explained, "Realizing the dangers of parochialism in a sectarian vocational service agency, the F.E.S. has sought to be as cooperative as possible in relation to its sister public and private agencies. Several of our staff members have been actively identified in the work of the Employment and Vocational Guidance Section of the Welfare Council of New York City, with its many committee activities designed to achieve an integrated community program."[94] In justifying its independent employment efforts, the Federation relied on the same arguments used in defending the ongoing viability of private Jewish philanthropy. Jewish leaders supported the legitimacy of meeting specific Jewish needs while at the same time emphasizing Jewish commitment to shared American concerns. In employment activities as well as in its broader program, the Federation struggled to balance sectarian interests with participation in American public projects.

While refuting any charges that their work was exclusionary, Jewish professionals increasingly emphasized the ethnic mission of the Federation and its agencies. During the Depression, concern with social and economic discrimination coupled with the need to defend the legitimacy of private Jewish philanthropy led communal leaders to stress the distinctly Jewish content of their work. While shifting the focus from material relief to personal and vocational counseling, Jewish professionals also envisioned a broader role for the Federation's agencies within the community. "Philanthropic efforts, designed to ameliorate the lot of victims of economic injustice are not enough," insisted Rabbi Eugene Kohn. "The sense of not being wanted which results from social and economic boycott is destructive of Jewish morale and must be countered by cultural activities that express and emphasize the ties of fraternal loyalty which unite Jews in a mutually responsible fellowship."[95] Seeking to preserve ethnic consciousness and community in a period of social and economic pressure, Jewish social service took responsibility for a far-reaching cultural program. Isaac Rubinow, who had foresightedly predicted the need for public relief and remained outspoken in his opinions about the role of private Jewish agencies, succinctly outlined the new direction of Jewish philanthropy. Within the welfare state, Rubinow argued, "Jewish responsibility is to be interpreted not merely in terms of collection and distribution of Jewish money, but in terms of an expanding program of Jewish social service, with a shift in emphasis from the submerged part of the community to the community as a whole and from merely physical and economic need to cultural and spiritual satisfaction."[96]

As Jewish social workers formulated their role within Depression-era America, they underlined the importance of strengthening ethnic culture and commitment. Noting the shifting tone at the annual Jewish social service conferences, one 1933 participant observed, "One speaker after another stressed the need for inculcating a broader interest in Jewish life into the Jewish group, veering from the emphasis of previous Conferences on the more philanthropic phases of social services." During the Depression, Jewish social workers formally included the promotion of cultural programs within their prescribed duties, resolving to "maintain community programs concerned with Jewish education, recreation and culture . . . as essential phases of Jewish social work."[97] Jewish social service emerged from the Depression as a profession devoted to ethnic persistence. As Samuel Kohs of the Graduate School for Jewish Social Work explained: "Jewish social work, if it is Jewish, is not merely a matter of social work with Jews. . . . Jewish social work is *Jewish* because it should concern itself with Jewish life, Jewish survival, Jewish cultural enrichment, and ministers to Jews individually and collectively so that they can wholesomely and positively adjust to the problems which their non-Jewish milieu presents without loss to their intellectual, cultural, and spiritual life."[98] The inroads of public welfare and the challenges posed by the Depression made the preservation of Jewish culture a priority within the social service agenda.

In part, the new emphasis on Jewish culture and education reflected an attempt to protect the viability of Jewish social service. By accepting responsibility for a broader Jewish agenda, Jewish social workers legitimated their continued importance to the community. With relief becoming the province of the state, Jewish professionals insisted that their contributions extended beyond material aid. "Jewish social work is concerned with the recognition and cultivation of those potentialities of the Jewish people which will make possible the richest expression of Jewish cultural life through the highest development of the individual Jew."[99] Yet, Jewish social workers were not motivated entirely by self-interest. During the Depression, Jewish communal leaders became convinced that ethnic knowledge, pride, and self-respect were just as essential to the Jewish future as relief and employment assistance. "Neither a common past nor common economic interests are sufficient to weld us into an inherently unified people," Mordecai Kaplan observed, calling for a positive Jewish program that would lead Jews to affirm their ethnic identity as something more than a "common fate of persecution."[100] Throughout the thirties, Jewish professionals urged the Federation to demonstrate its commitment to sustaining the ethnic community by allotting adequate funds to the city's religious, cultural, and educational institutions.

Yet, despite repeated calls to fortify ethnic culture and commitment as part of the mission of Jewish social service, funds for Jewish cultural and educational programs were not readily available. In a period of scarce financial resources and mounting debt, the Federation was forced to make difficult choices about which programs would take precedence in budgetary decisions. In fact, the Depression heightened a long-standing debate over whether the Federation adequately supported educational and cultural programs within the Jewish community. During the most severe years of the crisis, the Federation's board of trustees discussed revising bylaws in order to allow greater funding for relief programs. "The institutions which furnish food and shelter to the hungry and the needy," argued one board member, "should be recognized as having first option on the funds . . . available for distribution to the Jewish community instead of having equitable distribution among the character building, religious education and recreational agencies."[101] In outlining the 1933 budget, Federation board members initially proposed eliminating financial support for all Jewish educational institutions except the Bureau of Jewish Education.[102] At a time when the organized Jewish community faced a severe deficit, many leaders insisted that "Federation would have to give first consideration to the requirements of its relief agencies."[103]

That proposal elicited virulent opposition from Jews who maintained that cultural and educational programs were just as crucial to Jewish survival as financial assistance. Morris Waldman, a rabbi, social worker, and secretary of the American Jewish Committee, responded sarcastically, "Board members of Federations who have no Jewish *Weltanschauung* will say, 'Not one penny for Jewish schools; our primary and paramount duty is to feed and shelter our poor; isn't this the promise we made to Peter Stuyvesant?'"[104] Critics of the Federation denounced "the now familiar cry, '*in times of depression, what shall it be, bread or education?*'" as nothing more than "a dilemma . . . being posited by those in our community who are physically satiated, but Jewishly, spiritually starved."[105] One Federation board member, among the few who advocated continued support of Jewish education, agreed with the critics, insisting that the abandonment of Jewish education was "indefensible." "In decapitating all the Jewish educational work we would antagonize such a large part of the population that the damage to the Federation would be too great."[106] Ultimately, board members resolved not to enact their initial proposal. The Federation implemented drastic budget cuts but maintained its support of all but one of New York's Jewish educational agencies.[107] Yet, educational and cultural projects continued to suffer in national Federation budgets. All Federation institutions received fewer funds during the Depression; but whereas the percentage of Federation monies allotted to relief agencies steadily increased throughout the early thirties, the portion given to educational, recreational, and cultural programs declined during the same period.[108]

The controversy surrounding the education budget was only part of a larger debate about the Federation's communal role. In the 1930s, Federation board members remained a predominantly upper-class, German-Jewish group. The gulf between East European and German Jewish immigrants had significantly narrowed by the thirties; nevertheless, the advocates of Jewish culture continued to condemn the "spirit of . . . assimilationism which has always been animating the German Jews who are in control of the Jewish institutions."[109] According to critics, the Federation's "assimilationists" wanted to confine the role of Jewish philanthropy to caring for the Jewish poor and offered only limited support for Jewish cultural and educational projects. "The Jewish federations, as at present constituted," lamented Mordecai Kaplan, "take at best a benevolently neutral attitude toward all efforts to foster an affirmative Jewish life."[110] A vocal opponent of Federation policies, Kaplan worried that the Depression would further reduce the Federation's resolve to support cultural and educational programs. "There is no doubt that the philanthropic assimilationists who were talked into consenting to have Jewish education as part of Federation work, but who really have been opposed to any form of Jewish cultural work, are taking advantage of the present depression to display their true attitude," Kaplan complained. "They have raised the cry 'Bread before education.'"[111] The economic crisis rekindled a long-standing debate about the Federation's role within the Jewish community. Some Jewish leaders rejected any implication that a distinct Jewish culture could exist within the American environment, claiming that Jews differed from other Americans only in terms of religious faith. Although not all board members completely disavowed a broader ethnic identity, many continued to relegate cultural and educational projects to the bottom of the Federation's list of priorities. Yet, despite the attitudes expressed by some Federation leaders, the voices agitating for a more far-reaching cultural commitment from the Federation continued to grow stronger during the Depression years.[112]

Although Federation funding for educational and cultural programs remained scarce, a growing number of workers within Federation agencies pressured the Federation to assume a more forceful role in sustaining all aspects of Jewish life. In 1934, Joseph Willen, director of the Federation's Business Men's Council, reported that although "Federation leaders have never made any secret of their assimilationist proclivities, a number of

Jewish social workers and educators proceed from the assumption that the Federation should aim at the conservation of Jewish life."[113] The debate about the Federation's proper role in fostering Jewish cultural life was not fully resolved during the Depression years. As the economic crisis required the Federation to make difficult decisions about priorities, however, a growing number of Jewish educators and social workers mounted an increasingly insistent movement for a more comprehensive Federation agenda.

In fact, despite decreased funding from the Federation, certain cultural institutions thrived during the Depression years.[114] Although Jewish community centers experienced their share of financial problems in the thirties, they reported unprecedented levels of attendance. From 1929 until 1937, attendance doubled at the fifteen Jewish neighborhood and community centers affiliated with the New York and Brooklyn Federations.[115] Unemployment and increased leisure time brought many Jews, especially Jewish youth, to the centers. As the Ninety-Second Street YMHA Bulletin reported jokingly, "The depression, it seems, hasn't hit the market in requests for Sunday passes to the gym."[116] Officials estimated that half of those who regularly attended Jewish community centers were unemployed or on relief, looking to neighborhood centers as their only outlet for "a decent social life."[117] Jewish centers provided an ethnic setting for recreation, club activities, religious, social, and athletic programs. Critics argued that there was little Jewish content in Jewish center programs, yet many communal leaders noted the widespread appeal of neighborhood centers and considered them "a bulwark against the disintegration of character and a force sustaining the morale of our people."[118] Jewish social workers defended Jewish community centers as an important element in what they hoped would become a far-reaching Jewish cultural revival. "The Jewish Community Centre," declared Harry Glucksman, executive director of the Jewish Welfare Board, "is rapidly taking its place as a unifying factor in American Israel."[119] Throughout the Depression, Jewish leaders continued to champion the primacy of cultural and educational programs and to insist, often futilely, on greater funding from the Federation.

Ironically, public welfare lent ammunition to the advocates of Jewish culture. They argued that without the sole obligation to care for the poor, the Jewish community had greater resources for cultural and educational projects. During the 1930s, speakers at the annual Jewish social service conferences repeatedly urged that energy once expended in purely philanthropic endeavors be redirected to the cultural and educational arena. As early as 1930, social worker Jacob Billikopf heralded government welfare as an opportunity to fortify the cultural foundation of American Jewry. By relying on state funds for material relief, Billikopf argued, "we shall be able to release our energies, our moral support and everything that is within us to Jewish educational and cultural efforts, on the strength of which we are going to build up a sound Jewish body in America." The revised program for private Jewish philanthropy, sparked by public welfare and Depression-era challenges, emphasized the Jewish content and ethnic mission of Jewish social service. Nonsectarian work and wholehearted commitment to public projects remained a vital part of the Federation's agenda, but during the 1930s, its agencies dedicated their efforts not only to representing but also to sustaining the ethnic community.[120]

Throughout the Depression, Jewish communal leaders argued for an ethnic distinctiveness compatible with American democratic principles. The Federation aimed to achieve a "decent balancing of Jewish religious, ethical and other concepts with national American community organization and ideals."[121] In 1934, the Jewish Social Service Association celebrated its sixtieth anniversary with a special radio presentation on the Columbia Broadcasting Company's "March of Time" program. Dramatizing the work of the Jewish agency, the program portrayed the accomplishments of private Jewish social workers as they came to the aid of troubled clients. The presentation contained little reference to the Jewish content of the agency's work, but the fictitious clients were given Jewish names and ethnic dialects. At its conclusion, the program suggested that other private agencies might want to adopt the dramatic presentation and recommended that they change the names and dialects of the characters for their own purposes.[122] The message implicit in the Jewish Social Service Association's radio celebration was that private philanthropic work retained its legitimacy for American groups; the distinctive qualities of Jewish agencies were analogous, though not identical, to those of other communities. As long as ethnic communities remained an accepted part of the American landscape, private Jewish philanthropy secured its future as a representative of Jewish communal interests. As they reconfigured Jewish philanthropy within the welfare state, Jewish communal workers defended the importance of serving particular Jewish needs, placed their efforts within the legitimate panorama of ethnic expression in America, and portrayed the survival of Jewish organizations as a symbol of the enduring strength of the Jewish community.

Jewish leaders reiterated that there was nothing un-American about preserving a distinct ethnic community in New Deal America. Samuel Kohs spoke for most of the organized Jewish community when he insisted that "by arguing for greater Jewish content in Jewish social work, we are not arguing for anything unique or exceptional, or for something which we wish to claim for ourselves, but is denied or does not exist for other groups. All we ask for is the same right for 'self-determination' that is granted the majority, and that other minority groups may also rightfully claim for themselves."[123] Defending ethnic pluralism as a cornerstone of American values, Jews attempted to secure the ongoing legitimacy of private Jewish philanthropy. "I have never believed in a melting pot theory," declared Judge Joseph Proskauer only a month after the stock market crash. "I think we do that which is best for this America which we love if we preserve unsullied those spiritual traditions and ideals which come to us as the descendants of a great race and a great people."[124] While the celebration of American ethnic diversity was not new to the Depression era, it remained the basic tenet of Jewish communal philosophy throughout the 1930s.

Jews responded to public welfare as they had to other developments in American life—by reweaving the fabric of Jewish ethnicity into a thoroughly American pattern. Government programs that challenged enduring Jewish ideals were accommodated in a manner that preserved Jewish community but accepted emerging American norms. Through participation in the public welfare system, Jews discovered a vehicle for integration into American society. The New Deal galvanized Jewish support for social legislation even as it provided a new arena for Jewish solidarity beyond the bounds of private philanthropy. Jews extended the tradition of communal responsibility to American public policy, lending ethnic expression to support for government programs. At the same time, the foundations for Jewish community remained intact but were recast to meet the new conditions of American private philanthropy. With relief playing a diminished role in communal affairs, the organized Jewish community took responsibility for meeting other Jewish needs and promoting ethnic consciousness. Responding to both government welfare and the challenges of the Depression era, Jewish professionals rededicated their efforts to sustaining ethnic identity. Material relief became a smaller part of the Jewish communal program in the 1930s, but private Jewish philanthropy did not collapse in the welfare state. On the contrary, the Federation and its agencies emerged from the Depression with a more clearly defined ethnic mission. Private Jewish philanthropy not only survived the Depression; it emerged as a means to maintain the integrity of the ethnic community in a manner consonant with the new conditions of the welfare state.

The Federation survived the Depression as New York's representative Jewish communal institution. Although it continued to struggle for grassroots allegiance, the Federation remained the citywide symbol of an enduring ethnic community, growing stronger and gaining wider communal support in the post–World War II era. Yet, the Federation advocated a broad version of ethnic culture, rooted in Jewish tradition but not committed to any particular religious movement. In a decade of financial hardship and widespread religious indifference, the task of preserving Judaism and maintaining the religious dimension of American Jewish life fell to New York's synagogues.

# 7

# The Spiritual Depression

*We are suffering not only from financial depression; the depreciation in spiritual and religious values is evident at every hand. . . . The religious life of the Jewish people, its manifestation in synagog and home, is at a low ebb.*
—CCAR Yearbook

*Judaism is badly in need of a major operation. Send for the ambulance—or the undertaker.*
—*American Hebrew and Jewish Tribune*

In the history of the American synagogue, the 1930s stand between two periods of enormous synagogue expansion. The 1920s synagogue building boom ended with the onset of the Great Depression, and synagogue growth resumed only after World War II, when a new generation of Jews revived synagogue life on the suburban frontier. The Depression decade has generally been characterized as a period of stagnation and religious malaise in American synagogues. During the 1930s, synagogues struggled under heavy financial burdens and mortgage debts, watched their memberships shrink, and were often forced to curtail programs and dismiss personnel. And the fiscal crisis was only part of the problem facing Depression-era synagogues. Like their Christian counterparts, Jewish leaders identified a "spiritual depression" gripping the nation.[1] During the thirties, both Jewish and Christian clergy complained of dwindling attendance at worship services and widespread religious apathy. The Depression threatened both the economic health and substantive role of synagogues. As Jewish leaders contended with the financial problems plaguing their synagogues, they also searched for some means to combat spiritual lethargy and transform the synagogue into a vital communal institution.

The Depression-era programs initiated by New York synagogues reveal that the decade was much more than a brief interruption in the growth of the American synagogue. Concerned about the future of institutional Judaism, congregational leaders mounted a concerted effort to revitalize synagogue life. In many respects, the programs devised during the Depression represented a continuation of patterns established in the 1920s. During the twenties, second-generation Jews built elaborate synagogues that provided a modern setting for the practice of Judaism and offered a variety of social, cultural, and recreational programs. In the 1930s, New York congregations continued to broaden the scope of congregational activity, hoping to make the synagogue relevant and attractive to Jews during trying economic times. As they expanded social and cultural programs, synagogue leaders also responded to the political and social climate of the Depression, developing strategies to combat economic injustice and anti-Semitism, and even adopting New Deal rhetoric to address the problems of American Judaism. Although financial stringencies halted many synagogue programs and prompted a reassessment of congregational priorities, the economic crisis ultimately furthered the integration of the secular and the sacred within New York synagogues.[2]

The Depression was an arduous and uncertain period for Jewish congregations, but it was also a time when Jewish leaders reevaluated the synagogue's inner structure, communal role, and spiritual agenda against the backdrop of a changing American environment. The economic crisis did not radically transform American Judaism or dramatically alter the character of the synagogue, but the Depression experience significantly contributed to the ongoing development of institutional Judaism. Confronted with fiscal crisis and religious apathy, New York congregations responded by continuing to broaden the synagogue's role, by linking synagogue policy and programs with American social and political developments, and by addressing the evolving needs and interests of American Jews whose ethnic identities extended beyond strictly religious concerns. New York synagogues struggled through the Depression years and never succeeded in commanding widespread Jewish interest, but they emerged as institutions more acutely determined to build an expansive and relevant religious agenda.

When the Great Depression struck, American Jews had just completed a decade of unprecedented synagogue growth. During the 1920s, scores of new congregations were built, memberships grew, and synagogue programming reached new heights. From 1916 to 1926, the number of American synagogues almost doubled.[3] As middle-class Jews attained greater prosperity and moved to new neighborhoods, they created religious institutions that reflected their economic status and social aspirations. The late twenties saw New York Jews spend more than $12 million on synagogue construction, with a significant portion of that money funding the building of synagogue centers. The synagogue center, popularized by Mordecai Kaplan, provided social, educational, and recreational facilities, all under the religious auspices of the synagogue. Synagogue centers were created by a generation of Jews who wanted to maintain Jewish identification and to Americanize their religious and ethnic practices. Offering a range of programs beyond religious worship, the synagogue center affirmed the persistence of Judaism while also providing secular activities that appealed to acculturated Jews. Fulfilling both the Jewish communal needs and the middle-class aspirations of American-born Jews, the synagogue center blended religious expression with a broader secular and cultural program. The enormous growth in the number of synagogues and synagogue centers in the 1920s reflected the success and ethnic vision of second-generation Jews, but it also involved a hefty capital investment. Many New York congregations were both elaborate and costly. The Brooklyn Jewish Center, one of the largest in the city, housed a pool, restaurant, gymnasium, large synagogue, auditorium, and religious school. The construction of synagogue centers generally required at least $150,000, but more extravagant structures like the Brooklyn Jewish Center cost more than $1 million. Confident of future growth and increasing membership, middle-class Jewish communities invested heavily in their synagogues and expected them to thrive. In 1929 alone, New York Jews were financing the construction of twelve synagogue centers as well as building other congregations.[4]

The staggering financial problems of the 1930s stood in direct contrast to the enormous synagogue expansion that characterized the 1920s. The Depression brought an abrupt halt to a decade of synagogue growth and left congregations to contend with outstanding loans and formidable mortgage debts. After investing in elaborate buildings and expanding synagogue pro-

grams, many congregations suddenly had to struggle to remain fiscally solvent. At the height of the Depression, the president of the Brooklyn Jewish
Center candidly explained to congregants, "Our annual interest of $22,000 on
the $400,000 first mortgage is actually crushing us."[5] Synagogues throughout
the city experienced similar aftershocks from the 1920s building boom. Even
older, well-established synagogues had difficulty meeting interest payments.
In 1931, Congregation Kehilath Jeshurun, an elaborate Yorkville synagogue
built in 1902 by New York's most prosperous Orthodox Jews, owed $15,000
in interest on bank loans. After unsuccessful attempts to extend the payment
deadline and without other sufficient sources of income, the congregation
was finally forced to deepen its debt by taking another loan to cover the
mortgage interest. During the Depression, virtually every congregation suffered from an inability to meet financial obligations. A 1936 sample of 456
New York synagogues reported a collective debt of more than $14 million.[6]

The unfortunate combination of dwindling incomes and mounting
deficits characterized synagogue experience in the 1930s. Rabbi Abba Hillel
Silver, a leading figure in the Reform movement, pointedly assessed the state
of synagogue affairs: "I was once asked whether I thought that Judaism
would die in America. I answered no! the banks won't let it die! We built so
many of our institutions on borrowed money and mortgaged their future
incomes. So that in this depression the leaders of these institutions must
wear themselves out in heart-breaking efforts to meet budgets abnormally
swollen by huge interest and amortization charges."[7] In the 1920s, heavily
mortgaged synagogues expected to meet their debts with the dues from a
steadily growing membership. Instead, many found themselves with shrinking memberships, expensive facilities, and large deficits.[8] By 1935, American
synagogues were suffering so severely from the economic crisis that the
Reform movement's Union of American Hebrew Congregations (UAHC) distributed a guide entitled, "Financial Security for the Synagogue," which
offered budgetary suggestions as well as advice for attracting and retaining
members.[9]

The crisis prompted a reassessment of the previous decade's expansion.
Jewish leaders concluded that the progress of the 1920s had been illusory,
based on fleeting prosperity and grandiose synagogue construction rather
than a true commitment to Judaism. "We are beginning to realize," explained one Conservative movement publication, "that our duties and obligations to our religion are not satisfied completely by erecting buildings and
providing maintenance."[10] Rabbi Mordecai Kaplan, a pioneer of the synagogue center movement, acknowledged that "there is too much of a building
craze" and attacked the growing tendency "of relying upon the mere pres-

ence of the building to guarantee a Jewish future." Less than two months after the Wall Street Crash, Kaplan predicted that "the folly and the waste of putting up structures which are seldom used and which involve a tremendous overhead will sooner or later become too flagrant to be permitted to go on."[11] Reflecting on the hardships of the Depression, Rabbi Silver echoed those sentiments, suggesting that "perhaps in the future we shall learn to invest more in the essential qualitative purposes and programs of our institutions and less in brick and stone."[12]

As the Depression wore on, synagogues did reevaluate the content of their programming, but they had to contend first with urgent financial problems. Responses to the economic crisis varied according to the fiscal health of each institution and the economic status of its members. Like Kehilath Jeshurun, some congregations managed to secure bank loans, which kept them afloat despite creating greater debt.[13] More affluent synagogues, particularly those located on the Upper West Side's "gilded ghetto," were able to turn to prosperous members for support. At B'nai Jeshurun synagogue, several board members each loaned five hundred dollars to the congregation to ease its financial burdens. The Institutional Synagogue, an early forerunner of the Jewish center movement that had expanded from Harlem to the Upper West Side, also accepted loans from its synagogue directors to help meet expenses.[14] Few synagogues could rely on such generosity from members, however. Elias Cohen, president of nearby Anshe Chesed, explained to his board of directors, "Not by the use of the cash register will we survive, because we have now reached a state where we are flat broke and have no resources whatsoever."[15]

Whatever the economic status of their members, all congregations were forced to institute extensive, often painful, money-saving measures. Many congregations scaled down their choirs and limited synagogue hours and activities.[16] In more drastic budget cuts, synagogues frequently dismissed personnel, reduced salaries, and sometimes failed to pay their employees for months at a time. The Brooklyn Jewish Center "cut down expenses in each and every department to rock bottom," operating on what Rabbi Israel Levinthal called a "starvation diet." In addition to eliminating some of its maintenance and office staff, the center reduced wages to all remaining synagogue employees.[17] By 1931, the Society for the Advancement of Judaism had accumulated a $60,000 deficit and owed its staff thousands of dollars in back salaries.[18] Officials at Kehilath Jeshurun went without pay for as much as eight months at a time.[19] In 1932, Brooklyn's Kane Street synagogue told officers that they "would have to wait indefinitely for their back salaries." One year later, Kane Street abolished fixed wage scales entirely, determining its ability to pay employees on a month by month basis.[20] At Anshe Chesed, where finances were particularly strained, one board member recommended that "all persons with whom we have heretofore had obligations to serve for salaries should be told in a spirit of fair play and honesty that if they remain it must be with the understanding that at this time, and until some practical financial plan can be evolved, we are not in a position to pay salaries.[21] Even at the most affluent synagogues, officers, teachers, and staff routinely remained unpaid for months while their congregations struggled to stay afloat.

Salary cuts affected all those involved in the synagogue, including rabbis. Using tactful language, congregational minutes regularly reported that their rabbis had "declined" salary increases or "voluntarily contributed" their wages to the synagogue.[22] At the Society for the Advancement of Judaism, Mordecai Kaplan was forced to raise funds to pay his own salary and at one point offered to sacrifice part of his earnings to prevent sweeping budget cuts. In some cases, congregations could not afford to pay even drastically reduced rabbinic salaries and dismissed their clergy altogether. At the worst point of the Depression, Kaplan noted in his personal diary, "Among those who are bound to suffer most keenly from the demoralizing effect of the present economic depression are the rabbis, the superfluousness of whose calling has become more conspicuous than ever. Most of my colleagues are going through torments of hell."[23] The Reform movement's Central Conference of American Rabbis (CCAR), like the other rabbinical associations, expressed great concern about "the serious economic condition that faces many of the rabbinate of America." Rabbis grew apprehensive, not only about their own futures, but also about the bleak employment prospects that awaited newly ordained seminary graduates. Fearing that the economic crisis might produce a "rabbinical proletariat," the CCAR implored congregations to recognize "their duty to maintain spiritual leaders in a manner befitting their work and position." Despite all the warnings that they were "harming themselves and Judaism," however, congregations could not shield their rabbis from the realities of the Depression.[24]

Among the greatest obstacles facing synagogues was that they could no longer depend on a steady income from membership dues. During the Depression, synagogue memberships plummeted in virtually every congregation. At New York's prestigious Temple Emanu-El, home to the city's most affluent German Jews, membership decreased by 44 percent during the 1930s.[25] The Brooklyn Jewish Center had hoped to attract 1500 members by the mid-thirties but instead struggled to retain just over half that number.[26] The precipitous decline in membership resulted not simply from disinterest in synagogue life, but from the inability or unwillingness of many congregants to continue paying dues. During the Depression, many members formally resigned from synagogues or simply stopped paying dues. Some congregations, like Temple Emanu-El, refused to waive dues requirements for those who could not pay. Indeed, congregational minutes from the 1930s contain frequent reports of members being suspended for failure to pay dues. Most synagogues, however, allowed congregants at least a year's grace period before removing them from the membership rolls. As a rule, synagogues developed policies that gave consideration to their congregants' individual circumstances, frequently waiving and postponing membership fees. At the Kane Street synagogue, for example, one member wrote to the rabbi explaining that he could not afford to pay dues at the present time but pledging to resume regular payments "should conditions improve."[27] Synagogues desperately needed to retain congregants and in most cases, carried members on their books despite nonpayment. The UAHC supported the "method of 'personal adjustment,' that is handling each case separately," as the best way of "preventing by every possible means the withdrawal of members either permanently or temporarily."[28]

Hoping to stem the loss of membership, most synagogues instituted wholesale reductions in their dues. The Brooklyn Jewish Center had charged a steep one-hundred-dollar annual fee for married couples but slashed its dues requirement in half in 1933. "This radical step," explained the center's president, "was taken to lighten the burden of many of our members who are suffering from the prolonged, bitter depression. However, we [also] hoped that the smaller dues would attract many new members." Like most congregations, the Brooklyn Jewish Center altered its policy to allow members to pay their dues in installments rather than in one lump sum.[29] Virtually every congregation reduced its dues and some created new membership categories to entice prospective members to join. The Kane Street Synagogue, for example, charged married members twenty-five dollars but "in order to gain additional membership" also created a ten-dollar junior fee as well as other forms of limited membership.[30] Although new dues regulations did not prevent substantial losses in synagogue membership, they did aid in retaining and attracting some members. Despite significant attrition, 250 new members joined the Brooklyn Jewish Center in 1932. Speaking on behalf of the center, the president explained, "We are sure that if not for the reduction in dues they would not have joined. . . . We also feel certain that it has saved us a good many members who otherwise would have resigned."[31]

Congregations depended on their financially stable members to shoulder the fiscal burden in hard times, but in an age of economic contraction, many middle-class families viewed synagogue membership as an expendable luxury. In 1931, Kehilath Jeshurun's president proposed that certain well-to-do members increase their regular dues payments during the economic crisis. But three years later, the congregation's new president expressed outrage at the lack of member response. "I cannot believe," he insisted, "that the loyal members of Kehilath Jeshurun will take undue advantage in these times and withhold their generosity and obligation from the congregation that has every right and reason to expect it."[32] Rabbi Israel Goldstein of the Upper West Side's B'nai Jeshurun Synagogue firmly maintained that "there are very few people in our section of the city who cannot afford the minimum rates charged by Congregations."[33] At the Brooklyn Jewish Center, leaders expressed similar disgust with financially secure members who failed to participate in fund-raising drives. "There are many members of the Center," declared its president, "who, although quite able to help this institution in its distress, have turned a deaf ear to all our appeals." Center officials claimed that some congregants took advantage of the crisis, using it "merely as a cloak to conceal their selfishness and lack of public interest."[34] Mordecai Kaplan acknowledged that many members of the Society for the Advancement of Judaism were unable to contribute to the synagogue's annual fund-raising appeal but insisted that "in a number of cases there is no such excuse. They simply avail themselves of the general demoralization in communal life to shake off any sense of responsibility for the maintenance of the synagogue."[35] In a national discussion about the effects of dues reduction on congregations, one rabbi argued against the policy, maintaining that those unable to afford regular dues generally could not pay even a reduced fee, while those who would otherwise fulfill their usual obligation simply paid less.[36] Despite such concerns, dues reduction remained the norm in congregations throughout the 1930s, as did ongoing rebukes against members able but not willing to contribute to the synagogue.

The reasons for withdrawing from or declining to join synagogues varied enormously, as did the individual experiences of Jews during the Depression. Many Jews affiliated with synagogues only to celebrate life-cycle events. Sydney Evans, who grew up in Brooklyn, remembered that, "When the time came to be Bar-Mitzvahed, [my family] joined . . . and when it was over, it kind of faded away." Evans explained that his parents, like so many other Jews in the thirties, were too preoccupied with the daily struggles of securing work and raising children to take much interest in the synagogue.[37] Another Depression-era youth reported a different story, recalling that his father had attended synagogue regularly until his business failed. "With the Depression," he reflected, "things changed with my father even in religious practice. Before, he never failed to take us to the synagogue every single Saturday. After the crash he didn't seem to care anymore."[38] For other Jews, lack of participation in the synagogue was more a financial than a psychological matter. Edwin Shapiro, who grew up in Flatbush, remembered celebrating his Bar-Mitzvah in 1934 but noted that his parents did not belong to a synagogue because it "required some financial identity" that the family did not possess.[39] Financial considerations drove the synagogue choices of many Jews. Irving Howe recalled that in his Bronx neighborhood, "The nearest synagogue, in a once baroque structure, was also struggling through the Depression, and as if to acknowledge reduced circumstances my own bar mitzvah took place not there, since that would have cost too much and probably made us feel uncomfortable."[40] Resigning from a synagogue was not necessarily the result of impoverishment; many congregants simply chose to eliminate synagogue dues from strained household budgets. As Mordecai Kaplan observed in the mid-thirties, "There is a growing tendency to treat synagogue affiliation as a luxury to be enjoyed when times are good and money plentiful. But as soon as the financial status of the members slumps, the affiliation is one of the first luxuries to be surrendered."[41]

During the economic crisis, synagogues were often accused of placing financial concerns above a commitment to serve Jews and Judaism. Although by the 1930s most second-generation congregations had abolished the practice of raising funds by publicly auctioning synagogue honors, most continued to sell seats for High Holiday services. Many Jews attended synagogue only on Rosh Hashanah and Yom Kippur and purchased tickets for those days alone. Stanley Katz recalled that his family bought High Holiday tickets every year. "You had a special ticket fee you would pay," Katz explained, "and you could attend holiday services without having to be an annual member."[42] For Jews who had neither the income nor the desire to become regular synagogue members, High Holiday tickets provided a useful solution. But critics claimed that by charging for worship during Rosh Hashanah and Yom Kippur (the peak days for synagogue attendance), congregations discriminated against poorer Jews. A harsh editorial in the *American Hebrew* assailed synagogue practice:

> In a time when men's very souls are tried by calamity; in a time when men who for years were the very backbone of the synagogue find themselves helpless to carry on; in a time when men are apt to lose their faith in God and humanity, what did some of our synagogues do? They refused admission on Rosh Hashanah and Yom Kippur unless men either paid up their arrears or came to the office and made adequate explanation. . . . It was the most conspicuous act of stupidity, and lack of religious feeling, that the American synagogue has ever witnessed.[43]

Many congregations did make High Holiday services available to those who could not pay, but obtaining the free seats often required special application. The Institutional Synagogue, for example, explained that "upon application, unemployed people, home relief recipients and children will be given free seats."[44] Yet many Jews would not submit to the humiliation of formally declaring impoverishment in order to gain admission to the synagogue. Despite the best intentions of congregations to serve the Jewish poor, most synagogues remained, in the words of Mordecai Kaplan, "the exclusive clubhouse of a homogeneous group," often alienating the poor and working-class.[45]

For poor and unaffiliated Jews, "mushroom" synagogues—large auditoriums or theaters temporarily converted to houses of worship for the High Holidays—offered an alternative to established congregations. For years before the Depression, merchants eager to exploit the Jewish desire to attend High Holiday services had turned a profit by hiring amateurs to conduct worship and charging a reasonable two- to five-dollar admission fee. In response to an *American Hebrew* article entitled, "Religion at Bargain Prices," one reader wrote to the editor, questioning, "Why should not those who cannot afford [synagogues'] fancy prices . . . seek religion at bargain prices? . . . Are not mushroom synagogues, therefore, rendering a real service?"[46] Established synagogues vehemently opposed such sentiments. Jewish leaders believed that most Jews who attended mushroom synagogues were not impoverished but simply chose not to support regular congregations. Rabbi Israel Goldstein insisted that "many people who think nothing of spending $25.00 for a day's amusement, will balk at spending a similar sum in support of a house of worship. . . . I doubt whether such people deserve any sympathy or consideration."[47] Moreover, congregational leaders resented the profit-seekers who sponsored mushroom synagogues. The chairman of the United Synagogue's mushroom synagogue committee emphasized that "unburdened by the heavy expenses and upkeep which legitimate synagogues and temples must carry, [mushroom synagogues] are enabled to sell seats for the so-called high holiday services at a price below that which regular temples must charge."[48]

During the Depression, established congregations struggling to stay afloat attacked mushroom synagogues more virulently than ever before. Saddled with heavy financial burdens, synagogues could no longer afford to have their efforts undermined by profit-hungry competitors. High Holiday services were a chief source of income for congregations as well as their best opportunity to reach the Jewish public. To combat mushroom synagogues, some congregations organized additional services on the High Holidays, attempting to accommodate a larger number of worshippers. And in 1934, religious leaders persuaded the New York state legislature to pass a law making it a misdemeanor to sell tickets to services in "non-legitimate places of worship."[49] The battle against mushroom synagogues was an attempt to preserve the integrity of established congregations at a time when synagogues desperately needed moral and financial support.

Synagogues pursued several avenues to raise funds during the economic crisis. Congregations relied on traditional fund-raising tactics, such as selling memorial plaques and holding bazaars and appeals.[50] Almost without exception, synagogues also looked to their sisterhoods for financial help. Synagogue sisterhoods had always functioned as important behind-the-scenes fund-raisers, but during the Depression, they shouldered even greater responsibility. "The dire need of the Brooklyn Jewish Center," declared the center's president, "has compelled it to create additional sources of income. And where shall we turn to in time of need but to our own women?"[51] The Depression spurred a change in the sisterhood's role at the Brooklyn Jewish Center. Before 1929, the organization had limited its agenda to social, cultural, and religious activities. But, as the sisterhood's president explained, "the changes in the financial condition of the Center made it imperative for the women to come to the assistance of the officers and directors who were struggling to keep the institution functioning."[52] So great was the preoccupation with fund-raising that some women expressed concern that "sisterhoods have been so engrossed in decreasing the indebtedness of their Houses of Worship that they have not had the opportunity of increasing those spiritual activities for which these Houses of Worship stand."[53] Although women's organizations had always raised money for the synagogue, they considered their primary mission to provide spiritual and cultural programs. Sisterhood leaders worried that Depression-era fund-raising might take precedence over the broader religious agenda that women had constructed. Despite such fears, however, sisterhoods were forced by circumstance to join their fellow congregants in devoting unprecedented attention to financial matters.

As the Depression deepened, synagogue sisterhoods shouldered an increasing financial load and a greater responsibility for maintaining synagogue activities. In years past, religious leaders had often lamented the fact that the synagogue had become largely the province of women, but during the Depression, they usually described women's contributions as absolutely essential. The chairman of the UAHC's Commission on Synagogue Activities emphasized that "in these days of high pressure business and professional relationships that hold our men in such rigorous thralldom, many of the functions of the synagogue depend perforce on the leisure class, and the women, who are the most numerous components of that class."[54] Such appeals to women had a long tradition within American synagogues. Male congregational leaders had regularly depended on women's volunteer activities and charitable endeavors, particularly in times of crisis. When their congregations turned to them in the Depression, women responded. In 1934 alone, the Kane Street Synagogue Sisterhood contributed $1750 to the congregation's floundering treasury, a hefty sum in the midst of the Great Depression. But Jewish women did more than raise money for their synagogues; they also predominated in the ranks of religious school teachers, often working as unpaid volunteers. In congregations without the resources to pay teachers, many sisterhoods "charged themselves with the duty of organizing the Religious Schools and of teaching in them."[55] Sisterhood women answered their congregations' calls for help, but in the words of the president of the Brooklyn Jewish Center's Sisterhood, their efforts also eased women's transition to "active participation in the affairs of the institution."[56] In a dramatic sketch staged in 1939 by the Park Avenue Synagogue Sisterhood, Jewish women revealed how they perceived the value of their contributions to the congregation. Portraying a fictional scenario in which the synagogue board decided to relinquish control of congregational affairs to the sisterhood, one board official was scripted to exclaim, "Splendid. They're the only ones who have any money. They're the only ones who know how to raise money. They're the only ones who use the Synagogue anyway. . . . Well, then, why should we worry—let's vote to give the shuel to the sisterhood." While the comedic presentation was designed to elicit laughter, it also revealed that Jewish women understood the importance of their efforts in keeping Depression-era congregations afloat, even if male congregational leaders continued to regard their contributions as simply another example of female benevolence.[57]

Congregations depended on their female members to bolster the synagogue from within, but in the midst of the Depression, they also looked for new ways to broaden synagogue appeal, initiating several innovative publicity techniques. In 1931 on Yom Kippur, New York's Reform congregations distributed leaflets to all those attending services, urging the unaffiliated to become synagogue members. With the slogan, "Join the Temple in Your Neighborhood Today," Reform congregations advertised their product using the tactics of the commercial world.[58] Orthodox congregations also participated in mass membership and fund-raising campaigns. The Orthodox Religious Reconstruction Committee called on every Jew to donate one dollar to a central fund that supported synagogues and religious schools. The national drive culminated on the eve of Purim, a traditional holiday for charitable contributions. Yet, the campaign used modern propaganda tools, including a radio program aired nationwide on a National Broadcasting Company station.[59] In 1935, New York's Reform, Conservative, and Orthodox synagogues joined forces in the Into the Synagogue movement, a program intended "to stimulate interest in the synagogue and to increase congregational membership."[60]

In the age of radio, religious leaders recognized the vast audience that might be reached through judicious use of the airways. For example, Rabbi Israel Levinthal of the Brooklyn Jewish Center often contributed his oratorical skills to radio programs addressing Jewish topics. Jewish political leaders also sometimes engaged in religious propaganda. In 1931, Manhattan borough president Samuel Levy broadcast a radio appeal to second-generation Jews, urging them "to adhere to the faith of their fathers."[61] Jewish programming of all varieties filled New York stations, including regular broadcasts of worship services. Religious leaders hoped, probably mistakenly, that mass exposure would bring Jewish listeners from their radios to the synagogue. The use of radio, leafleting, and large-scale campaigns testified to the new commercial tactics adopted by the synagogue in its quest to attract a new generation of American Jews. Throughout the 1930s, Jewish leaders relied on publicity and propaganda to "sell" the synagogue and its religious message to a wider segment of the Jewish community.[62]

Religious renewal efforts gained momentum with the implementation of the New Deal, as congregations mimicked and capitalized on the spirit of Roosevelt's recovery programs. In 1933, Rabbi Herbert Goldstein of the Institutional Synagogue urged Jewish leaders to seize the moment and initiate a meaningful revival program. "While the entire nation has enlisted in the very worthy cause of restoring economic prosperity to the United States, little has been done to repair the depleted state of our religious institutions," Goldstein insisted. "The best minds in the country have been drafted in the noble effort to bring back prosperity, but no religious or lay leaders have taken any steps to revive our weakened institutions." In the years after Roosevelt's election, religious leaders hoped to create a movement for spiritual renewal. Taking their cue from New Deal programs, Jewish, Catholic, and Protestant organizations united in a Drive for Religious Recovery. The campaign urged complete attendance in churches and synagogues during one weekend in October of 1935. Known as "loyalty days," the two days of worship were advertised as a means "to show united leadership in spiritual recovery." Jewish organizations promoted the day as "loyalty Sabbath," using the slogan, "Every Jew Present and Accounted For."[63] There is little evidence to suggest the realization of a religious revival, but Jewish leaders persisted nonetheless, hoping to capture for the synagogue what Roosevelt had promised for the nation.

Among all New Deal initiatives, no Roosevelt program sparked as much rhetoric in religious circles as did the National Recovery Administration (NRA). Established in 1933 as a tool for economic recovery, the NRA negotiated codes for industries, determining hours, wages, and rates of production. Jewish commentators seized upon the political terminology of the New Deal as a way to demonstrate Jewish commitment to the national recovery effort and to emulate Roosevelt's far-reaching renewal tactics within religious life.

For religious leaders, the NRA not only epitomized the spirit of revitalization but, equally important, promoted the five-day work week. Jewish organizations hoped that Jews who were freed from Saturday employment would embrace the opportunity to observe the Sabbath. "The NRA will . . . revolutionize the Sabbath," declared the United Synagogue, which represented Conservative congregations, "the new standard of working hours for the individual means that the Sabbath will be a real day of rest."[64] Representatives from all branches of Jewish life welcomed the promise of the NRA. Like many other rabbis, Herbert Goldstein made the NRA the subject of his 1933 Rosh Hashanah sermon, proclaiming to the congregation: "I regard the NRA as singularly Providential for the restoration of the observance of the Sabbath. It will bring on I am sure (if only we seize its possibilities), a religious revival to both Jew and Christian. Work and physical enjoyment were rapidly supplanting rest and the religious exhilaration of the Sabbath. With the introduction of the five day work week throughout the nation, there will be one day for the recreation of the body and the other for the recreation of the soul."[65] Other Jewish leaders echoed Goldstein's sentiment, declaring that "the opportunity for which countless Sabbath-loving Jews have been hoping is at hand. . . . Now the 'I-would-if-I-could' Jew can, if he will, observe Shabboth [sic]."[66] The NRA met with similar enthusiasm from leaders throughout the Jewish community. The Synagogue Council of America, representing the three major bodies of American Judaism, hailed the NRA as a spiritual antidote, capable of "bringing the Sabbath back to the Jews."[67] In fact, the NRA brought no discernible change in Sabbath observance; American Jews rarely attended synagogue or set aside the Sabbath as a day of rest. The fervent enthusiasm about the NRA and the five-day work week revealed much more about changes in synagogue strategy and rhetoric than it did about general patterns of religious observance.

The possibility for greater Sabbath observance was not the only benefit that religious leaders hoped to reap from the NRA. They also wanted to build a mass movement for religious recovery modeled after Roosevelt's sweeping economic programs. As Israel Levinthal proclaimed in his 1933 Rosh Hashanah sermon, "We need an NRA in American Jewish life, a resolve on the part of every Jew to bring about a recovery of those ideals that have given strength and vitality to Jewish life in all the ages past." Levinthal outlined the symbolism of each letter of the NRA acronym, explaining that the N represented the nationality of Israel, both in Palestine and throughout the world; the R stood for the religion of Israel, which he claimed required a "New Deal" in order to survive; finally, the A emphasized the importance of action, of demonstrating Jewish commitment through deed.[68]

Jewish leaders capitalized on the spirit of national recovery, using the NRA as a springboard for promoting religious revival. In the fall of 1933, the United Synagogue told its constituents that "the synagogue should meet the challenge presented by the NRA. It should initiate the new era with the proclamation of a Spiritual Recovery Act." Declaring its efforts an "historic event in the life of American Jewry," the United Synagogue organized a National Recovery Assembly with representatives from more than 750 Conservative congregations and associations. The major issues addressed by the assembly—reviving the Sabbath, channeling new leisure time produced by the NRA into Jewish educational, cultural, and spiritual pursuits, and democratizing the synagogue in order to attract a broader constituency—represented the central concerns of congregations from all branches of American Judaism.[69]

The pressing need for most synagogues was to attract the interest of the Jewish public. Critics of synagogue behavior emphasized that the Jew "does not . . . reject the synagogue; he ignores it."[70] During the Depression, religious leaders worked to change synagogue atmosphere and address contemporary issues in an effort to appeal to a broader segment of the Jewish population. They also attempted to destroy the image of the synagogue as an elitist institution. With the spirit of social democracy permeating New Deal politics, congregations emphasized the need to apply democratic principles to synagogue life. Bringing democracy to the synagogue meant accepting members regardless of financial status and including them fully in congregational affairs. At the National Recovery Assembly, the United Synagogue resolved to create membership categories "so as to enable the man and woman of the smallest means to share in the honors and responsibilities of the synagogue." The organization further declared that "financial and social snobbery should have no place in the synagogue. A true spirit of old-fashioned Jewish democracy should permeate every synagogal activity."[71] In fact, the democratic spirit had never been a vital element in American synagogues, which were generally supported and governed by an economic and social elite. The new emphasis on equality in the synagogue represented a conscious attempt to broaden the base of congregational support, but equally important, it underlined the commonality of Jewish and American ideals and championed the cause of democracy. As Europe fell victim to right-wing political movements in the 1930s, American Jews became more concerned than ever about preserving the principles of American democracy. The UAHC's president insisted that the synagogue, "cannot afford to overlook the trends and tendencies of present-day American life. In these days when democracy is everywhere on the defensive, we Jews must more than ever affirm it—and especially in the synagogue."[72] By calling for democracy in Jewish congregations and mimicking New Deal programs, synagogues portrayed the essential harmony of Jewish and American pursuits. The attempt to bring democracy to Jewish congregations was, then, both an effort to attract a larger synagogue constituency as well as part of the synagogue's response to the political and social climate.

The endeavor to heighten synagogue appeal and create relevant programming also included a new emphasis on the Jewish working class. "The bane of the synagogue in this country," insisted Mordecai Kaplan, "has been its confinement to the middle class."[73] At the National Recovery Assembly, United Synagogue representatives discussed ways to draw the masses of Jewish workers to the synagogue. They not only stressed the importance of attracting Jewish laborers but also declared that "the synagogue must take an active interest in all problems affecting the worker, such as the relationships between employer and employee, exploitation of labor, [and] general problems of social justice."[74] The Reform movement acted most vigorously in the field of social justice, accelerating its efforts during the Depression years. As early as 1931, the Central Conference of American Rabbis (CCAR) formally endorsed federal public works projects, relief programs, unemployment insurance, and even encouraged industry profit-sharing. In order to implement its social justice program within the synagogue, the CCAR recommended that congregations employ only those firms that supported organized labor and collective bargaining.[75] None of these programs succeeded in attracting large numbers of working-class Jews to the synagogue. Nevertheless, the explicitly political role outlined for the synagogue represented a significant innovation.

The themes of social justice and economic reform were not limited to the resolutions of national organizations but were also reiterated in individual synagogue programs and rabbinic sermons. Several congregations responded to the call for social justice with volunteer projects and fund-raising efforts for the unemployed. With the implementation of relief programs, New York synagogues often served as unofficial liaisons between the jobless and the city's relief offices.[76] In addition, rabbis used their pulpits to draw lessons from the Depression experience. Israel Levinthal, known for applying Jewish teachings to contemporary issues, told his audience that the "whole social structure needs revision. There is something radically wrong with an economic system that keeps men, who want and are able to work, out of employment." According to Levinthal, lobbying for social and economic reform could be equated with pursuing the religious goal of *mishpat*, justice. A few years later, Levinthal put his theories into action by helping to mediate a labor dispute at Brooklyn's Beth Moses Hospital.[77]

Not all rabbis agreed that the pulpit was the proper place to discuss contemporary social and economic concerns. As one Orthodox publication proclaimed, "We believe that the rabbi should not stoop to the discussion . . . of economic problems, for then he generally becomes sophomoric. He is not a teacher of economics, but of religion. What we need today is to make our people understand that our economic, social and political problems are basically personal religious ones."[78] But despite some detractors, the trend toward extending the realm of synagogue concerns to include the social and political arena persisted.

Although they differed about the extent to which rabbis and congregations should address contemporary social problems, religious leaders agreed that the synagogue should provide comfort and inspiration in times of crisis. Congregational minutes from the Depression report a mood of despondency hovering over synagogue activities. The Brooklyn Jewish Center's social committee repeatedly complained that members were too preoccupied to take interest in its programs. "The depressed feeling prevailing throughout the world has had its effect on the work of the Social Committee," explained the committee chairman in 1934.[79] During the Depression, rabbinic sermons frequently addressed the pervasive feeling of despair, offering consolation and hope. "The great tragedy," Israel Levinthal told his congregation, "is that we have lost our moral[e]. . . . We see only darkness. We are overwhelmed by the rising tide of unemployment—bankruptcy—the very breakdown of economic structure." Encouraging his congregants to remain steadfast through the crisis, Levinthal exhorted them "not to lose faith nor hope" but rather "to have faith in a better day and to fight for it."[80] Synagogue leaders hoped that congregants would turn to religion for strength and solace. "In the midst of our present depression," proclaimed the Institutional Synagogue's president, "we have seen and learned that those who possessed a religious background may have been down but they were never out."[81]

Some Jewish leaders anticipated that the economic crisis might revive religious enthusiasm. In both Jewish and Christian circles, hopes for a return to religion increased with the onset of the Depression. "Some religious leaders actually hailed the depression with rejoicing," explained a Chicago Theological Seminary professor, "since they had the idea that previous depressions had 'driven men to God' and felt that the time was overdue for men again to be reminded of the need to let the spiritual dominate the materialistic order."[82] Synagogue officials similarly hoped that the crisis might spark a spiritual renewal among American Jews. In 1932, the CCAR's president reminded his rabbinic colleagues that "the rehabilitation of a disordered world presents to religious leaders an opportunity and a challenge." He urged synagogue leaders to "furnish the dynamic spiritual force to maintain the morale of people in these trying days," insisting that "if we religious leaders are equal to the task, the ultimate result of this depression will yet be a gain for things of the spirit."[83]

Despite such public proclamations, many Jewish leaders feared that the Depression would only erode devotion to Judaism. Mordecai Kaplan worked to revitalize Jewish life throughout the 1930s, yet privately he confessed, "It is only through the exertion of strenuous mental effort that I manage to expel from my mind temporarily the apprehension of almost certain demise of Judaism in this country. . . . In my heart of hearts I know that with the insane and stupid economic order under which we are living, it is absolutely fatuous to expect the millions of people who are starving to take life religiously."[84] In fact, the economic crisis did not precipitate a mass religious return. While some Jews undoubtedly found comfort in the synagogue, enthusiasm for Roosevelt and the New Deal and the daily challenges of Depression-era life far eclipsed religious concerns for most Jewish Americans. In examining the religious response to the Depression, the *Christian Century* reported that most Americans attributed the Depression to "the failure of human intelligence or the blind power of entrenched privilege, or both." Therefore, they opted to look for solutions in the human rather than in the divine realm. The Depression did more to rally fundamentalist and reactionary movements rather than to reinvigorate mainstream religion. In the field of religion, the thirties are best remembered as the era of such leaders as Father Coughlin, William Pelley, Gerald L. K. Smith, and Father Divine.[85] In 1937, New York's Social Science Research Council reported the meager accomplishments of organized religion during the Depression, concluding that the country's religious movements had not "reaped a large harvest during these lean years of economic life."[86]

Jewish leaders joined the chorus lamenting the decline of religious devotion during the Depression years. As early as 1931, the Orthodox Rabbinical Association identified a "'spiritual depression' in American religious life" and vowed to prevent the economic crisis from bringing about a complete "moratorium on religion."[87] Evaluating the sentiment of second-generation Jews in the late thirties, one rabbi remarked, "the faith of their fathers is *with* their fathers; it is no longer with them."[88] While pronouncements of doom about the imminent decay of Jewish life and impassioned pleas for greater religious commitment were hardly new to the American Jewish community, the Depression brought a sense of urgency to apprehensions about the Jewish future. Rabbis and synagogue leaders seized on the metaphor of recovery, in part, because they perceived their institutions to be as morally and financially bankrupt as the nation as a whole. In the mid-thirties, one Jewish sociologist went so far as to claim that "the Jewish religion as a social institution is losing its influence for the perpetuation of the Jewish group" and predicted "the total eclipse of the Jewish church in America."[89] As synagogue memberships plummeted, congregations struggled to remain fiscally solvent, and Jews looked elsewhere for personal and political solutions, the future of institutional Judaism looked particularly grim.

The Great Depression did not bring about a sudden disinterest in Judaism, but rather exposed long-term trends in American Jewish life. Even before the Depression, only a minority of American Jews were affiliated with synagogues and fewer attended regularly. In 1935, three-quarters of New York's Jewish youth reported that they had not attended any religious services during the past year.[90] A 1929 study revealed that almost 80 percent of Jewish children in New York City received no religious training whatsoever and had never learned the Hebrew alphabet.[91] The lack of interest in the synagogue was nothing new to the American Jewish community; even during the enormous synagogue expansion of the 1920s, only a minority of Jews joined, supported, or attended congregations. But in the twenties, despite ongoing concerns about religious apathy, synagogues were able to carry out and even expand congregational programming. The Depression revealed the narrow base of synagogue support and brought to light the precariousness of relying on a small group to sustain these institutions. For years, congregations had underlined the importance of reaching a broader constituency, but the economic crisis made that need even more pressing. The Depression forced synagogue leaders to search

for a way to revitalize congregations and make them relevant and respon-
sive to the needs of Depression-era Jews.

Rabbi Mordecai Kaplan, the leading proponent of synagogue reform in
the 1930s, had argued for sweeping changes in the synagogue long before
the Depression. In the 1910s, Kaplan founded the Jewish Center in Manhattan which served as a model for the synagogue center movement. Claiming
that a narrow definition of Judaism as religion was insufficient to assure
Jewish survival in the American environment, Kaplan promoted the synagogue center as a home for all the leisure activities of the Jew. Deriving his
ideas from a variety of sociologists and philosophers, including Emile Durk-
heim and John Dewey, as well as leading Jewish thinkers such as Ahad
Ha-am and Simon Dubnow, Kaplan maintained that the synagogue ought to
embrace the gamut of Jewish needs and concerns.[93] "Public worship," he
insisted, "should be one of the functions of the synagogue, but by no means
the only one, nor even the principal one." In order for Judaism to become a
way of life rather than a narrow belief system, Kaplan argued, synagogues
had to participate in the social, cultural, political, economic, recreational as
well as the religious lives of American Jews. He faulted existing synagogues
for failing to meet Jewish needs, in part, because they focused solely on
worship. According to Kaplan, the synagogue, "should be a neighborhood
center to which all Jews to whom it is accessible would resort for all religious,
cultural, social and recreational purposes."[93] Although he had formulated his
ideas years earlier, Kaplan published his magnum opus, *Judaism as a Civilization*, in 1934, lending theoretical expression to the drive to incorporate
secular concerns into the religious agenda.[94]

By the time the Depression struck, New York synagogues had already
adopted at least some elements of Kaplan's vision of American Judaism.[95]
Whether or not they subscribed to his philosophy, congregations of all
denominations had discovered the benefits and the necessity of broadening
the scope of synagogue programs. By the late 1920s, social functions had
become an integral part of synagogue life in congregations throughout the
city and the nation. As Rabbi Israel Levinthal succinctly explained in 1936,
providing extra-religious activities was the best way to draw Jews to the
synagogue. "It is true that many will come for other purposes than to
meet God," he admitted. "But let them come."[96] Not all Jewish leaders
were quite as enthusiastic about the emerging synagogue center movement.
The prominent Reform rabbi, Abba Hillel Silver, a sharp critic of Kaplan
and of his vision of the synagogue center, argued that "it is futile and
altogether confusing to attempt to bring the whole of Jewish life under
the roof of the synagogue." Attacking the path that synagogues had taken,

Silver added that "if the Jewish community no longer needs the God of the synagogue, the worship of the synagogue and the spiritual and ethical preachment of the synagogue, it certainly does not need the swimming pool of the synagogue, or its dances or its theatricals."[97] But despite some detractors, the trend toward blending secular and religious functions continued unabated. That trend had begun before the 1930s, but the Depression ensured its continuation, as congregations struggled for ways to attract the Jewish public.

The Great Depression was by no means the first time that congregations had offered social and recreational activities, but unemployment and limited working hours created more leisure time, breathing new life into the synagogue's secular programming. During the Depression, Jewish centers that housed pools and gymnasiums found their facilities taxed to capacity. Between 1931 and 1935, while the Brooklyn Jewish Center experienced dramatic losses in general membership, more than four thousand new members came to use its gym.[98] Jews flocked to synagogue centers to use physical education facilities and also to participate in social and cultural activities. "We have more social, literary, and athletic clubs . . . today than ever before in our history," declared Rabbi Goldstein, assessing the Institutional Synagogue's programs in 1934. "This is due," he added, "to the present unemployment situation. Our young people have more leisure now than ever before." Goldstein further explained that by offering a range of activities under religious auspices, the synagogue helped to protect Jewish youth from "communistic and other destructive forces."[99] Depression-era synagogues underlined the importance of making the synagogue a gathering place for youth, noting that "this leisure will shape the character of the individual for good or bad." Since increased leisure time affected adults as well as youth, several congregations initiated adult education programs. At Congregation Beth Elohim in Brooklyn, Rabbi Isaac Landman founded the Academy of Adult Jewish Education, which received state accreditation in 1933. That same year, the Brooklyn Jewish Center inaugurated the Institute of Adult Jewish Studies under Israel Levinthal's guidance; it attracted more than three hundred students who wanted "to utilize the extra leisure hours to some useful purpose."[100] The city's large Jewish centers sponsored the widest array of leisure activities for both young and old, but even the smallest congregations organized social programs, youth groups, sporting events, and cultural activities. The United Synagogue insisted that Jewish congregations owed it to their members to alter programming in response to Depression-era conditions and "to step in and see that this leisure is used for spiritual and character building purposes."[101]

As the Depression wore on, New York congregations became more convinced than ever that expansive synagogue programming answered the needs of Depression-era Jews and provided a prescription to heal Jewish disinterest in the synagogue.

Ironically, in the midst of the Depression, as synagogues continued to broaden their reach, Mordecai Kaplan began to express doubts about the synagogue center idea that he had once advocated so passionately. Kaplan had conceived the synagogue center as one means to counteract apathy toward congregational life and preserve Jewish community in America. By 1935, however, he confessed, "At first I thought that if the synagogue were transformed into a center that would house the leisure activities of our people, the problem of Jewish life in this country would be solved. Before long I realized this was far from enough." Kaplan was disappointed that leisure activities had taken precedence over more far-reaching efforts to revitalize American Judaism.[102] In his personal diary, Kaplan revealed his profound discouragement: "What a Sisyphus affair, this trying to keep Judaism alive in this country," he lamented.[103] In his own congregation, he noticed that Jewish youth had almost completely abandoned organized worship, leaving prayer services as the sole province of the older generation. "As for American-Jewish life," Kaplan wrote in 1935, "I have come to a point where I feel as though I were choking for lack of air to breathe. It is almost a physical sensation with me and never so painful as on Sabbath mornings at the services of the S.A.J. when I sit on the platform and watch the few old timers going through mechanically the services."[104] Kaplan believed that the Depression would only accelerate the decline of American Jewish life. "The inevitable submergence of Judaism," he concluded, "is only apt to be confirmed by the growing economic and moral deficit in every one of the Jewish institutions.[105] Paradoxically, as Kaplan expressed increasing misgiving about the direction of American synagogues, his original formulation of a broadly based synagogue agenda was becoming more firmly entrenched in American congregations with each successive year of the Depression.[106]

Filling increased leisure time was only one way that Depression-era synagogues hoped to widen their appeal. Many congregations also initiated practical programs to improve Jewish economic status and employment options. Just as the New York Jewish Federation recognized the paramount importance of sponsoring Jewish employment bureaus during the Depression, so too, synagogues sought to address the economic concerns of their members. Many religious leaders believed that by actively working to better the Jewish economic condition, synagogues could capture a central role in the lives of American Jews. "In the direction of economic life, there is a great opportunity for the Synagog," one rabbi proclaimed. "When men and women, young and old, will see that the Synagog is alive to their needs in the economic area of life," he optimistically and mistakenly predicted, "their allegiance and devotion to Judaism will become much stronger and more enduring." Responding according to their own ideological positions, religious organizations proposed various solutions to ease the Jewish economic burden. At the 1937 meeting of the Reform movement's rabbinical conference, Rabbi Samuel Wohl proposed the creation of Jewish Economic Councils that would operate under the auspices of the synagogue. By helping to "normalize" Jewish employment, by encouraging Jews to consider alternatives to white-collar professions, and by urging Jewish employers to hire Jewish workers, the synagogue might exercise its influence in the daily economic concerns of its members. Wohl's proposal received some discussion at the CCAR convention but was never implemented.[107] His belief that organized religion should play a role in aiding the Jewish economy was, however, echoed by many Jewish leaders.

Because of their concern with maintaining Sabbath observance, Orthodox synagogues initiated some of the best organized efforts to help Jews find jobs that would not require Saturday work. As early as 1930, Orthodox congregations in the Bronx joined forces to compile lists of employers willing to hire Sabbath-observant workers.[108] New York's Young Israel, a modern Orthodox movement designed to appeal to American-born youth, provided more far-reaching employment services. The Young Israel Employment Bureau, first organized in 1925, expanded its activities during the Depression, offering both job placement and vocational training. Acknowledging that "in a world of depression and despondency, . . . the unemployed Sabbath-observer of today finds himself in a precarious predicament," Young Israel set out to find jobs for religiously observant Jews.[109] Young Israel's employment bureau targeted native-born, well-educated youth and sought to combine traditional observance with the economic realities of the day. The number of young Jews whose employment problems stemmed from a refusal to work on Saturdays was admittedly small. Nevertheless, Young Israel's efforts to secure jobs for Jews reflected the Orthodox movement's attempt to address Depression-era economic needs in accordance with its religious agenda. In the 1930s, synagogues across the Jewish spectrum not only brought secular programming into the house of worship but also extended religious endeavors into the political and economic realm.

Behind religious employment efforts and various synagogue proposals to aid the Jewish economy lay real fears about Jewish status and security in

29. *Through its Sabbath-observant employment bureau,*
*Young Israel attempted to bolster both religious practice*
*and Jewish economic prospects. Courtesy of the American*
*Jewish Historical Society, Waltham, Massachusetts.*

America. Jewish employment bureaus and attempts to diversify the Jewish
economic profile were, in part, a response to job discrimination and prejudice.
Many nonobservant Jews came to the Young Israel Employment Bureau
because it offered protection from anti-Semitism and job discrimination.[110]
National and citywide organizations played the most prominent role in combating anti-Semitism, but synagogues also responded to the growing threat.
As anti-Semitism peaked in the 1930s, religious organizations worked even
harder to maintain Jewish support—not only by devising schemes to preserve
Jewish economic health, but also by arguing that participation in synagogue

life helped to fortify Jewish self-respect in the face of anti-Semitism. In 1933, the UAHC provided a sample letter that congregations could send to members who had resigned from the synagogue. The letter emphasized that no matter what economic hardships members had endured, they could not afford "*not* to be a member of the Temple" because of the threat of anti-Semitism. The synagogue reminded withdrawing members that anti-Semites "are capitalizing the fact that a number of Jews are in the confidence of the Federal Administration and they are capitalizing the fact that men such as you and I have been reasonably successful in our respective fields." Retaining synagogue membership, according to the UAHC, was crucial in order for Jews to demonstrate loyalty and pride in the face of prejudice.[111]

As the Depression wore on, synagogues became more concerned with raising Jewish self-respect. Religious leaders worried that anti-Semitism would place "the stigma of inferiority" on American Jews and further undermine commitment to Jewish life. Jewish leaders knew too well that some Jews had resorted to changing their names and denying their identity in order to secure employment and avoid anti-Semitism.[112] Given the economic and cultural pressures facing Depression-era Jews, synagogues made it part of their mission to fortify a positive Jewish identity. "It is exceedingly difficult for the Jew to maintain his self-respect under modern conditions," insisted Rabbi Eugene Kohn. "He is a member of a minority group that is disliked and regarded as inferior. . . . To exorcise this Jewish inferiority complex, there is needed . . . a cultural program which will develop an appreciation of Jewish achievement in the past and afford the opportunity for creative Jewish activity in the present."[113] Mordecai Kaplan advocated much the same approach to combating anti-Semitism. He considered anti-Semitism a force that ultimately helped to preserve Jewish consciousness and group cohesion, noting that Jews were often "impelled to rise to new heights of spiritual achievement because of the threat of annihilation." During the Depression, synagogues joined that battle against anti-Semitism, hoping, often without success, that the struggle would produce "a more concentrated social energy and a finer spirituality."[114]

Religious leaders considered education the best means to preserve Jewish self-respect. "A sound educational system," declared Bernard Revel, president of Yeshiva College, "is the only power American Jewry can bring to bear upon the perplexing problem of spiritual survival."[115] Synagogues directed their greatest educational efforts toward Jewish youth. Almost every Depression-era congregation offered supplementary Jewish education through a variety of afternoon Hebrew school and Sunday school programs. A few synagogues even launched Jewish day schools during the Depression. In

1937, Kehilath Jeshurun founded and generously supported the Ramaz Academy day school. Despite ongoing financial difficulties, the Brooklyn Jewish Center maintained a day school, Sunday school, and afternoon Hebrew school.[116] During the thirties, the field of Jewish education became increasingly professionalized; the Jewish Education Association initiated official licensing of Hebrew school teachers and encouraged the use of modern pedagogic techniques in Jewish classrooms.[117] Professional Jewish educators, such as Samson Benderly and Alexander Dushkin, along with advocates of Jewish culture, including Mordecai Kaplan, underlined the importance of Jewish education for "sustaining self-respect and self-confidence" among young Jews who were facing the social and economic perils of the Depression. Without a knowledge of their heritage and culture, claimed Jewish educators, Jewish children would grow "into baffled, groping, denatured Jews."[118]

Impassioned pleas for the importance of Jewish education grew stronger as financial hardships and dwindling enrollments threatened the future of Jewish schools. During the Depression, student enrollments drastically declined. Without steady income from tuition, synagogues had difficulty supporting programs and paying teacher salaries. In 1931, the Institutional Synagogue owed nine thousand dollars in back salaries to teachers who remained unpaid for four to seven months at a time. Like many congregations, the Kane Street synagogue could not fund a paid teaching staff and relied on volunteers (usually women) to serve as teachers in its Sunday school.[119] Many professional educators denounced the practice of hiring unskilled volunteer teachers and were particularly incensed when congregations made school budgets the primary victims of money-saving efforts. Reform, Conservative, and Orthodox rabbinical organizations publicly protested the decisions of congregations and Federations to allot Jewish education secondary status in budgetary decisions. But the insistent clamor about the need to preserve Jewish education was often futile in the face of shrinking student enrollments, unpaid tuition bills, and the general fiscal distress plaguing New York synagogues.[120]

Nevertheless, despite the serious toll the Depression took on religious schools, Jewish education remained a centerpiece of synagogue programming throughout the 1930s. Although officials at the Brooklyn Jewish Center admitted that "the apathy prevailing in the field of Jewish education" had resulted in a significant loss of students and a growing number of unpaid tuition fees, the center was proud of its ability to sustain educational programs "despite hard financial conditions."[121] The Institutional Synagogue's Talmud Torah experienced similar difficulties but also managed to stay afloat. "Though our Talmud Torah Department has lost greatly through removals," explained Rabbi Goldstein, "we still educate from 250 to 300 children." The Institutional Synagogue claimed to "have the largest percentage of poor children . . . than any [other] Talmud Torah in Greater New York," with more than 70 percent of its students unable to pay any tuition. Using the motto, "a religious education for every child, regardless of financial circumstances," the Institutional Synagogue school, like most in the city, struggled but did not collapse during the Depression years.[122]

On the whole, religious schools conducted under synagogue auspices fared better than independent parochial Jewish schools, which were utterly devastated by the economic crisis. Unlike synagogue schools, New York's private Talmud Torahs relied almost entirely on tuition and voluntary contributions. Facing a half-million-dollar deficit and owing an estimated two hundred thousand dollars in teacher salaries, several New York parochial schools created a united federation and initiated joint fund-raising drives in the midst of the Depression, but their efforts met with little success.[123] Yeshiva teachers, whose wages were meager even in better economic times, often worked without pay for months at a time. Lauding the efforts of Talmud Torah teachers, Albert Schoolman, director of New York's Central Jewish Institute, explained, "Without salary, heavily in debt, and truly on the brink of destitution, they have held on faithfully and devotedly to their tasks, making every personal sacrifice, and aiming only to prevent, as long as possible, the complete collapse of their respective schools." Yeshiva teachers did not always respond passively when their salaries were slashed or withheld for months at a time. During the Depression, Talmud Torah instructors conducted several strikes and work stoppages to protest pay cuts and low wages. In 1933, in response to recurrent disputes with teachers and searching for ways to raise funds, the Federation of Yeshivas and Talmud Torahs resorted to a very traditional Jewish fund-raising tactic. The federation attempted to impose a tax on religious articles to be used for teacher salaries and to keep the city's small Yeshivas afloat. Premodern European Jewish communities had supported Jewish education through a system of mandatory taxation. Depression-era Talmud Torahs adopted that tradition in an attempt to overcome the "diminution of voluntary contributions." In the American environment, however, taxes on religious articles required voluntary cooperation from merchants and consumers and ultimately did not prove particularly effective in correcting the budget shortfalls in Jewish parochial schools. Most of New York's independent Jewish schools survived the economic crisis, but they were among its most severe casualties, suffering far more acutely than synagogue-sponsored schools.[124]

Along with the financial difficulties experienced by Jewish schools in the Depression also came substantive changes within the core curriculum. In virtually every Depression-era synagogue school, Zionism became a central focus. "Palestine . . . gives tone to everything that we do educationally," declared the president of the National Council for Jewish Education in 1934. "It is the leit motif in all our cultural efforts."[125] The 1930s were a turning point in American Zionism, a decade that witnessed widespread support for the Zionist cause among both Jewish laity and professionals. In 1937, the Reform movement reversed its previous anti-Zionist stand, formally declaring support for Palestine as a center of Jewish culture. Joining the Conservative and Orthodox movements in accepting Zionism as part of its religious program, Reform leaders gave official sanction to an already popular grassroots Zionist sentiment. By 1930, an estimated one in five Jewish families had at least one member who had joined a Zionist organization.[126] The American Zionist movement, which included a range of convictions from religious Zionism to Socialist Zionism to cultural Zionism, grew substantially in the Depression decade, as American Jews responded to the crisis of European Jewry and came to believe that Palestine could provide both a refuge for Jews and a center for Jewish culture. Within American Jewish life, Zionism was not a movement that required Jews to relocate to Palestine, but rather an ideology that offered a foundation for Jewish identity and ethnic survival in America. Given the concern with maintaining Jewish identity and culture in Depression-era America, Jewish educators seized on Zionism as a tool for Jewish renewal.[127]

New York synagogues, like congregations throughout the country, promoted a Jewish identity infused with the Zionist message. Zionist themes pervaded rabbinic sermons, cultural and social activities, and school curricula in the 1930s.[128] "The drama of restoring a Jewish homeland . . . constitutes today the greatest single force in strengthening and preserving the Jewish spirit," insisted one Zionist leader.[129] At a time when synagogues had little success in reviving religious devotion, Zionism offered a program capable of eliciting Jewish support and enthusiasm. "Jewish life . . . is precisely in the stage of trying to find itself—trying to find a new point of view to live today," declared one Jewish professional in 1933, claiming that "Zionism seems to offer the only possible substitute."[130] In the midst of the Depression, historian Jacob Marcus observed that "Zionism has prevented the *morale* of many from completely collapsing . . . Zionism brings [Jews] comfort; it instills new hope in them by emphasizing the fact that they belong spiritually, at least, to a group with whom they share a tradition of a courageous past and the hope for a better future."[131] For Jewish leaders searching for some means to invigorate American Judaism, Zionism offered a strong cultural message with far greater appeal than calls for renewed religious commitment.

The enormous expansion of Jewish youth groups in the 1930s testified to the power of the Zionist cause. Zionist-oriented youth groups grew rapidly in the Depression years, attracting thousands of new members. Radical politics continued to command much greater allegiance from Jewish youth than did the Zionist movement, a fact that constantly frustrated Zionist leaders. Nevertheless, American Zionism did make significant inroads in the 1930s.[132] Jewish youth who demonstrated little interest in religious worship often responded to the Zionist message, which was often infused with a Socialist spirit and a program for economic justice. Synagogue officials who lamented that Jewish youth were "indifferent to the spiritual intensity of their forebears," became convinced that cultural Zionism, with its emphasis on Jewish peoplehood and ethnic persistence, was uniquely capable of sustaining Jewish identity in the next generation.[133]

During the 1930s, the shared notion of Jewish national identity and culture provided the most likely foundation on which to build Jewish life in America. Some Jewish leaders remained opposed to political Zionism and others worried about focusing too much attention on Jewish nationalism at the expense of other aspects of Jewish life. Most Jewish observers, however, insisted that "whether [one] personally sympathizes with the Zionist ideal or not, the concept of the unity of the Jewish people which underlies that ideal" could only strengthen Jewish culture and promote Jewish survival.[134] Describing the contributions of one Zionist organization, Judah Shapiro of the Bronx YMHA declared that, "It is not the Zionism in this program which I regard as most important, but its definite social stand and its interest in the preservation of the Jewish group."[135] Alexander Dushkin, a leading Jewish educator, echoed those sentiments, explaining that regardless of whether it was labeled Zionism, the concept of Jewish peoplehood was a cohesive force in Jewish life. "The bond which unites Jewry is not knowledge and not beliefs and not proofs but it is kinship," Dushkin claimed. "It is what I would call nationalism, but somebody else would call ethnic grouping."[136] American Zionist ideology was highly malleable, capable of veering from strict adherence to the rebuilding of Palestine to encompass general support for Jewish cultural survival. Mordecai Kaplan referred to the nationalist movement as "spiritual Zionism, the purpose of which is to keep the Jews of the world united and creative."[137] Zionism certainly did not draw most Jews back to the synagogue, but it was quickly embraced as a key component of Depression-era synagogue life. By incorporating Zionism within the synagogue agenda, congregations broadened their message to reach a generation of Jews whose ethnic identities extended beyond religious concerns. As the Depression decade drew to a close, Zionism was poised to become a foundation for Jewish identity, preserving and enhancing ethnic consciousness both inside and outside the synagogue walls.

The Depression was a time of both crisis and consolidation in American synagogues, less a dramatic turning point than a period of hardship that accelerated ongoing trends in congregational life. The economic crisis neither heralded the demise of the synagogue as skeptics had predicted nor precipitated the religious revival for which leaders had hoped. In the 1930s, New York synagogues endured financial problems, loss of members, and spiritual malaise, but few congregations collapsed and most "displayed a remarkable resilience."[138] In 1933, Isidor Fine, president of the Brooklyn Jewish Center, jokingly remarked that despite the crisis, "the Brooklyn Jewish Center [had] kept its head above water . . . [and] in this respect we did better than Mr. Hoover."[139] The "religious depression" that preoccupied Jewish leaders during the 1930s was the combined product of sudden fiscal distress and heightened concern for the future vitality of American Judaism. The survival strategies of New York synagogues included economic cutbacks and fund-raising efforts as well as a crucial reassessment of the role of the synagogue in Jewish communal life. The Depression forced synagogues to confront the emerging religious and ethnic patterns of American-born Jews and to refine their purpose and programs to meet changing needs and values. As synagogues struggled to incorporate social and ethnic needs within the religious agenda, they played a formative role in the evolution of twentieth-century American Judaism.

After World War II, American Jews initiated another synagogue building boom that eclipsed the level of growth produced in the 1920s. In the post–World War II era, synagogue affiliation and religious school enrollment peaked as a new generation of Jews moved from urban centers to the suburbs.[140] The fiscal crisis that characterized synagogue experience in the Depression years disappeared in the postwar prosperity, but the lessons of the 1930s remained important to American congregations. Depression-era synagogues reaped few benefits from their efforts to heighten synagogue appeal by extending the religious umbrella to embrace social and secular concerns. Yet, the much-heralded post–World War II religious revival owed much to the synagogue's expansive religious vision. American Jews of the 1940s and 1950s joined synagogues in unprecedented numbers, but attending worship services remained a minority phenomenon. The postwar revival was primarily a reflection of the Jewish desire to maintain ethnic identity, to associate with other Jews, and to educate Jewish children in the basic principles of Judaism. Although the blueprint for integrating the secular and the sacred emerged before the Depression, synagogues survived a decade of religious apathy and stagnation by refining the parameters of an inclusive religious agenda, laying the groundwork for an institutional Judaism in which religion and ethnicity were inextricably intertwined.

# 8

## American Jews and the American Dream

*We trailed in our search for freedom and the better life. . . . We never got wealthy,*
*we never made any money . . . the great American dream was always the dream,*
*you were pursuing it like it was a movie screen ahead of you somewhere.*
—Sam Levenson, Oral history

*For the majority of Jewish young people, things looked bright in the late 1940s and*
*the future even brighter. . . . They had made it into American Society.*
—Peter I. Rose, "The Ghetto and Beyond"

Mired in the turmoil of the Great Depression, New York Jews had good cause
to experience the futility and frustration of pursuing the American Dream.
Only fifteen years later, this mood of uncertainty and despair had been
replaced by hope and confidence in the future. Prosperity returned in the
postwar era, accompanied by a decrease in anti-Semitism and a renewal of
Jewish mobility. Yet, to view the 1930s from the perspective of hindsight
distorts the reality of the Depression experience. For Jews who had endured
the trials of immigration, seen their fortunes improve in the twenties, and

believed that their children would reap even greater rewards, the Depression came as a shock, raising serious doubts about Jewish prospects in America. "The economic conditions of our country," reflected one Jewish immigrant in the late-thirties, "instead of improving, went contrary to our expectations. We are frank to say we became dubious and despaired of a successful culmination of our endeavors."[1] Just as some individual Jews watched their fortunes decline, synagogues, community centers, and Jewish philanthropic organizations plunged from unprecedented prosperity and expansion in the 1920s to the verge of bankruptcy and collapse. New York Jews could not have imagined that their individual and communal fates would so rapidly improve in the next decade. From the vantage point of Jews who faced the setbacks of the 1930s, the Great Depression was not a brief aberration in the American Jewish experience, but rather an uncertain and anxious period when the promise of Jewish life in America seemed more tenuous than ever.

The challenge to Jewish faith in America was an overriding theme of the Depression decade. Economic losses and stalled mobility combined with job discrimination and the sharp rise in anti-Semitism shook the confidence of many Depression-era Jews. "Suddenly some of us have become afraid and seem willing to abandon to the fear and the uncertainty of the moment," confessed the *American Hebrew* during the worst part of the crisis.[2] Jews never completely relinquished their belief in America, but the Depression weakened the image of America as a "Golden Land," undermining an ideal that had dominated Jewish aspirations through the 1920s. As much as the Depression precipitated financial despair, personal disappointment, and a crisis in Jewish institutions, it also called into question Jewish convictions about the security and opportunity of America.

The mood among American Jews in the 1930s was characterized more by fear than by hope. Depression-era adversity had particular meaning within the Jewish community, as Jews assessed their own fates amid the apparent collapse of American ideals and institutions. The disillusionment with America found expression within several Jewish movements. The Depression gave rise to radical campaigns across the nation, yet Jewish radicals retained a distinct perspective on the failures of the American system. Michael Gold's *Jews Without Money* offered a scathing critique, not only of American capitalism, but of Jewish experience in the United States. His dismal portrait of Jews striving but failing to attain the promise of American life, confronting the dual pressures of working-class oppression and anti-Semitic discrimination, became a rallying cry for Jewish Communists. As the Depression lingered, Jewish radicals insisted that America's capitalist society had not only failed on a national level but had betrayed its Jewish citizens. During the Depression, before the Hitler-Stalin pact destroyed Jewish belief in the Soviet system, Jewish Communists pointed out that Jews living in the Soviet Union enjoyed comparatively greater levels of security. "In the Soviet system," one Jewish Communist publication announced, "the burning Jewish questions have been solved. Anti-Semitism is a crime, punishable by fine and imprisonment. The U.S.S.R. has given the Jews opportunity, security, and a respectable life."[3] For a brief moment in the 1930s, Communists could argue that Jewish prospects looked brighter in the Soviet Union than in the United States. While only a handful of Jewish Communists ever promoted migration to the Soviet Union or supported a full-scale worker's revolution in the United States, the Communist platform provided a running commentary on the inadequacies of Jewish life in America. To be sure, Jewish Communists were a minority voice within the community, but they offered one of the most powerful expressions of Jewish disappointment and doubt in Depression-era America.

Taking a different approach, the American Zionist movement offered its own critical assessment of American Jewish life even as it provided an ideology of hope and renewal. It was the latter aspect of the movement that captured the allegiance of most Jewish Americans. The growing popularity of Zionism in the thirties was primarily the result of American Jews looking to provide a refuge for European Jews and to bolster Jewish identity on the homefront. The majority of American Jews embraced Zionism as a movement that strengthened rather than challenged Jewish life in the United States. But a small faction within the Zionist movement advocated a more radical program. Some Zionist organizations, particularly Habonim and Hashomer Hatzair, supported the ideal of settlement and pioneering in the Jewish homeland, urging American Jews to immigrate to Palestine. The pioneer movement in America was admittedly small, but its appeal grew in the Depression decade, spurred by the rise of Hitler in Europe and the economic crisis gripping the United States. As they stressed the many benefits of rebuilding the Jewish homeland, Zionist pioneers also issued frequent attacks on the failures of America. In the midst of the Depression, one Labor Zionist publication quipped:

Goodbye, America
Goodbye, Yankee fashion
I'm going to Palestine
To hell with the Depression[4]

The radical Zionist organization, Betar, told Depression-era Jews that "the myth of equality of opportunity has been exploded" for Jews living in the United States and insisted that "America as a land of opportunities, a country

where the lowliest may rise to the most exalted position no longer exists."
Rejecting the notion that only persecuted European Jews needed Palestine
as a refuge, Betar leaders claimed that Jews who suffered from anti-Semitism and economic despair in America could build a better life in Palestine.
"The time has come," declared the *Betar Monthly*, "when the American boy
and girl must seriously consider settling in Palestine."[5] Of course, most
Zionist organizations supported no such rejection of America. More typical
of Zionist sentiments in the United States, the Young Judaea movement
endorsed a program committed to rebuilding Palestine, fortifying Jewish
culture, and developing a "vital, creative American Jewry."[6] The dominant
coalition of American Zionists expressed ongoing confidence in the United
States even in the face of the multiple challenges of the Depression. But
minority dissension within the Zionist movement and widespread Jewish
fears about anti-Semitism in the United States shaped the tone of American
Zionism throughout the decade.

The threat of anti-Semitism provided a constant source of anxiety for
Depression-era Jews. American Jews had always firmly believed that the
prejudices of Europe would not take root in America. Although anti-Semitism had been present in many forms since the first arrival of Jews in the
United States, Jews had never before encountered such a dramatic growth
of anti-Semitism on American soil. As employment discrimination escalated
and the number of organized hate groups multiplied, Jews witnessed a
disturbing rise in domestic prejudice, steadily fortified by Nazism abroad and
a desperate economy at home.[7] Resurgent anti-Semitism in the United
States fueled Jewish fears about their future in America. Jews had come to
expect anti-Semitism in European nations, "but that something of the same
spirit should appear in the United States . . . came to us as a shock,"
confessed one Jewish publication.[8] Depression-era anti-Semitism precipitated a painful discussion about whether America might yet succumb to
anti-Semitic forces. "European experience has already revealed how handily
the Jew can serve as scapegoat," warned one communal leader. "It would be
a miracle if the disease of anti-Semitism prevalent in fascist countries were
not to make serious inroads in our own country," added another Jewish
observer.[9] The combination of economic adversity, job discrimination, and
mounting anti-Semitism shook the faith of even those Jews who trusted
wholeheartedly in the promise of American democracy.

American Jews had ample cause for doubt and concern in the midst of the
Depression, but they evaluated their experiences in the United States
against the backdrop of the situation of Jews worldwide. Immigrant Jews
were particularly attuned to the relative benefits of American life. "They do

a lot of injustices here, too," admitted one Depression-era immigrant, "but still, if you would have been there [Europe], you think this is paradise."[10] As they watched Europe become an increasingly hostile and desperate environment for Jews with each successive year of the Depression, most American Jews believed that the United States offered them the safest and most promising alternative. The Jewish future in America may have seemed uncertain and even menacing at times, but the Jewish situation in Europe was decidedly worse. Despite genuine fears, disillusionment, and skepticism about their adopted homeland, most Jews believed that "here in America the Jews at least had a chance."[11] As the Depression wore on, American Jews shared a collective anxiety about their future, worried about their declining economic fortunes, and feared the growth of anti-Semitism, but most never completely abandoned their belief in America as the best locus of Jewish security and opportunity.

The Great Depression did not destroy Jewish belief in the American Dream, but that brief period in the 1930s changed Jewish perspectives about the promise and potential of America. In a few short years, the collapse of Europe would reassure American Jews that their faith in the American system had not been misplaced. American anti-Semitism waned in the coming decades and Jewish economic fortunes markedly improved. But America no longer seemed completely and irrevocably immune to the forces that had decimated European Jewry. If American Jews clung tenaciously to the belief that America was different, they understood more than ever the precariousness of that distinction.

As New York Jews emerged from the Depression and plunged into the turbulence of World War II, they stood at a cultural threshold, about to enter a new phase in American Jewish life. The immigrant world that survived throughout the 1930s had virtually disappeared by 1945, and Jewish life became solidly dominated by a generation of Jews whose ethnic identities and communal institutions reflected their American roots. In the postwar years synagogues multiplied, communal institutions expanded, and American Jews attained an unprecedented level of prosperity. The Holocaust had marked the painful end of a thriving European Jewish community, but postwar successes rejuvenated Jewish belief in the promise of America. Even as American Jews celebrated the birth of the Jewish state, they reiterated their unwavering loyalty to America. Support for Israel reinforced Jewish identity and bolstered ethnic pride, but American Jews confidently placed their hopes for the future in the United States. In less than a decade, the struggles of the Great Depression had receded and been replaced by the triumphs of the postwar era.

But the challenges of the Depression decade left an enduring legacy for the postwar Jewish community. During the crisis of Depression, New York Jews refined the contours of Jewish identity and community on American soil. The 1930s witnessed several obvious turning points in American Jewish life—the final chapter of a flourishing East European immigrant culture, the emergence of a predominantly American-born Jewish population, and the formation of a lasting Jewish commitment to the Democratic Party. At the same time, many of the most critical developments of the Depression era were more subtle, evident less in demographic changes and voting patterns than in the delicate balance between ethnic survival and further integration into American society. As they coped with the fiscal challenges, anti-Semitic threats, and social and political innovations of the Depression years, New York Jews reshaped the character of Jewish lifestyles, politics, and institutions. Adjusting ethnic patterns to fit the changing circumstances of American life, Depression-era Jews fashioned a Jewish community capable of sustaining ethnic identity in a nation transformed by new economic, social, and political realities.

In this respect, the Depression crisis reveals an overriding theme of the American Jewish experience. The evolution of Jewish life during the Depression years reflected an ongoing process of Jewish acculturation. Adapting but not relinquishing ethnic identity, Depression-era Jews reconciled the maintenance of Jewish culture with the pursuit of full participation in American society. The continual reconstruction of American Jewish ethnicity was particularly apparent in the urgent campaigns to keep Jewish communal institutions afloat and the heightened anxiety about the Jewish future. In the turmoil of the Great Depression, New York Jews ensured the persistence of Jewish identity and community by tailoring Jewish ethnicity to American norms.

Patterns established during the Depression years endured for decades within the American Jewish community. Within Jewish families, the 1930s clearly marked a transitional period, as immigrant parents raised an American-born generation to adulthood. The economic crisis that accompanied the generational transition and temporarily stalled the progress of New York Jews contributed to lasting alterations in Jewish family life. Ronald Berman, who remembered the upheaval of the thirties, went so far as to claim that

> the depression—which I think is one of the two or three definitive experiences for modern Jews—transformed their evolution. It didn't bring families together as televised mythology tends fondly to believe, although at times it did bring out remarkable individual acts of human kindness and human goodness. . . . But in

the large the depression encouraged multiple employment in families; finished the job of disintegrating parental authority; [and] delegitimized those skills and trades that had attached the generations.[12]

Depression-era Jews came of age in Jewish households very different from those they would create in later years. The children of the thirties emerged from the Depression, not only with a new occupational profile, but also with a tendency to pursue higher education, delay marriage, and have fewer children—patterns that continue to define American Jewry to the present day.[13]

New York's Jewish neighborhoods eased both the generational transition and the economic hardships of the Depression years, nurturing a sense of Jewish community while paving the road to Jewish integration. In working-class enclaves, where the Depression dealt its harshest blow, neighborhood support networks preserved Jewish morale and offered critical material aid. While middle- and upper-class Jews seldom required the financial supports of their neighborhoods, Jewish residential clustering encouraged ethnic persistence for Jews at all economic levels. In a decade when Jews, like other Americans, were beginning to look beyond their ethnic communities and toward the federal government to provide for their needs, the neighborhood lent ethnic tone to the fabric of daily life. During the 1930s, New York's Jewish neighborhoods provided an ethnic foundation that bolstered Jewish participation in the larger social and political movements of Depression-era America.

Jewish politics reflected the evolving dynamic of Jewish ethnicity during the Great Depression. The long-standing Jewish tradition of grassroots neighborhood activism retained its strength throughout the 1930s, regaining momentum as economic conditions deteriorated. Even as the New Deal and the welfare state transformed ethnic politics and altered the tactics of Jewish activists, a distinct Jewish political culture remained intact. New York Jews rallied behind Roosevelt and the Democratic Party, celebrating New Deal social programs as a realization of Jewish ideals. In the political realignment of the Depression years, Jewish political culture not only survived but grew stronger as it led New York Jews from the neighborhood into the new Democratic coalition.

By the postwar era, Jewish political values had become so tightly interwoven with Democratic liberalism that American Jews could hardly disentangle the two. In the 1940s and 1950s, when upwardly mobile New York Jews moved their ethnic enclaves from urban centers to the suburbs, they adopted liberalism as a virtual Jewish creed. During the 1930s, American

Jews had forged such a strong link between their ethnic ideological commitment and the Democratic liberal agenda that the ascendancy of liberalism reinforced the sense of ethnic solidarity. Far from excluding Jews from the American mainstream, the maintenance of a distinct ethnic political profile facilitated Jewish integration in the years following the Depression. Sociologist Steven Cohen has argued that "Jewish liberalism—as much as modern Orthodoxy, Zionism, assimilationism, and so forth—should be seen as a reflection (if not, sometimes, a strategy) of the entry and integration of Jews into modern society."[14] In the wake of the Depression, Jewish political liberalism emerged as a symbol of both ethnic distinctiveness and the successful assimilation of American Jews, setting the stage for an enduring brand of American Jewish politics.

The Depression also produced lasting alterations in the character of Jewish communal institutions. In addition to the financial burdens it endured during the economic crisis, New York's Federation of Jewish Philanthropies struggled to defend its legitimacy and redefine its role within the new welfare state. As public welfare shook the foundation on which American Jewish charities had previously operated, New York Jews reshaped private Jewish philanthropy to meet the new conditions of American life. Like so many other developments of the Depression decade, the changes within private Jewish philanthropy reflected the Jewish quest to sustain the ethnic community without appearing clannish or isolated from the American mainstream. Jewish leaders carefully balanced the maintenance of separate ethnic agencies with wholehearted participation in the national recovery effort. Championing public welfare as a sign of American progress as well as a fulfillment of Jewish precepts of communal responsibility, New York Jews emphasized the essential harmony of Jewish and American ideals. With the state assuming the bulk of relief work, private Jewish philanthropy emerged from the Depression as a vehicle for strengthening ethnic culture and commitment. The evolution of Federation priorities during the Depression laid the groundwork for future years, when Jewish philanthropy virtually ceased to provide relief services for American Jews and became instead an expression of ethnic identity and solidarity.

In the postwar years, Jewish philanthropy grew more complex and became a dominant arena of Jewish activity. Responding to the trauma of the Holocaust and the creation of Israel as a Jewish state, national organizations mobilized large-scale overseas relief efforts. As American Jews rallied to assist the international campaign, philanthropy became a cornerstone of American Jewish expression. Providing material support for Jews abroad fortified the ethnic resolve of Jews at home. The New York Federation, which retained its independence as the citywide representative of the local Jewish community, reflected the new dynamic of American Jewish ethnicity. In the postwar era, the Federation expanded religious and cultural programming, dedicating its efforts not only to representing but also to sustaining the ethnic community. Pursuing a path that had been forged in the Depression years, American Jewish philanthropy became a symbol and an instrument of ethnic persistence.

New York synagogues survived the Depression as institutions devoted as much to preserving ethnic consciousness as to providing religious worship. The fiscal crisis that plagued Jewish congregations throughout the 1930s quickly disappeared in the next decade, but institutional Judaism continued to reflect the expansive agenda refined by synagogues during their most trying years. The seeds of synagogue behavior that had been planted in the 1920s and cultivated throughout the drought of Depression flourished in the postwar era. Jewish leaders discovered that integrating the secular and the sacred, which had kept synagogues afloat during a decade of economic hardship and religious apathy, was also an effective program in a period of prosperity and religious revival.

In the years after World War II, American Jews participated actively in the highly touted national religious revival. From the end of the war until the close of the 1950s, New York Jews founded more than 150 new congregations, as the synagogue rapidly became the central institution of Jewish life.[15] Explaining this trend, Will Herberg argued that religious affiliation had become the chief expression of group identity in postwar America. "To find a place in American society increasingly means to place oneself in one or another of these religious communities," Herberg explained. "Religion has become a primary symbol of 'heritage,' and church membership the most appropriate form of 'belonging' under contemporary American conditions."[16] Synagogue membership soared in the postwar years, yet attendance at worship services remained small. Jews joined synagogues in order to associate with other Jews, to preserve a sense of Jewish community, and to demonstrate their commitment to ethnic survival. As Rabbi Eugene Borowitz observed, most Jews became synagogue members "because there are few if any acceptable alternatives to synagogue affiliation for one who wants to maintain his Jewish identity and wants his children to be Jewish, in some sense, after him."[17] Depression-era Jewish leaders had lamented the lack of religious enthusiasm in the 1930s, but ethnic sensibility rather than religious conviction continued to define American Jewish identity even during the so-called religious revival. American synagogues rebounded dramatically from the financial hardships of the Depression and appeared to have reinvented themselves in the postwar era, but they remained remarkably similar institutions.

The challenges of the Great Depression prompted significant realignments within the Jewish community but also reinforced ongoing trends in American Jewish life. Many Depression-era developments reflected patterns that predated the thirties and continued throughout the economic crisis. With or without the Depression, the immigrant character of Jewish life would have gradually faded, replaced by increasingly Americanized forms of Jewish identity and communal organization. By the close of the 1920s, second-generation Jews had already built the foundations for a Jewish community constructed according to American norms. Throughout the adversity of the Depression, New York Jews maintained their central ethnic institutions and their desire to synthesize Jewish and American values. The sweeping changes of the Depression decade did not overturn long-standing Jewish goals and patterns, but instead forced New York Jews to refine the formula for balancing ethnic survival with acceptance and integration into American society.

In the midst of their bleakest and most desolate years, New York Jews redefined the parameters of American Jewish ethnicity. For American Jews, the Great Depression was a time of creativity and innovation as well as uneasiness and frustration. The economic hardships and enormous social and political changes of the 1930s upset both individual and communal Jewish strategies, forcing alterations in American Jewish life. In a decade of economic, social, and political upheaval, New York Jews redesigned their ethnic community using the blueprints of both Jewish tradition and New Deal America. The personal and communal struggles of the Depression decade faded in the postwar era, but the creative ferment of Depression-era Jewry provided an enduring structure for later generations of American Jews.

# Appendix

## Report of the Survey of 7,775 Applications to the Federation Employment Service from September 1934 to May 1935

*Table 1. Age Distribution*

| | | | | Percent Distribution | | |
|---|---|---|---|---|---|---|
| Age | Total | Male | Female | Total | Male | Female |
| | 7775 | 4765 | 3010 | 100 | 100 | 100 |
| 16–17 | 165 | 112 | 53 | 2.1 | 2.4 | 1.8 |
| 18–19 | 1276 | 749 | 527 | 16.4 | 15.7 | 17.5 |
| 20–24 | 3116 | 1925 | 1191 | 40.1 | 40.0 | 39.6 |
| 25–34 | 2231 | 1279 | 952 | 28.7 | 26.8 | 31.6 |
| 35–44 | 667 | 427 | 240 | 8.6 | 9.2 | 8.0 |
| 45–54 | 233 | 190 | 43 | 3.0 | 4.0 | 1.4 |
| 55–64 | 87 | 83 | 4 | 2.1 | 1.7 | .1 |

Source for all tables: Occupational Adjustment Problems Presented by 7,775 Applicants of a Jewish Employment Bureau, Federation Employment Service Reports, 1935, Federal Employment and Guidance Service Records, Ninety-second Street YMHA Archives, New York. This survey contains additional data not reprinted in these tables.

*Table 2. Residence by New York City Health Center Districts*

| Health District° | Total | Male | Female | Percent Distribution Total | Male | Female |
|---|---|---|---|---|---|---|
| | 7775 | 4765 | 3010 | 100 | 100 | 100 |
| Riverside | 428 | 237 | 191 | 5.5 | 4.9 | 6.3 |
| Washington Heights | 236 | 130 | 106 | 3.0 | 2.7 | 3.5 |
| Flatbush | 157 | 77 | 80 | 2.0 | 1.6 | 2.6 |
| Fordham-Riverdale | 90 | 51 | 39 | 1.2 | 1.0 | 1.3 |
| Tremont | 1778 | 1127 | 651 | 22.8 | 23.7 | 21.6 |
| Corona | 13 | 7 | 6 | 0.2 | 0.1 | 0.2 |
| Bayridge | 309 | 163 | 146 | 3.9 | 3.4 | 4.8 |
| Pelham Bay | 253 | 165 | 88 | 3.2 | 3.5 | 2.9 |
| Williamsbridge-Westchester | 77 | 50 | 27 | 0.9 | 1.0 | 0.9 |
| Lower Flatbush | 252 | 150 | 102 | 3.2 | 3.2 | 3.3 |
| Flushing | 27 | 19 | 8 | 0.3 | 0.3 | 0.2 |
| Central Harlem | 9 | 6 | 3 | 0.1 | 0.1 | 0.1 |
| Jamaica West | 35 | 20 | 15 | 0.4 | 0.3 | 0.5 |
| Bedford | 381 | 222 | 159 | 4.9 | 4.7 | 5.3 |
| Morrisania | 579 | 391 | 188 | 7.4 | 8.4 | 6.2 |
| Astoria-L.I.C. | 79 | 50 | 29 | 1.0 | 1.0 | 0.9 |
| Jamaica East | 8 | 5 | 3 | 0.1 | 0.1 | 0.1 |
| Sunset Park | 386 | 208 | 178 | 4.9 | 4.3 | 5.9 |
| Mott Haven | 237 | 151 | 86 | 3.0 | 3.2 | 2.8 |
| Maspeth-Forest Hills | 34 | 22 | 12 | 0.4 | 0.3 | 0.4 |
| Kips-Bay-Lenox Hill | 128 | 73 | 55 | 1.6 | 1.5 | 1.5 |
| Fort Greene | 268 | 162 | 106 | 3.4 | 3.4 | 3.5 |
| Brownsville | 393 | 243 | 150 | 5.1 | 5.0 | 5.0 |
| Richmond | 21 | 9 | 12 | 0.3 | 0.2 | 0.4 |
| Lower West Side | 136 | 78 | 58 | 1.7 | 1.6 | 1.6 |
| Red Hook-Gowanus | 177 | 120 | 57 | 2.3 | 2.5 | 1.6 |
| Bushwick | 196 | 117 | 79 | 2.5 | 2.4 | 2.6 |
| East Harlem | 204 | 117 | 87 | 2.6 | 2.4 | 2.9 |
| Williamsburg-Greenpoint | 117 | 83 | 34 | 1.5 | 1.8 | 1.1 |
| Lower East Side | 619 | 436 | 183 | 7.8 | 9.1 | 6.1 |
| Surburban°° | 148 | 76 | 72 | 1.9 | 1.6 | 2.4 |

°These districts are arranged in rank order from 1 to 30 on the basis of median monthly rent as compiled by the Committee on Neighborhood Health Development from the 1930 census.
°°Not including in the ranking

*Table. 3. Father's Occupation*

| | Total | Male | Female | Percent Distribution | | |
| --- | --- | --- | --- | --- | --- | --- |
| | | | | Total | Male | Female |
| | 4993 | 3209 | 1784 | 100 | 100 | 100 |
| Professional | 262 | 154 | 108 | 5.3 | 4.8 | 6.1 |
| Business | 1038 | 597 | 441 | 20.8 | 18.6 | 24.7 |
| Clerical and Sales | 530 | 303 | 227 | 10.6 | 9.4 | 12.7 |
| Skilled Manual | 2247 | 1545 | 702 | 45.0 | 48.3 | 34.3 |
| Semi-skilled | 564 | 365 | 199 | 11.3 | 11.4 | 11.2 |
| Unskilled | 274 | 196 | 78 | 5.5 | 6.1 | 4.4 |
| Retired | 80 | 51 | 29 | 1.6 | 1.6 | 1.6 |

*Table 4. Educational Background*

| Years at School | Total | Male | Female | Percent Distribution | | |
| --- | --- | --- | --- | --- | --- | --- |
| | | | | Total | Male | Female |
| | 7616 | 4653 | 2963 | 100 | 100 | 100 |
| Academic | | | | | | |
| 1 | 0 | 0 | 0 | 0.00 | 0.00 | 0.00 |
| 2 | 5 | 5 | 0 | 0.10 | 0.10 | 0.00 |
| 3 | 3 | 2 | 1 | 0.04 | 0.04 | 0.03 |
| 4 | 5 | 4 | 1 | 0.10 | 0.10 | 0.03 |
| 5 | 3 | 2 | 1 | 0.04 | 0.04 | 0.03 |
| 6 | 36 | 25 | 11 | 0.50 | 0.50 | 0.40 |
| 7 | 39 | 30 | 9 | 0.50 | 0.60 | 0.30 |
| 8 | 603 | 429 | 174 | 7.91 | 9.20 | 5.87 |
| 9 | 157 | 124 | 33 | 2.06 | 2.70 | 1.10 |
| 10 | 283 | 216 | 67 | 3.72 | 4.60 | 2.30 |
| 11 | 260 | 210 | 50 | 3.41 | 4.50 | 1.70 |
| 12 | 1315 | 865 | 450 | 17.27 | 18.60 | 15.00 |
| 13 | 406 | 273 | 133 | 5.33 | 5.90 | 4.50 |
| 14 | 413 | 299 | 114 | 5.42 | 6.40 | 3.80 |
| 15 | 220 | 174 | 46 | 2.88 | 3.70 | 1.60 |
| 16 | 556 | 342 | 214 | 7.30 | 7.40 | 7.22 |
| Commercial | | | | | | |
| 9 | 147 | 67 | 80 | 1.93 | 1.40 | 2.70 |
| 10 | 313 | 155 | 158 | 4.11 | 3.30 | 5.30 |
| 11 | 260 | 131 | 129 | 3.41 | 2.80 | 4.40 |

*Table 4.  (continued)*

| | | | | Percent Distribution | | |
|---|---|---|---|---|---|---|
| Years at School | Total | Male | Female | Total | Male | Female |
| 12 | 1266 | 346 | 820 | 16.62 | 7.40 | 27.70 |
| 13 | 326 | 109 | 217 | 4.28 | 2.30 | 7.30 |
| 14 | 179 | 111 | 68 | 2.35 | 2.40 | 2.30 |
| 15 | 137 | 10 | 127 | 1.80 | 0.20 | 4.28 |
| 16 | 33 | 27 | 6 | 0.43 | 0.50 | 0.20 |
| 17 | 12 | 7 | 5 | 0.16 | 0.15 | 0.20 |
| 18 | 8 | 7 | 1 | 0.11 | 0.15 | 0.03 |
| | | | Trade | | | |
| 9 | 33 | 21 | 12 | 0.43 | 0.45 | 0.40 |
| 10 | 59 | 43 | 16 | 0.77 | 0.92 | 0.54 |
| 11 | 57 | 53 | 4 | 0.75 | 1.13 | 0.13 |
| 12 | 102 | 87 | 15 | 1.33 | 1.86 | 0.50 |
| | | | Technical | | | |
| 13 | 60 | 46 | 14 | 0.80 | 0.99 | 0.47 |
| 14 | 37 | 30 | 7 | 0.49 | 0.60 | 0.23 |
| 15 | 24 | 23 | 1 | 0.32 | 0.40 | 0.03 |
| 16 | 44 | 37 | 7 | 0.58 | 0.80 | 0.23 |
| 17 | 19 | 16 | 3 | 0.25 | 0.30 | 0.10 |
| 18 | 5 | 4 | 1 | 0.10 | 0.09 | 0.03 |
| 19 | 1 | 1 | 0 | 0.01 | 0.02 | 0.00 |
| - | 1 | 1 | 0 | 0.01 | 0.02 | 0.00 |
| | | | Professional | | | |
| 15 | 29 | 15 | 14 | 0.38 | 0.30 | 0.47 |
| 16 | 114 | 76 | 38 | 1.50 | 1.60 | 1.28 |
| 17 | 48 | 40 | 8 | 0.63 | 0.80 | 0.26 |
| 18 | 27 | 23 | 4 | 0.35 | 0.40 | 0.13 |
| 19 | 5 | 5 | 0 | 0.10 | 0.10 | 0.00 |
| 20 | 10 | 10 | 0 | 0.12 | 0.20 | 0.00 |

# Abbreviations

| | |
|---|---|
| AJC | American Jewish Committee, New York |
| *AJH* | *American Jewish History* |
| *AJHQ* | *American Jewish Historical Quarterly* |
| AJHS | American Jewish Historical Society, Waltham, Massachusetts |
| *AJYB* | *American Jewish Yearbook* |
| BJC | Brooklyn Jewish Center |
| CCAR | Central Conference of American Rabbis |
| CJFWF | Council of Jewish Federations and Welfare Funds Collection, American Jewish Historical Society |
| FEGS | Federation Employment and Guidance Service Records, Ninety-second Street YMHA Archives, New York |
| FJP | Federation of Jewish Philanthropies of New York City |
| *JDB* | *Jewish Daily Bulletin* |
| *JDF* | *Jewish Daily Forward* |
| *JSSQ* | *Jewish Social Service Quarterly* |
| JTSA | Jewish Theological Seminary of America, New York |
| NYPL | New York Public Library |
| *NYT* | *New York Times* |
| *PNCJSS* | *Proceedings of the National Conference of Jewish Social Service* |

PNCJSW    *Proceedings of the National Conference of Jewish Social Welfare*
WPA       Works Progress Administration: Historical Records Survey: Federal
          Writers Project, Municipal Archives, New York
WWOHL     William Weiner Oral History Library, now part of the Jewish Division
          of the New York Public Library

# Notes

INTRODUCTION

1 "Jews in America," *Fortune* 13 (February 1936): 79, 141.
2 This is the interpretation offered by most Jewish historians and repeated most recently in Henry L. Feingold, *A Time for Searching: Entering the Mainstream, 1920–1945* (Baltimore, Md.: Johns Hopkins University Press, 1992), 146–54.
3 Examples of this scholarship include: Arthur D. Morse, *While Six Million Died: A Chronicle of American Apathy* (New York: Random House, 1967); Henry Feingold, *The Politics of Rescue: The Roosevelt Administration and the Holocaust, 1938–1945* (New Brunswick, N.J.: Rutgers University Press, 1970) and his "Who Shall Bear the Guilt for the Holocaust: The Human Dilemma," *AJH* (March 1979): 261–83; David Wyman, *Paper Walls: America and the Refugee Crisis, 1938–1941* (Amherst: University of Massachusetts Press, 1971). See also Moshe R. Gottlieb, *American Anti-Nazi Resistance, 1933–1941: An Historical Analysis* (New York: KTAV Publishing, 1981); Shlomo Shafir, "American Jewish Leaders and the Emerging Nazi Threat, 1928–January, 1933," *American Jewish Archives* (November 1979): 150–83. For a different approach, see Deborah E. Lipstadt, *Beyond*

*Belief: The American Press and the Coming of the Holocaust, 1933–1945* (New York: Free Press, 1986).

4 To date, the most comprehensive analysis of American anti-Semitism is Leonard Dinnerstein, *Anti-Semitism in America* (New York: Oxford University Press, 1994), esp. 105–27. Studies of anti-Jewish quotas include Marcia Graham Synott, *The Half Opened Door: Discrimination and Admissions at Harvard, Yale, and Princeton, 1900–70* (Westport, Conn: Greenwood Press, 1979); Harold S. Wechsler, *The Qualified Student: A History of Selective College Admission in America* (New York: John Wiley, 1977). Works dealing with Father Coughlin's anti-Semitism include: Charles Tull, *Father Coughlin and the New Deal* (Syracuse: Syracuse University Press, 1965); Sheldon Marcus, *Father Coughlin: The Tumultuous Life of the Priest of the Little Flower* (Boston: Little, Brown, 1973); a more recent treatment is Alan Brinkley, *Voices of Protest: Huey Long, Father Coughlin and the Great Depression* (New York: Vintage Books, 1982).

Other forms of domestic anti-Semitism also arose during the Depression era. See Donald Strong, *Organized Anti-Semitism in America: The Rise of Group Prejudice During the Decade 1930–1940.* (Washington, D.C.: American Council on Public Affairs, 1941) Also useful is, Ronald H. Bayor, *Neighbors in Conflict: The Irish, Germans, Jews, and Italians of New York City, 1929–1941* (Baltimore, Md.: Johns Hopkins University Press, 1978).

5 Alfred Kazin, *Starting Out in the Thirties* (Boston: Little, Brown, 1965; reprint, Ithaca, N.Y.: Cornell University Press, 1989); Alfred Kazin, *A Walker in the City* (New York: Harcourt Brace Jovanovich, 1951); Michael Gold, *Jews Without Money* (New York: Horace Liveright, 1930); Irving Howe, *A Margin of Hope: An Intellectual Autobiography* (New York: Harcourt Brace Jovanovich, 1982).

The New York Intellectuals have received a great deal of scholarly attention. Three of the most recent studies are: Terry A. Cooney, *The Rise of the New York Intellectuals, Partisan Review and Its Circle* (Madison: University of Wisconsin Press, 1986); Alan M. Wald, *The New York Intellectuals: The Rise and Decline of the Anti-Stalinist Left from the 1930s to the 1980s* (Chapel Hill: University of North Carolina Press, 1987); Alexander Bloom, *Prodigal Sons: The New York Intellectuals and Their World* (New York: Oxford University Press, 1986). See also Daniel Aaron, *Writers on the Left* (New York: Harcourt, Brace and World, 1961); Marcus Klein, *Foreigners: The Making of American Literature, 1900–1940* (Chicago: University of Chicago Press, 1981).

6 A detailed discussion of the Jewish labor movement in this period can be found in Joseph Brandes, "From Sweatshop to Stability: Jewish Labor Between the Two World Wars," *YIVO Annual of Jewish Social Science* 16 (1976): 1–149. Two general essays on the Jewish labor movement are: Moses Rischin, "The Jewish Labor Movement in America: A Social Interpretation," *Labor History* 4, no. 3 (Fall 1963): 227–47, and Lucy S. Dawidowicz, "The Jewishness of the Jewish Labor Movement in the United States," in Jonathan Sarna, ed., *The American Jewish Experience* (New York: Holmes and Meier, 1986), 158–66; see also Arthur Liebman, *Jews and*

*the Left* (New York: John Wiley, 1979) and his "The Ties that Bind: The Jewish Support for the Left in the United States," *AJHQ* 66 (December 1976): 285–321.

The entrance of Jews into government during the Roosevelt administration is addressed by Lloyd Gartner, "The Midpassage of American Jewry," in Sarna, ed., *The American Jewish Experience*, 228–30; see also Leonard Dinnerstein, "Jews in the New Deal," *AJH* 72 (June 1983): 461–76. On the history of Jewish liberalism, see Moses Rischin, "The Jews and the Liberal Tradition in America," *AJHQ* (September 1961): 3–16; Ben Halpern, "The Roots of American Jewish Liberalism," *AJHQ* (December 1976): 190–215. For an excellent discussion of Jewish commitment to the Democratic party in New York, see Deborah Dash Moore, *At Home in America: Second Generation New York Jews* (New York: Columbia University Press, 1981), 200–230. Lawrence H. Fuchs provides a useful but disputed analysis of Jewish political behavior in *The Political Behavior of American Jews* (Glencoe, Ill.: Free Press, 1956).

7 Meyer Liben, "CCNY—A Memoir," in Betty Rizzo and Barry Wallenstein, eds., *City at the Center: A Collection of Writings by CCNY Alumni and Faculty* (New York: City College of New York, 1983), 47.

8 Marcus Arkin, *Aspects of Jewish Economic History* (Philadelphia: Jewish Publication Society of America, 1975), 210; Chaim I. Waxman, *America's Jews in Transition* (Philadelphia: Temple University Press, 1983), 67.

9 Gartner, "The Midpassage of American Jewry," 230; Abraham G. Duker, "Socio-Psychological Trends in the American Jewish Community Since 1900," *YIVO Annual of Jewish Social Science* 9 (1954): 167.

10 H. S. Linfield, "The Jews of the United States: Number and Distribution, Preliminary Figures For 1937," *AJYB* 41 (1940): table 5, 185–86.

11 Ira Rosenwaike, *Population History of New York City* (Syracuse, N.Y.: Syracuse University Press, 1972), 100–112.

12 A 1935 survey placed 47 percent of New York Jewish households in the white-collar category. Nettie Pauline McGill, "Some Characteristics of Jewish Youth in New York City," *JSSQ* 14, no. 2 (December 1937): 255, 263–65; Thomas Kessner, "Jobs, Ghettoes, and the Urban Economy, 1880–1935," *AJH* 71 (December 1981): 234–37. Jewish employment patterns during the Depression are discussed in greater detail in chapter 1.

13 The division of American Jewish history into generational stages, although problematic in several respects, has become an almost universal standard of periodization in the field. (This paradigm, commencing with the East European migration, assumes that the earlier Sephardic and German migrations were overshadowed by the massive influx of Jews from Eastern Europe.) Two examples of the many works that periodize American Jewish history according to this model are Waxman, *America's Jews in Transition,* and Arnold M. Eisen, *The Chosen People in America* (Bloomington: Indiana University Press, 1983).

A slightly modified generational model was proposed by one scholar who suggested that the year 1925, when the percentage of foreign-born Jews began its steady decline, marked the onset of a new period in American Jewish history characterized by the domination of native-born Jews. Duker, "Socio-Psychological Trends in the American Jewish Community Since 1900," 166–67.

Three useful methodological discussions of the generational paradigm are Alan Spitzer, "The Historical Problem of Generations," *American Historical Review* 78 (December 1973): 1353–85; Vladimir C. Nahirny and Joshua A. Fishman, "American Immigrant Groups: Ethnic Identification and the Problem of Generations," *Sociological Review* 13 (1965): 311–26; Annie Kriegel, "Generational Difference: The History of an Idea," *Daedalus* (Fall 1978): 23–38. See also the collection of essays presented in Peter Kivisto and Dag Blanck, eds., *American Immigrants and Their Generations: Studies and Commentaries on the Hansen Thesis After Fifty Years* (Urbana: University of Illinois Press, 1990).

14  Peter I. Rose, "The Ghetto and Beyond," in Peter I. Rose, ed., *The Ghetto and Beyond: Essays on Jewish Life in America* (New York: Random House, 1969), 9; Moore, *At Home in America*, 9–11. Deborah Dash Moore's work presents a thorough historical analysis of second-generation Jewry.

15  Moore, *At Home in America*, 16.

16  For a succinct description of the conflict between Uptown and Downtown Jews in the immigrant generation, see Moses Rischin, *The Promised City: New York's Jews, 1870–1914* (Cambridge, Mass.: Harvard University Press, 1962), 95–111.

17  Moore discusses all these Jewish communal developments of the 1920s in *At Home in America*.

18  Maurice J. Karpf, *Jewish Community Organization in the United States: An Outline of Types of Organizations, Activities, and Problems* (New York: Bloch Publishing, 1938), 136.

19  A few of the many works that cover the immigrant period include Rischin, *The Promised City*; Irving Howe, *World of Our Fathers: The Journey of the East European Jews to America and the Life They Found and Made* (New York: Simon and Schuster, 1976); Arthur Goren, *New York Jews and the Quest for Community: The Kehillah Experiment, 1908–1922* (New York: Columbia University Press, 1970). Two more recent works that address this period are Susan A. Glenn, *Daughters of the Shtetl: Life and Labor in the Immigrant Generation* (Ithaca, N.Y.: Cornell University Press, 1990); Andrew R. Heinze, *Adapting to Abundance: Jewish Immigrants, Mass Consumption, and the Search for American Identity* (New York: Columbia University Press, 1990).

20  One of the few rigorous studies of the post–World War II period can be found in Deborah Dash Moore's, *To the Golden Cities: Pursuing the American Jewish Dream in Miami and L.A.* (New York: Free Press, 1994). See also Edward S. Shapiro, *A Time for Healing: American Jewry Since World War II* (Baltimore, Md.: Johns Hopkins University Press, 1992). Most scholarly accounts of the postwar period have been offered by sociologists rather than historians. See, for example, Marshall Sklare and Joseph Greenblum, *Jewish Identity on the Suburban Frontier* (Chicago: University of Chicago Press, 1967), and Steven M. Cohen, *American*

*Modernity and Jewish Identity* (New York: Tavistock Publications, 1983). For a popular discussion of postwar Jewish life, see Charles E. Silberman, *A Certain People: American Jews and Their Lives Today* (New York: Simon and Schuster, 1985).

CHAPTER 1: AN ETHNIC ECONOMY

Note to epigraph: Howe, *A Margin of Hope*, 10–11.

1 Judd Teller, *Strangers and Natives: The Evolution of the American Jew from 1921 to the Present* (New York: Delacorte Press, 1968), 113–15; Howard M. Sachar, *A History of the Jews in America* (New York: Alfred A. Knopf, 1992), 428–29.

2 *NYT*, 13 December 1930, 14.

3 *JDF*, 12 December 1930, 6.

4 *NYT*, 12 December 1930, 2; 13 December 1930, 14; 19 December 1930, 22; Frederick Powell, *Depositors Paid in Full* (New York: Arbitrator Press, 1931), 96–111.

5 *NYT*, 19 December 1930, 1, 22.

6 *The Day*, 11 January 1931, 4.

7 Ibid., 12 December 1930, 4.

8 Thomas Kessner, *Fiorello H. LaGuardia and the Making of Modern New York* (New York: McGraw-Hill, 1989), 400.

9 For a discussion of Jewish occupational characteristics, see Thomas Kessner, *The Golden Door: Italian and Jewish Immigrant Mobility in New York City, 1880–1915* (New York: Oxford University Press, 1977), 59–65. In the federal census, immigrant occupations such as peddling and owning small businesses and stores were listed as white-collar, making the Jewish occupational portrait somewhat deceptive. It remains relevant, however, that Jews were underrepresented in manual and unskilled labor and heavily concentrated in skilled and white-collar employment.

10 Leonard Dinnerstein, "Education and the Advancement of American Jews," in Bernard J. Weiss, ed., *American Education and the European Immigrant: 1840–1940* (Urbana: University of Illinois Press, 1982), 53.

11 Sachar, *A History of the Jews in America*, 428.

12 McGill, "Some Characteristics of Jewish Youth in New York City," 255. The Welfare Council study interviewed young people between the ages of sixteen and twenty-five at one of each one hundred residences in the city. The survey included information only about the occupations of fathers. Irwin Rosen, "The Economic Position of Jewish Youth," *JSSQ* 13, no. 1 (September 1936): 72.

13 Will Herberg, "The Jewish Labor Movement in the United States," *AJYB* 53 (1952): 53–54.

14 McGill, "Some Characteristics of Jewish Youth in New York City," 263–64.

15 Kessner, "Jobs, Ghettoes, and the Urban Economy," 234–237. A breakdown of New York's unemployed population revealed that professional, proprietary, and

clerical workers comprised 19.7 percent of the jobless; skilled workers, 27.3 percent; semiskilled, 27.1 percent; and unskilled, 25.9 percent. Ibid., 234.

16  Nettie Pauline McGill and Ellen Nathalie Matthews, *The Youth of New York City* (New York: MacMillan, 1940), 45. The percentage of Jewish youth on relief was 12.2, compared with 11.9 percent of the white Protestant sample.

17  Howe, *A Margin of Hope,* 6.

18  Yiddish Writers' Group of the Federal Writers' Project of the Works Projects Administration in the City of New York, *Jewish Families and Family Circles of New York* [Yiddish] (New York: Yiddish Writers' Union, 1939), 71.

19  Personal interview, Sydney Evans, 18 August 1991, New Haven, Conn.

20  Amram Ducovny, Oral history, 20, wwohl.

21  Brandes, "From Sweatshop to Stability," 61–67; Rosen, "The Economic Position of Jewish Youth," 71–72; Sachar, *A History of the Jews in America,* 428.

22  Kazin, *A Walker in the City,* 38–39.

23  Rosen, "The Economic Position of Jewish Youth," 71; Kessner, "Jobs, Ghettoes, and the Urban Economy," 234.

24  The differences between income levels and occupational status are highlighted in Kessner, *The Golden Door.*

25  *The Coops: The United Workers Cooperative Colony 50th Anniversary, 1927– 1977* (New York: Semi-Centennial Coop Reunion, 1977), 9.

26  Rosen, "The Economic Position of Jewish Youth," 70.

27  ymha *Bulletin* [published by the Ninety-second Street ymha], 5 May 1933, 3.

28  "Jews in America," 133, 141, 130.

29  Harriet Schneiderman, cited in Kessner, "Jobs, Ghettoes, and the Urban Economy," 236.

30  Kessner, *Fiorello H. LaGuardia,* 399–401; Bayor, *Neighbors in Conflict,* 24–28.

31  Dinnerstein, *Anti-Semitism in America,* 127.

32  *Brooklyn Tablet* editorial, cited in Bayor, *Neighbors in Conflict,* 28.

33  Personal interview, Jean Margolies, 27 August 1991, New Haven, Conn.

34  The American Jewish Congress published comprehensive surveys of economic discrimination in the 1930s. See Jacob X. Cohen, *Jews, Jobs, and Discrimination: A Report on Jewish Non-Employment* (New York: American Jewish Congress, 1937); J. X. Cohen, *Helping to End Economic Discrimination: Second Report on Jewish Non-Employment* (New York: American Jewish Congress, 1937); J. X. Cohen, *Towards Fair Play for Jewish Workers: Third Report on Jewish Non-Employment* (New York: American Jewish Congress, 1938). See also Heywood Broun and George Britt, *Christians Only: A Study in Prejudice* (New York: Vanguard Press, 1931); A. L. Severson, "Nationality and Religious Preferences as Reflected in Newspaper Advertisements," *American Journal of Sociology* 44 (1939): 540–42; a limited study is: Emanuel Federated Employment Service, "Resumé of the Preliminary Survey of the Problem of Discrimination Against Jews in Employment in New York City," Prepared for the Committee on the Study of Racial and Religious Problems in Employment (September 1931), nypl.

35 Ruth Jacknow Markowitz, *My Daughter, The Teacher: Jewish Teachers in the New York City Schools* (New Brunswick, N.J.: Rutgers University Press, 1993), 30. Many Depression-era Jews turned to government jobs and civil service employment in an effort to avoid discrimination in private firms. See, for example, the oral histories of Paul A. Freund, and Louis Weiser, WWOHL.

36 Marcia Graham Synnott, "Anti-Semitism and American Universities: Did Quotas Follow the Jews?" in David Gerber, ed., *Anti-Semitism in American History* (Urbana: University of Illinois Press, 1987), 250–53, 260.

37 "Jews in America," 141.

38 Synnott, "Anti-Semitism and American Universities," 258–59; Feingold, *A Time for Searching,* 148; Melvin M. Fagen, "The Status of Jewish Lawyers in New York City," *Jewish Social Studies* 1 (January 1939): 73–104.

39 Synnott, "Anti-Semitism and American Universities," 259.

40 Feingold, *A Time for Searching,* 151.

41 Among the many Jewish organizations that offered employment services were the Emanuel Federated Employment Service, the Fellowship House, the Hebrew Orphan Asylum, the Sabbath Alliance, and others throughout the city. See Organization Meeting Report, 19 April 1934, Board of Directors Minutes, 1934, FEGS.

B'nai B'rith also demonstrated an interest in helping young Jews secure employment and created the Vocational Service Bureau in 1938. Deborah Dash Moore, *B'nai B'rith and the Challenge of Ethnic Leadership* (Albany: State University of New York Press, 1981), 157–58. In 1939, several Jewish organizations pooled their efforts and established the Jewish Occupational Council, which remained essentially a paper organization. See Federation Employment Service, "Towards Occupational Adjustment—Summary of Activities," Federation Employment Service, 1939, 14, FEGS.

42 Irwin Rosen, "The Vocational Adjustment of Jews: A Contribution Towards Understanding the Problems Involved and Towards Communal Planning," *JSSQ* 11, no. 1 (September 1934): 40.

43 Constitution and By-Laws, Federation Employment Service, 28 June 1934, FEGS. The Federation Employment Service coordinated the efforts of several but not all of the city's Jewish employment bureaus. In 1934, the six cooperating agencies were the Ninety-second Street YMHA, Jewish Board of Guardians, Hebrew Orphan Asylum, Brooklyn Jewish Federation, Fellowship House, and the Emanuel Sisterhood of Personal Service. Organizations such as the Employment Bureau for Sabbath Observers and others chose to remain independent. On the establishment of a central Jewish employment bureau, see Rosen, "The Vocational Adjustment of Jews," 42–43. Bureau of Jewish Social Research, *Jewish Social Work* (1933), 29.

44 For an overview of the officers and organizational structure of the Federation Employment Service, see "Announcing a New Service for Employers . . . The Federation Employment Service," 1934, FEGS.

45  Federation Employment Service Board of Directors Minutes, 19 April 1934, 28 June 1934, FECS; for a detailed description of the Business Men's Council, see Moore, *At Home in America,* 153–57.

46  Federation Employment Service—Highlights of the Annual Report for the Year 1937, 5, Federation Employment Service Reports, 1937, FECS.

47  YMHA *Bulletin,* 30 June 1930, 12 September 1930.

48  In the 1930s, psychological testing was considered a scientific means of determining the character traits necessary for particular vocations. In addition, Rosen used such tests to compare the psychological traits of Jews with those of a non-Jewish sample. As a corollary to anthropological studies conducted to prove that Jews, as a group, demonstrated no distinct physical traits, Rosen's research was an attempt to demonstrate that Jews also had no distinct psychological characteristics. "If enough statistical evidence can be found to support the contention that there is no such thing as a 'racial type,' an important blow will have been struck against the difficulty that faces most Jewish workers and would-be workers. The success of this unusual venture will mean the explosion of myths and the destruction of prejudice." YMHA *Bulletin,* 20 February 1931, 1.

49  Report of the Employment Department, Ninety-second Street YMHA, February 1932, Ninety-second Street YMHA Archives.

50  Ibid., March 1931. Irwin Rosen compiled detailed statistics and monthly reports chronicling the activities of the Y's employment bureau. A collection of 1,500 registration cards submitted by male applicants to the bureau has survived and is housed in the Ninety-second Street YMHA archives. Rosen's detailed reports and statistical studies compiled at both the Ninety-second Street Y and the Federation Employment Service provide an excellent source for analyzing Jewish employment patterns and preferences in the Depression era.

51  For a discussion of the Federation Employment Service study, see Irwin Rosen, "Occupational Adjustment Problems Among Jews," *JSSQ* 12, no. 1 (September 1935): 15–19.

52  Report of the Employment Department, Ninety-second Street YMHA, July 1931, Ninety-second Street YMHA Archives.

53  McGill, "Some Characteristics of Jewish Youth in New York City," 264.

54  "Jews in America," 141.

55  Ben M. Selekman, "Planning for Jewish Economic Welfare," *JSSQ* 11, no. 1 (September 1934): 30. The concern with Jewish occupational maldistribution was a central feature of Jewish modernity. Enlightenment thinkers had hoped that emancipation would destroy Jewish occupational tendencies and integrate Jews within the general economy. The need to restructure the Jewish economy was a key aspect of both Enlightenment thought and Zionist ideology which emphasized the importance of productive labor. See Jacob Katz, *Out of the Ghetto: The Social Background of Jewish Emancipation, 1770–1870* (New York: Schocken Books, 1978), esp. 176–90; Arthur Hertzberg, *The Zionist Idea* (New York: Atheneum, 1984).

56  A. A. Liveright, "Problems in Community Organization of Vocational Services," *PNCJSW* (1939): 153.

57  Jewish Social Service Association, Annual Report, 1935, 22.

58  Selekman, "Planning for Jewish Economic Welfare," 31.

59  Selig Perlman, "Present Day Economic Trends and Their Effect on Jewish Life in America," *JSSQ* 11, no. 1 (September 1934): 14. The Depression was not the first time that agricultural movements had emerged among American Jews. See Uri D. Herscher, *Jewish Agricultural Utopias in America, 1880–1910* (Detroit: Wayne State University Press, 1981).

60  For more on the call for Jews to return to manual labor, see, for example, Isaac Rubinow, "The Economic and Industrial Status of American Jewry," *JSSQ* 9, no. 1 (December 1932): 35.

61  Selekman, "Planning for Jewish Economic Welfare," 31.

62  Rosen, "Occupational Adjustment Problems Among Jews," 19, 18; see also Rosen, "The Economic Position of Jewish Youth," 67–79.

63  Liveright, "Problems in Community Organization of Vocational Services," 152.

64  Morris D. Waldman, "Effects of Hitlerism in America," Paper presented at the meeting of the American Jewish Committee, Chicago, Ill., 10 June 1934, 3–4, American Jewish Committee Papers, Chronological File, June–August 1934, Box 3, AJC.

65  Report of the Employment Department, Ninety-second Street YMHA, May 1932, Ninety-second Street YMHA Archives.

66  Samuel A. Goldsmith, "Jewish Economic Adjustment: Integrated Approaches to Jewish Economic Adjustment," *PNCJSS* (1937): 201.

CHAPTER 2: A FAMILY AFFAIR

Note to epigraph: Kazin, *A Walker in the City,* 55.

1  Personal interview, Stanley Katz, 23 August 1991, New Haven, Conn.

2  Howe, *A Margin of Hope,* 4.

3  A few of the many studies that emphasize the importance of family networks in immigrant life are Judith E. Smith, *Family Connections: A History of Italian and Jewish Immigrant Lives in Providence, Rhode Island, 1900–1940* (Albany: State University of New York Press, 1985); Virginia Yans-McLaughlin, *Family and Community: Italian Immigrants in Buffalo, 1880–1920* (Ithaca, N.Y.: Cornell University Press, 1978); John Bodnar, "Immigration, Kinship, and the Rise of Working-Class Realism," *Journal of Social History* 14 (Fall 1980): 46–65; Corine Azen Krause, "Urbanization Without Breakdown: Italian, Jewish, and Slavic Immigrant Women in Pittsburgh, 1900–1945," *Journal of Urban History* 4 (May 1978): 291–305.

4  Sydelle Kramer and Jenny Masur, eds., *Jewish Grandmothers* (Boston: Beacon Press, 1976), 155.

5  Legislation enacted in 1924 drastically reduced immigration quotas. See John

Higham, *Send These To Me: Jews and Other Immigrants in Urban America* (New York: Atheneum, 1975), 43–58. In the 1930s, Jewish immigration to the United States reached its lowest ebb. See Mark Wischnitzer, *To Dwell in Safety: The Story of Jewish Migration Since 1800* (Philadelphia: The Jewish Publication Society of America, 1948), 289.

6  Gartner, "The Midpassage of American Jewry," 230; Arthur Hertzberg, *The Jews in America: Four Centuries of an Uneasy Encounter: A History* (New York: Simon and Schuster, 1989), 280; J. B. Maller, "A Study of Jewish Neighborhoods in New York City," *JSSQ* 10, no. 4 (June 1934): 272, 274; *JDB*, 7 March 1933, 1.

7  McGill, "Some Characteristics of Jewish Youth in New York City," 255. For further evidence of the tendency of Jews in their twenties to live at home during the 1930s, see the statistical data compiled by the Federation Employment Service.

8  Paula Hyman, "Gender and the Immigrant Experience in the United States," in Judith Baskin, ed., *Jewish Women in Historical Perspective* (Detroit: Wayne State University Press, 1991), 224–25.

9  Between 1910 and 1925, the percentage of Jewish women in the labor force continued to decline as Jewish men attained a higher socioeconomic status and Jewish women came to accept American behavioral norms celebrating a married woman's role within the home. For more on the Eastern European tradition of married women working and the role of Jewish wives in the American labor force, see Paula Hyman, "Culture and Gender: Women in the Immigrant Jewish Community," in David Berger, ed., *The Legacy of Jewish Migration: 1881 and Its Impact* (New York: Brooklyn College Press, 1983), 157–68; see also Hyman, "Gender and the Immigrant Experience in the United States," 225–26; Kessner, *The Golden Door*, 76; see statistical comparison of several ethnic groups in Elizabeth H. Pleck, "A Mother's Wages: Income Earning Among Married Italian and Black Women, 1896–1911," in Nancy F. Cott and Elizabeth H. Pleck, eds., *A Heritage of Her Own: Toward A New Social History of American Women* (New York: Simon and Schuster, 1979), 372.

10  For a detailed discussion of the economic contributions of married Jewish women and the tendency of Jewish daughters rather than wives to assume wage-paying work, see Susan A. Glenn, *Daughters of the Shtetl: Life and Labor in the Immigrant Generation* (Ithaca, N.Y.: Cornell University Press, 1990), 50–89.

11  Rose S., cited in Sydney Stahl Weinberg, *The World of Our Mothers: The Lives of Jewish Immigrant Women* (Chapel Hill: University of North Carolina Press, 1988), 229.

12  Personal interview, Rebecca Augenstein, 26 August 1991, New Haven, Conn.

13  Weinberg, *The World of Our Mothers*, 235.

14  Rose S., cited ibid., 229.

15  *JDF*, 4 April 1935, 9.

16  Ibid., 18 June 1931, 8.

17  Susan Glenn briefly discusses the conflicts that the daughters of immigrants felt about married women's work. Glenn, *Daughters of the Shtetl*, 238–240.

18 Susan Ware, *Holding Their Own: American Women in the 1930s* (Boston: Twayne Publishers, 1982), 27.

19 Lois Scharf, *To Work and to Wed: Female Employment, Feminism, and the Great Depression* (Westport, Conn.: Greenwood Press, 1980), 43–65. Scharf presents a detailed analysis of the many issues surrounding married women's participation in the labor force during the Depression.

20 Ruth Milkman, "Women's Work and the Economic Crisis: Some Lessons from the Great Depression," in Cott and Pleck, eds., *A Heritage of Her Own,* 510–20; Samuel A. Stouffer and Paul F. Lazarsfeld, *Research Memorandum on the Family in the Depression,* Social Science Research Council Bulletin no. 29 (New York: Social Science Research Council, 1937), 28–34. See also the survey results reported in the *NYT*, 25 December 1938, section 2: 5.

21 Alice Kessler-Harris, *Out to Work: A History of Wage-Earning Women in the United States* (New York: Oxford University Press, 1982), 257–59.

22 Winifred D. Wandersee Bolin, "The Economics of Middle-Income Family Life: Working Women During the Great Depression," *Journal of American History* 65, no. 1 (June 1978): 73. In her analysis of middle-income working women, Bolin observes that some working wives may have entered the labor force not only out of economic necessity but also in order to provide the "extras" needed to maintain middle-class living standards.

23 Pearl Bernstein, Oral history, 27, WWOHL.

24 *JDF*, 12 November 1930, 6.

25 Ibid., 12 April 1933, 3.

26 Personal interview, Stanley Katz, 23 August 1991, New Haven, Conn.; Personal interview, Ida Barnett, 1 September 1991, New Haven, Conn.

27 Glenn, *Daughters of the Shtetl,* 240.

28 Personal interview, Tillie Spiegel, 22 August 1991, New Haven, Conn.

29 Kate Simon, *A Wider World: Portraits in an Adolescence* (New York: Harper and Row, 1986), 110, 109.

30 Personal interview, Rebecca Augenstein, 26 August 1991, New Haven, Conn.

31 Personal interview, Jean Margolies, 27 August 1991, New Haven, Conn.

32 Eli Ginzberg, "Urban Jewish Immigrants: The Bergers," case history included in David A. Shannon, ed., *The Great Depression* (Englewood Cliffs, N.J.: Prentice Hall, 1960), 162.

33 Ibid.

34 *The Coops,* 10.

35 *Inside Information* [published by the Jewish Social Service Association], 1, no. 2 (June 1934), 2.

36 Personal interview, Jean Margolies, 27 August 1991, New Haven, Conn.

37 Personal interview, Louis Kfare, 26 August 1991, New Haven, Conn.

38 Ginzberg, "Urban Jewish Immigrants," 161.

39 Personal interview, Jean Margolies, 27 August 1991, New Haven, Conn.

40 Lillian Gorenstein, unpublished memoirs, in possession of the author. I wish to

thank Aryeh Goren for providing me with his mother's rich reminiscences of the Depression.

41 The Welfare Council estimated that 92 percent of Jewish youth under the age of twenty-five continued to live in their parents' homes. McGill, "Some Characteristics of Jewish Youth in New York City," 255–56.

42 Yiddish Writers' Group, *Jewish Families and Family Circles of New York*, 70.

43 Nathan C. Belth, Oral history, 11, Oral History Project, FJP.

44 Kramer and Masur, *Jewish Grandmothers*, 97.

45 McGill and Matthews, *The Youth of New York City*, 28.

46 Personal interview, Anna Kfare, 18 August 1991, New Haven, Conn. Anna Kfare and Louis Kfare are husband and wife; the couple married in 1937.

47 Personal interview, Louis Kfare, 26 August 1991, New Haven, Conn.

48 Smith, *Family Connections*, 82.

49 *Notes and News* [published by the Bureau of Jewish Social Research], 7 March 1933, 8.

50 Bess B. Spanner, "The Unattached Woman—Discussion," *JSSQ* 10, no. 1 (September 1933): 57.

51 Howe, *A Margin of Hope*, 4.

52 In 1934, the Bureau of Jewish Social Research found that in seven large American cities, Jews comprised between 2.3 and 10.8 percent of white families receiving public assistance. *Notes and News*, 20 December 1934, 14.

53 Personal interview, Ida Barnett, 1 September 1991, New Haven, Conn.

54 *The Coops*, 41.

55 Personal interview, Jean Margolies, 27 August 1991, New Haven, Conn.

56 Smith, *Family Connections*, 122; see also Stouffer and Lazarsfeld, *Research Memorandum on the Family in the Depression*, 98–102.

57 Howe, *A Margin of Hope*, 6.

58 Mark Naison, "From Eviction to Rent Control: Tenant Activism in the Great Depression," in Ronald Lawson, ed., *The Tenant Movement in New York City* (New Brunswick, N.J.: Rutgers University Press, 1986), 100.

59 Personal interview, Sydney Evans, 18 August 1991, New Haven, Conn.

60 Ibid.

61 Personal interview, Stanley Katz, 23 August 1991, New Haven, Conn.

62 Personal interview, Ida Barnett, 1 September 1991, New Haven, Conn.

63 Howe, *A Margin of Hope*, 7

64 H. L. Lurie, "The Jewish Family Agency in the Post-Depression Period," *JSSQ* 9, no. 1 (December 1932): 98.

65 On Jewish vacations in the immigrant period, see Heinze, *Adapting to Abundance*, 125–32; on reduced vacation rates during the Great Depression, see the representative advertisements in *The Young Judaean* (June 1932): 22–23; Stefan Kanfer, *A Summer World* (New York: Farrar Straus Giroux, 1989), 125–26.

66 Kazin, *Starting Out in the Thirties*, 40.

67 Sociologists of the 1930s who studied the Depression's effect on families con-

cluded that prior family stability usually predicted the Depression-era response. Using categories such as family organization, integration, and adaptability, sociologists attempted to analyze the factors that contributed to the relative cohesion or disruption of households during the economic crisis. Robert Cooley Angell, *The Family Encounters the Depression* (New York: Charles Scribner's Sons, 1936); Ruth Shonle Cavan and Katherine Howland Ranck, *The Family and the Depression: A Study of One Hundred Chicago Families* (Chicago: University of Chicago Press, 1938); Winona L. Morgan, *The Family Meets the Depression: A Study of a Group of Highly Selected Families* (Minneapolis: University of Minnesota Press, 1939); Mirra Komarovsky, *The Unemployed Man and His Family: The Effect of Unemployment upon the Status of the Man in Fifty-Nine Families* (New York: Institute of Social Research, 1940); E. Wight Bakke, *Citizens Without Work: A Study of the Effects of Unemployment upon the Workers and Social Relations and Practices* (New Haven: Yale University Press, 1940); for a more contemporary approach, see Glen Elder, Jr., *Children of the Great Depression* (Chicago: University of Chicago Press, 1974).

68 Jewish Social Service Association, Annual Report, 1935, 10, 3.

69 The court experienced frequent name changes in its history. Originally established as the Jewish Arbitration Court, it later became the Jewish Conciliation Court and finally the Jewish Conciliation Board. During most of the 1930s, it was called the Jewish Conciliation Court, which is the designation I will use in my discussion.

The New York State Arbitration Law of 1920 helped pave the way for the establishment of the court. The legislation upheld the legality of third-party agreements and rendered such decisions enforceable in the same manner as the decisions of civil courts. Three accounts of the formation and activities of the court are Samuel Buchler, *"Cohen Comes First" and Other Cases* (New York: Vanguard Press, 1933); James Yaffe, *So Sue Me! The Story of a Community Court* (New York: Saturday Review Press, 1972); Israel Goldstein, *Jewish Justice and Conciliation: History of the Jewish Conciliation Board of America, 1930–1968* (New York: KTAV Publishing, 1981).

70 *JDB*, 12 January 1933, 2.

71 *NYT*, 11 January 1934, 7.

72 *JDF*, 19 August 1937, 11.

73 Ibid., 1 February 1935, 4.

74 See, for example, *JDF*, 12 January 1937, 1, 9. Throughout the 1930s, the *Forward* carried regular reports of cases brought before the Jewish Conciliation Court.

75 *The Day*, 22 February 1931, 8.

76 *American Hebrew and Jewish Tribune*, 30 March 1934, 408.

77 Yaffe, *So Sue Me!* 10.

78 Simon, *A Wider World*, 123.

79 *JDF*, 16 November 1930, section 2: 1.

80 Robert and Helen Lynd, *Middletown in Transition: A Study in Cultural Conflicts* (New York: Harcourt, Brace and Company, 1937), 178–79.

81  Jewish Social Service Association, Annual Report, 1935, 15. The report presents this case as fictitious but representative of actual client cases.

82  Howe, *A Margin of Hope,* 7.

83  Arthur Granit, *The Time of the Peaches* (New York: Abelard-Schuman, 1959), 10.

84  *The Day,* 15 March 1931, 8.

85  Jewish Social Service Association, Annual Report, 1935, 15.

86  Howe, *A Margin of Hope,* 14.

87  Smith, *Family Connections,* 75–76; Elizabeth Ewen, *Immigrant Women in the Land of Dollars: Life and Culture on the Lower East Side, 1890–1925* (New York: Monthly Review Press, 1985), 94–109.

88  Komarovsky, *The Unemployed Man and His Family,* 49.

89  Reena S. Friedman, "'Send Me My Husband Who Is in New York City': Husband Desertion in the American Jewish Community, 1900–1926," *Jewish Social Studies* 44, no. 1 (Winter 1982): 4, 1–18.

90  For articles on the decline of desertion during the Depression, see *JDF,* 29 November 1930, 12; 1 February 1934, 4; on the tendency of Jewish husbands to remain with their families during the Depression, see Gerald Sorin, *The Nurturing Neighborhood: The Brownsville Boys Club and Jewish Community in Urban America, 1940–1990* (New York: New York University Press, 1990), 63–64.

91  *JDF,* 29 November 1930, 12.

92  Ware, *Holding Their Own,* 7; Dixon Wecter, *The Age of the Great Depression, 1929–1941* (New York: Macmillan, 1948), 198.

CHAPTER 3: STARTING OUT IN THE THIRTIES

Note to epigraph: Irving Rosenthal, "Rumblings of Unrest and Empty Stomachs," in Rizzo and Wallenstein, eds., *City at the Center,* 55.

 1  Howe, *A Margin of Hope,* 10.

 2  Kazin, *A Walker in the City,* 21.

 3  Paula S. Fass, *Outside In: Minorities and the Transformation of American Education* (New York: Oxford University Press, 1989), 65; Markowitz, *My Daughter, the Teacher,* 108; John Modell, *Into One's Own: From Youth to Adulthood in the United States, 1920–1975* (Berkeley: University of California Press, 1989), 122–29; David Tyack, Robert Lowe, and Elisabeth Hansot, *Public Schools in Hard Times: The Great Depression and Recent Years* (Cambridge, Mass.: Harvard University Press, 1984), 144–50. See also Ruth E. Eckert and Thomas O. Marshall, *When Youth Leave School* (New York: The Regents' Inquiry, 1938); McGill and Matthews, *The Youth of New York City,* 54.

 4  McGill, "Some Characteristics of Jewish Youth in New York City," 258; Moore, *At Home in America,* 95–100, 103.

 5  Kazin, *A Walker in the City,* 22.

 6  Howe, *A Margin of Hope,* 30.

7 *Lincoln Landmark*, Abraham Lincoln High School Yearbook, 1935, 11; *Aurora*, Thomas Jefferson High School Yearbook, 1933.

8 *The Oriole*, Evander Childs High School Yearbook, 1938.

9 *Aurora*, 1934, n.p.; *Lincoln Landmark*, 1934, 7.

10 See, for example, *Lincoln Landmark*, 1935, 14–33.

11 *Lincoln Landmark*, 1932, 69; Ibid., 1934, 11.

12 *Aurora*, 1932, 105.

13 *Lincoln Landmark*, 1932, 66.

14 Howe, *A Margin of Hope*, 28.

15 Sorin, *The Nurturing Neighborhood*, 84.

16 Charles L. Mulligan, "Mass Recreation," WPA, Jews of New York, Box 4, Folder 126.

17 Report of the Physical Education Department, Ninety-second Street YMHA, March 1934, Ninety-second Street YMHA Archives; YMHA *Bulletin*, 12 May 1935, 1; Jewish Welfare Board, Study of the Jewish Community of Brooklyn for the YMHA of Brooklyn, 1935, 42, Jewish Welfare Board Collection, AJHS.

18 *Federation Illustrated* 3, no. 2 (June 1937), n.p.

19 Yiddish Writers' Group, *Jewish Families and Family Circles of New York*, 75.

20 Harold M. Kase, Oral history, 10–11, Oral History Project, FJP.

21 Moore, *At Home in America*, 102–3; for an overview of American Jewish educational patterns, see Leonard Dinnerstein, "Education and the Advancement of American Jews," in Bernard J. Weiss, ed., *American Education and the European Immigrant: 1840–1940* (Urbana: University of Illinois Press, 1982), 44–60; see also *JDF*, 16 November 1930, English section, 1; Markowitz, *My Daughter, The Teacher*, 49.

22 McGill and Matthews, *The Youth of New York City*, 155–56.

23 Modell, *Into One's Own*, 121–29; see Stouffer and Lazarsfeld, *Research Memorandum on the Family in the Depression*, 28, 34–37.

24 McGill, "Some Characteristics of Jewish Youth in New York City," 264.

25 *The Day*, 15 March 1931, 8.

26 Ibid.

27 McGill, "Some Characteristics of Jewish Youth in New York City," 259.

28 Ibid., 256–60; The Welfare Council survey reveals two interesting features of the Jewish educational profile. The study found that college graduation was four times greater among Jewish men and two to three times greater among Jewish women than among their non-Jewish counterparts. The Jewish group also demonstrated the greatest disparity between the genders, however, with the difference between men's and women's college attendance surpassing that of any other group. Ibid., 258.

29 Ibid., Jacob Rader Marcus, *The American Jewish Woman, 1654–1980* (New York: KTAV Publishing, 1981), 132. By the 1920s, Jewish women had already demonstrated a disproportionate college attendance rate. Dinnerstein, "Education and the Advancement of American Jews," 47.

30 Markowitz, *My Daughter, the Teacher*, 14, 31.

31  Ibid., 21.

32  Morris Freedman, "ccny Days," in Rizzo and Wallenstein, eds., *City at the Center,* 64, 63.

33  Markowitz, *My Daughter, the Teacher,* 31.

34  Louis Weiser, Oral History, 7, wwohl.

35  Freedman, "ccny Days," 64.

36  Robert Cohen, *When the Old Left Was Young: Student Radicals and America's First Mass Student Movement, 1929–1941* (New York: Oxford University Press, 1993), 68–71. Cohen offers the most comprehensive analysis to date of Depression-era activism on college campuses.

37  *The Broeklundian* (1935), as cited in Markowitz, *My Daughter, The Teacher,* 51.

38  Howe, *A Margin of Hope,* 10. For more on the Jewish Left in this period, see Liebman, *Jews and the Left,* esp. 357–443. For a classic piece of proletarian literature produced by this generation of Jews, see Michael Gold, *Jews Without Money.*

39  Liben, "ccny—A Memoir," 49; for a detailed discussion of campus movements, see Cohen, *When the Old Left Was Young.*

40  Howe, *A Margin of Hope,* 9–10.

41  Liben, "ccny—A Memoir," 48.

42  William Barrett, *The Truants: Adventures Among the Intellectuals* (Garden City, N.Y.: Anchor Press/Doubleday, 1982), 22.

43  "The Jew in Sports," wpa, Jews of New York, Box 3, Folder 123.

44  Liben, "ccny—A Memoir," 50.

45  *The Mercury,* December 1932, 23.

46  City College, *Microcosm,* 1933, 162.

47  Ibid., 1937, 31.

48  Berrol, "Public Schools and Immigrants: The New York City Experience," in Weiss, ed., *American Education and the European Immigrant,* 40; Modell, *Into One's Own,* 121–26.

49  For examples, see *JDF,* 12 June 1932, section 2: 2; 17 June 1934, section 2: 2; 26 June 1938, section 2: 1.

50  Jewish Social Service Association, Annual Report, 1935, 17.

51  Yiddish Writers' Group, *Jewish Families and Family Circles of New York,* 75.

52  Employment Department Records, Ninety-second Street ymha, April 1932, May 1932, Ninety-second Street ymha Archives. A collection of registration cards for the employment bureau is also housed in the archives of the Ninety-second Street ymha.

53  Yiddish Writers' Group, *Jewish Families and Family Circles of New York,* 75.

54  Roland Baxt, Oral history, 11, Oral History Project, fjp.

55  William Stern, Oral history, 13, wwohl; Feingold, *A Time for Searching,* 148.

56  Louis Weiser, Oral history, 8, wwohl.

57  As cited in Suzanne Rachel Wasserman, "The Good Old Days of Poverty: The Battle over the Fate of New York City's Lower East Side During the Depression," (Ph.D. diss., New York University, 1990), 238.

58  *The Day,* 24 January 1932, 8. A somewhat contradictory critique that also existed

in the 1930s denounced Jewish parents, not for placing too many demands on their children, but for coddling them. This critique, directed almost exclusively at Jewish mothers, argued that children must be taught self-reliance and toughness in order to face the pressures of contemporary life. The *American Hebrew,* for example, carried an article about Jewish summer camps which proclaimed: "Not the least of the things the camp does is to separate the child from its sometimes too-doting mother. After all, every one of these children must in the years to come face life for itself, as an individual, hew out its own destiny, meet its own problems." The author argued that over-protective Jewish mothers prevented children from learning to "carry their own freight." *The American Hebrew and Jewish Tribune,* 11 March 1932, 432, 447.

59 *The Day,* 27 March 1932, 8. The author of this article, a Jewish woman, portrayed the secondary status of Jewish daughters as the norm in Jewish families.

60 Howe, *A Margin of Hope,* 10.

61 Report of the Employment Department, Ninety-second Street YMHA, February 1932, Ninety-second Street YMHA Archives.

62 Jewish Social Service Association, Annual Report, 1935, 23.

63 Report of the Physical Education Department, Ninety-second Street YMHA, March 1934, Ninety-second Street YMHA Archives.

64 Judge Albert Cohen, "What the Center Can Do for Youth," *Jewish Center* 15, no. 2 (June 1937): 23.

65 Gartner, "The Midpassage of American Jewry," 226.

66 Kazin, *Starting Out in the Thirties,* 7.

67 Milkman, "Women's Work and the Economic Crisis," 523.

68 McGill and Matthews, *The Youth of New York City,* 30.

69 McGill, "Some Characteristics of Jewish Youth in New York City," 255–56.

70 McGill and Matthews, *The Youth of New York City,* 31.

71 Harry M., cited in David Leviatin, *Followers of the Trail: Jewish Working-Class Radicals in America* (New Haven: Yale University Press, 1989), 176–77.

72 Personal interview, Jean Margolies, 27 August 1991, New Haven, Conn.

73 Personal interview, Louis Kfare, 26 August 1991, New Haven, Conn.

74 *JDF,* 28 February 1933, 4. For other examples of articles about declining marriage rates, see *JDF,* 18 January 1931; 28 May 1934, 3; 24 July 1931, 4.

75 Ibid., 28 May 1934, 3.

76 Kazin, *Starting Out in the Thirties,* 78.

77 Roland Baxt, Oral history, 15, Oral History Project, FJP.

78 Modell, *Into One's Own,* 132–40. Modell offers useful insights into the different marriage patterns among various occupational groups. See also his provocative discussion about the development of the notion of engagement during the Depression years, 140–53.

79 Ware, *Holding Their Own,* 7.

80 Calvin Goldscheider and Alan S. Zuckerman, *The Transformation of the Jews* (Chicago: University of Chicago Press, 1984), 177.

81 Arthur A. Goren, *The American Jews: Dimensions of Ethnicity* (Cambridge, Mass.: Belknap Press of Harvard University Press, 1980), 76; Sidney Goldstein, "Jews in the United States: Perspectives from Demography," in Marshall Sklare, ed., *American Jews: A Reader* (New York: Behrman House, 1983), 58–59, 63, 70.

82 *JDF*, 28 May 1934, 3.

83 Ware, *Holding Their Own*, 7; John D'Emilio and Estelle B. Freedman, *Intimate Matters: A History of Sexuality in America* (New York: Harper and Row, 1988), 244–46; Linda Gordon, *Woman's Body, Woman's Right: A Social History of Birth Control in America* (New York: Penguin Books, 1976), 301–40. See also Gordon's discussion of the ideological and tactical shift in the birth control movement during this period.

84 Sergio Della Pergolla, cited in Goldstein, "Jews in the United States," 70.

85 Regine K. Stix and Frank W. Nottestein, *Controlled Fertility: An Evaluation of Clinic Service* (Baltimore, Md.: Williams and Wilkins Company, 1940), 10–12, 28–29.

86 Raymond Pearl, *The Natural History of Population* (New York: Oxford University Press, 1939), 242–43.

87 *Men's Club Tattler* 1, no. 4 (May 1937), 1, Box 11, Brooklyn Jewish Center Collection, Joseph And Miriam Ratner Center for the Study of Conservative Judaism, JTSA.

88 *JDB*, 9 March 1933, 2.

89 *Bronx Home News,* 25 January 1932, 4. Although Rabbi Bril's condemnation of birth control in Jewish families was harsh, it should be noted that, before the Holocaust, the discourse about replacement levels in the Jewish population had not yet reached the feverish pitch that would characterize the discussion of Jewish birthrates in the post–World War II era.

90 Scharf, *To Work and to Wed*, 145–46.

91 Kazin, *A Walker in the City*, 56, 55.

92 *The Day*, 1 February 1931, 8; 1 March 1931, 8.

93 Ibid., 1 March 1931, 8; see also ibid., 3 April 1932, 8; 18 October 1930, 16.

94 Ibid., 8 March 1931, 8.

95 Ibid. The majority of letters argued that a mother should not work for wages. There were notable exceptions, however. For a letter written by a Jewish woman that supported a mother's right to work, see ibid., 3 April 1932, 8.

96 Ibid., 1 March 1931, 8.

97 Ibid.

CHAPTER 4: THE LANDSCAPE OF JEWISH LIFE

1 Personal interview, Louis Kfare, 26 August 1991, New Haven, Conn.

2 Kazin, *A Walker in the City*, 11.

3 Howe, *A Margin of Hope*, 28.

4  Nathaniel Zalowitz, "The Future of the Ghetto in the United States," *JDF*, 4 July 1926, section E: 2.

5  Moore, *At Home in America*, 30–31. This chapter builds on Moore's detailed discussion of the development and character of second generation Jewish neighborhoods. See ibid., 18–87.

6  Morris C. Horowitz and Lawrence J. Kaplan, *The Estimated Jewish Population of the New York Area, 1900–1975* (New York: Federation of Jewish Philanthropies of New York, 1959), 1–25.

7  Milton Klonsky, "The Trojans of Brighton Beach," *Commentary* (May 1947): 462.

8  Zalowitz, "The Future of the Ghetto in the United States."

9  Bureau of Jewish Social Research, *First Section: Studies in the New York Jewish Population. Jewish Communal Survey of Greater New York* (New York: Bureau of Jewish Social Research, 1928), 8; Horowitz and Kaplan, *The Estimated Jewish Population of the New York Area*, 133, 209, 239; McGill and Matthews, *The Youth of New York City*, appendix B, table 6.

10  Personal interview, Jean Margolies, 27 August 1991, New Haven, Conn.

11  Moore, *At Home in America*, 65–68; Jenna Weissman Joselit, *New York's Jewish Jews: The Orthodox Community in the Interwar Years* (Bloomington: Indiana University Press, 1990), 9–10.

12  Report on Photographic Study of the Lower East Side of New York City, n.d.; J. B. Lightman and A. J. Simon, Research Diary, Photographic Study of the Lower East Side, 1, Graduate School for Jewish Social Work, Collection I-7, Box 5, AJHS.

    The Lower East Side study and similar projects sponsored by the Graduate School for Jewish Social Work demonstrate that Jews, like other Americans of the period, felt the documentary impulse of the Depression era. As a cultural production, the Lower East Side study clearly falls within the documentary genre that emerged in the 1930s. See William Stott, *Documentary Expression and Thirties America* (New York: Oxford University Press, 1973) and the essays by Lawrence W. Levine and Alan Trachtenberg, in Carl Fleischhauer and Beverly Brannan, eds., *Documenting America, 1935–1943* (Berkeley: University of California Press, 1988).

13  Gold, *Jews Without Money*, 215, 225, 248.

14  McGill and Matthews, *The Youth of New York City*, appendix B, table 6.

15  Lillian Elkins, Oral history, 6, WWOHL.

16  Alter F. Landesman, "A Neighborhood Survey of Brownsville," 1927, 5–9, NYPL; Sorin, *The Nurturing Neighborhood*, 15.

17  Kazin, *A Walker in the City*, 38.

18  Sorin, *The Nurturing Neighborhood*, 17–19.

19  Kazin, *A Walker in the City*, 12.

20  William Poster, "'Twas A Dark Night in Brownsville: Pitkin Avenue's Self-Made Generation," *Commentary* 9 (May 1950): 461; Sorin, *The Nurturing Neighborhood*, 16, 14.

21  Gerald Green, cited in Sorin, *The Nurturing Neighborhood*, 14.

22 Ibid., 17, 12.

23 Kazin, *A Walker in the City*, 10.

24 Jewish Welfare Board, Study of the Jewish Community of Williamsburg, Brooklyn, New York, 1936, 6, Jewish Welfare Board Papers, AJHS; McGill and Matthews, *The Youth of New York City*, appendix B, table 6.

25 George Kranzler, *Williamsburg: A Community in Transition* (New York: Philipp Feldheim, 1961), 17–18, 166–69; Joselit, *New York's Jewish Jews*, 16–18.

26 Kazin, *A Walker in the City*, 9.

27 G. S. Roth, cited in Joselit, *New York's Jewish Jews*, 18.

28 Ibid; *New York City Market Analysis* (New York: *New York Herald Tribune, The News,* and *The New York Times,* 1933); Moore, *At Home in America,* 79–80.

29 *New York City Market Analysis*; Moore, *At Home in America,* 66, 78–79; McGill and Matthews, *The Youth of New York City,* appendix B, table 6.

30 Jewish Welfare Board, Study of the Jewish Community of Brooklyn for the YMHA of Brooklyn, 1935, Jewish Welfare Board Papers; Moore, *At Home in America,* 78–79. Moore's work offers a detailed discussion of the formation of a middle-class Jewish identity in this period.

31 Sorin, *The Nurturing Neighborhood,* 34.

32 Kazin, *A Walker in the City,* 9.

33 Federal Writers Project, *New York City Guide* (New York: Random House, 1939), 517.

34 "Just Plain Jews," WPA, Jews of New York, Box 3632.

35 Personal interview, Debby Kirschenbaum, 27 August 1991, New Haven, Conn.

36 Welfare Council of New York City, Research Bureau, *Housing and Rentals, New York City,* 1930, Health Districts 10, 15, 16, 22, 23, 33, Bronx; also cited in Selma C. Berrol, "The Jewish West Side of New York City, 1920–1970," *Journal of Ethnic Studies* 13, no. 4 (1987): 30.

37 Ruth Glazer, "West Bronx: Food, Shelter, Clothing," *Commentary* (June 1949): 578–85; Moore, *At Home in America,* 76–78.

38 Howe, *A Margin of Hope,* 2.

39 *The YMHA Bulletin,* 8 April 1932, 2.

40 Daniel G. Sullivan, "1940–1965: Population Mobility in the South Bronx," in *Devastation/Resurrection: The South Bronx* (New York: Bronx Museum of the Arts, 1979), 37.

41 Graenum Berger, Oral history, 4, Oral History Project, FJP; see also Jewish Welfare Board, Study of Council House and Its Immediate Area in the Borough of the Bronx, 1934, and Study of Council House and Its Immediate Area in the Borough of the Bronx, 1939, Jewish Welfare Board Papers.

42 Lucy S. Dawidowicz, *From That Place and Time: A Memoir, 1938–1947* (New York: W. W. Norton, 1989), 6.

43 *New York City Market Analysis*; Bayor, *Neighbors in Conflict,* 159; Moore, *At Home in America,* 73–74.

44 Howe, *A Margin of Hope,* 3–4.

45 Ibid., 2, 9.

46 Jewish cooperative housing projects were sponsored by several organizations, including the Amalgamated Clothing Workers of America, the Labor Zionist Farband, the Jewish Butchers Union, and the Typographical Union. Moore, *At Home in America*, 53–55, 80; Calvin Trillin, "U.S. Journal—The Bronx," *New Yorker*, 1 August 1977, 49; *The Coops; 30 Years of Amalgamated Cooperative Housing, 1927–1957* (New York: James Peter Warbasse Memorial Library, 1958).

47 Approximately 5 percent of New York's Jews lived in Queens in 1930. Horowitz and Kaplan, *The Estimated Jewish Population of the New York Area*, 22.

48 Joselit, *New York's Jewish Jews*, 9–14.

49 Bayor, *Neighbors in Conflict*, 150–55; Jeffrey S. Gurock, *When Harlem Was Jewish, 1870–1930* (New York: Columbia University Press, 1979), 151. The history and communal developments of German Jewish refugees lie outside the scope of this study. See Steven M. Lowenstein, *Frankfurt on the Hudson: The German-Jewish Community of Washington Heights, 1933–38, Its Structure and Culture* (Detroit: Wayne State University Press, 1989).

50 Mordecai Kaplan cited in Joselit, *New York's Jewish Jews*, 14–15.

51 *New York City Market Analysis*; Welfare Council of New York City, Research Bureau, *Housing and Rentals, New York City*, 1930, Manhattan Health Districts 27–35; also cited in Berrol, "The Jewish West Side of New York City," 30.

52 Berrol, "The Jewish West Side of New York City," 30–32, 36; see also Berrol, "Manhattan's Jewish West Side," *New York Affairs* 10, no. 1 (Winter 1987): 13–32.

53 Berrol, "The Jewish West Side of New York City," 32–33. The experience of New York synagogues during the Depression is discussed in detail in chapter 7.

54 Personal interview, Louis Kfare, 26 August 1991, New Haven, Conn.

55 Kazin, *A Walker in the City*, 36–37.

56 Milt Kirschner, cited in Sorin, *The Nurturing Neighborhood*, 30.

57 Kazin, *A Walker in the City*, 84.

58 Gerry Lenowitz, cited in Sorin, *The Nurturing Neighborhood*, 14.

59 "Just Plain Jews," WPA, Jews of New York, Box 3632; also cited in Moore, *At Home in America*, 83.

60 Howe, *A Margin of Hope*, 28.

61 Personal interview, Jean Margolies, 27 August 1991, New Haven, Conn.

62 Howe, *A Margin of Hope*, 3–4.

63 Ginzberg, "Urban Jewish Immigrants," 161.

64 Personal interview, Tillie Spiegel, 22 August 1991, New Haven, Conn.

65 Personal interview, Rebecca Augenstein, 26 August 1991, New Haven, Conn.

66 Ginzberg, "Urban Jewish Immigrants," 161.

67 Arthur Granit, *I Am from Brownsville* (New York: Philosophical Library, 1985), 83.

68 Personal interview, Louis Kfare, 26 August 1991, New Haven, Conn.

69 Lizabeth Cohen offers a detailed discussion of the fate of independent store

owners and the expansion of chain stores during the Great Depression. Lizabeth Cohen, *Making a New Deal: Industrial Workers in Chicago, 1919–1939* (New York: Cambridge University Press, 1990), 234–38.

70 Roland S. Vaile, *Research Memorandum on Social Aspects of Consumption in the Depression,* Social Science Research Council Bulletin no. 35 (New York: Social Science Research Council, 1937), 37; for comments about the effects of chain stores on small Jewish merchants, see I. M. Rubinow, "The Economic and Industrial Status of American Jewry," *JSSQ* 9, no. 1 (December 1932): 33.

71 Cohen, *Making a New Deal,* 237–38.

72 Mordecai Kaplan recorded these observations during a 1934 visit to Washington, D.C. Mordecai M. Kaplan Diaries, 17 June 1934, 199, Rare Book Room, JTSA.

73 Vaile, *Research Memorandum on Social Aspects of Consumption in the Depression,* 37.

74 Personal interview, Rebecca Augenstein, 26 August 1991, New Haven, Conn.

75 Personal interview, Jean Margolies, 27 August 1991, New Haven, Conn.

76 Howe, *A Margin of Hope,* 26; Kazin, *A Walker in the City,* 169.


CHAPTER 5: FROM NEIGHBORHOOD TO NEW DEAL

Notes to epigraphs: Kazin, *A Walker in the City,* 144–45; anonymous interview subject, cited in Jonathan Rieder, *Canarsie: The Jews and Italians of Brooklyn Against Liberalism* (Cambridge, Mass.: Harvard University Press, 1985), 25.

1 Cohen, *When the Old Left Was Young*; Mark Naison, "From Eviction Resistance to Rent Control: Tenant Activism in the Great Depression," in Ronald Lawson, ed., *The Tenant Movement in New York City, 1904–1984* (New Brunswick, N.J.: Rutgers University Press, 1986), 94–133; Howe, *World of Our Fathers,* 339–41; Cohen, *Making a New Deal,* 308–9.

2 Feingold, *A Time for Searching,* 189–224; Howe, *World of Our Fathers,* 287–394; Moore, *At Home in America,* 201–30.

3 Kazin, *Starting Out in the Thirties,* 4.

4 Harvey Klehr, *The Heyday of American Communism: The Depression Decade* (New York: Basic Books, 1984), 163. The Jewish role in radical political parties has been discussed in other scholarly works and is not the primary concern of this study. See Arthur Liebman, *Jews and the Left*; Melech Epstein, *The Jew and Communism* (New York: Trade Union Sponsoring Committee, 1959); Gerald Sorin, *The Prophetic Minority: American Jewish Immigrant Radicals, 1880–1920* (Bloomington: Indiana University Press, 1985); Paul Buhle, "Jews and American Communism: The Cultural Question," *Radical History Review* 23 (Spring 1980): 9–33; Louis Ruchmanes, "Jewish Radicalism in the United States," in Rose, ed., *The Ghetto and Beyond,* 228–52.

5 Rent strikes and consumer boycotts were a regular feature of immigrant Jewish neighborhoods. Jenna Weissman Joselit, "The Landlord as Czar: Pre–World War I Tenant Activity," in Lawson, ed., *The Tenant Movement in New York City,*

39–50; Paula E. Hyman, "Immigrant Women and Consumer Protest: The New York City Kosher Meat Boycott of 1902," *AJH* 70, no. 1 (September 1980): 91–105; Dana Frank, "Housewives, Socialists, and the Politics of Food: The 1917 New York Cost-of-Living Protests," *Feminist Studies* 11 (Summer 1985): 255–86.

6 Howe, *A Margin of Hope*, 24.

7 Naison, "From Eviction Resistance to Rent Control," 105, 100–112. See also Mark Naison, *Communists in Harlem During the Depression* (Urbana: University of Illinois Press, 1983).

8 Howe, *A Margin of Hope*, 2.

9 Personal interview, Jean Margolies, 27 August 1991, New Haven, Conn.

10 Naison, "From Eviction Resistance to Rent Control," 100.

11 Kazin, *A Walker in The City*, 78.

12 Norman Goroff, as cited in Sorin, *The Nurturing Neighborhood*, 54.

13 Personal interview, Louis Kfare, 26 August 1991, New Haven, Conn.

14 Ibid.

15 Norman Goroff, as cited in Sorin, *The Nurturing Neighborhood*, 54.

16 Alter F. Landesman, "Guide for Club Leaders in the Hebrew Educational Society of Brooklyn," 1934, 34, NYPL.

17 For a provocative discussion of the ways that immigrant Jews translated religious teachings into radicalism, see Sorin, *The Prophetic Minority*.

18 Roy Rosenzweig, "Organizing the Unemployed: The Early Years of the Great Depression, 1929–1933," *Radical America* 10, no. 4 (July–August 1976): 40.

19 Kazin, *A Walker in the City*, 143.

20 Irving Howe and Lewis Coser, *The American Communist Party* (Boston: Beacon Press, 1957), 192. For a detailed discussion of the Communist movement in the 1930s, see Klehr, *The Heyday of American Communism*, 49–68.

21 Daniel J. Leab, "'United We Eat': The Creation and Organization of the Unemployed Councils in 1930," *Labor History* 8 (1967): 300–315. The national unemployed movement, led by the Communist Party, commenced in earnest with the demonstrations that took place throughout the country on 6 March 1930. In New York, the unemployed demonstration was particularly violent. See Rosenzweig, "Organizing the Unemployed," 41.

22 Naison, "From Eviction Resistance to Rent Control," 105.

23 *Bronx Home News*, 23 January 1932, 3.

24 *JDF*, 23 January 1932, 1; 29 January 1932, 1, 9; *NYT*, 23 January 1932, 4.

25 *The Coops*, 10–11.

26 Naison, "From Eviction Resistance to Rent Control," 102–5.

27 Kate Simon, *A Wider World: Portraits in an Adolescence* (New York: Harper and Row, 1986), 13.

28 *Bronx Home News*, 29 January 1932, 3; for a variety of accounts of the Allerton Avenue rent strike, see: *JDF*, 29 January 1932, 1, 9; 2 February 1932, 1, 10; *NYT*, 30 January 1932, 19; 9 February 1932, 18; *Bronx Home News*, 8 February 1932, 3; see also Naison, "From Eviction Resistance to Rent Control," 103–5.

29 *NYT*, 9 February 1932, 18. For an account of earlier Jewish women's political activism within the neighborhood, see Hyman, "Immigrant Women and Consumer Protest."

30 *JDF*, 21 January 1932, 3; the *Forward* article went so far as to suggest that men involved in the strike should learn from the example of commitment and militancy set by the women.

31 *NYT*, 27 February 1932, 17.

32 *JDF*, 21 January 1932, 3.

33 Simon, *A Wider World*, 13.

34 Interview, Anna Taffler, 8 January 1978, Oral History of the American Left Collection, Tamiment Library, New York University. Reports of arrests, carried in virtually every newspaper report, showed that women were regular, even predominant, participants in neighborhood protests. Newspaper reports also included the ages of those arrested, indicating that protesters ranged from adolescents to middle-aged men and women. Jewish women's informal networks had been crucial to neighborhood politics since the early twentieth century, see Hyman, "Immigrant Women and Consumer Protest."

35 Marshall Sklare, "Jews, Ethnics, and the American City," *Commentary* (April 1972): 72. Deborah Dash Moore presents a detailed discussion of the role of Jewish builders and property owners in creating Jewish neighborhoods in Brooklyn and the Bronx. Moore, *At Home in America*, 18–58.

36 Joseph A. Spencer, "New York City Tenant Associations and the Post–World War I Housing Crisis," in Lawson, ed., *The Tenant Movement in New York City*, 70–72.

37 *Bronx Home News*, 7 February 1932, 1.

38 *NYT*, 30 January 1932, 32.

39 *Real Estate News*, 13 (March 1932): 80.

40 See the *Forward*'s interview with Max Osinoff, *JDF*, 29 January 1932, 1, 9; *Bronx Home News*, 7 February 1932, 1; *NYT*, 10 February 1932, 15; *JDF*, 8 February 1932, 1; 9 February 1932, 1, 8; *The Day*, 9 February 1932, 1; Naison, "From Eviction Resistance to Rent Control," 104–5.

41 The New York Kehillah survived from 1908 until 1922 and, despite its many accomplishments, could not unite the diverse interests of New York Jews nor exert any coercive power within America's open and voluntary society. Kehillah leaders and its Bureau of Industry successfully intervened in several labor disputes, see Goren, *New York Jews and the Quest for Community*, 196–213.

    During previous New York rent strikes, the city government had made attempts at arbitration. In 1919, Captain Charles Goldsmith headed the Mayor's Committee arbitration panel, which successfully resolved some landlord-tenant disputes. Spencer, "New York City Tenant Organizations and the Post–World War I Housing Crisis," 61.

42 *Bronx Home News*, 3 February 1932, 2; 7 February 1932, 1; 14 February 1932, 1; *The Day*, 9 February 1932, 1.

43 Naison, "From Eviction Resistance to Rent Control," 100; Saul Parker, "Unemployed Organizations of the 1930s," Panel discussion at the 1983 New York State Labor History Association, 30 April 1983, Tape of the session housed at the Oral History of the American Left Collection.

44 Norman Goroff, cited in Sorin, *The Nurturing Neighborhood*, 196.

45 *NYT*, 27 February 1932, 17.

46 *The Day*, 27 February 1932, 1; *JDF*, 27 February 1932, 1; *NYT*, 27 February 1932, 17; 13 March 1932, 27; Naison, "From Eviction Resistance to Rent Control," 105–7.

47 *Real Estate News*, 13 (April 1932): 124; ibid., (March 1932): 90–91.

48 The best accounts of the Sholem Aleichem strike can be found in the local New York press. See *JDF*, 29 August 1932, 5; 1 September 1932, 3, 7; 11 September 1932, section 1: 8; 13 September 1932, 10; 15 September 1932, 10; 16 September 1932, 1, 6; 19 September 1932, 3; 20 September 1932, 1, 8; 22 September 1932, 12; 24 September 1932, 1, 16; 27 September 1932, 10; 29 September 1932, 3, 7.
  *NYT*, 1 September 1932, 23; 2 September 1932, 17; 13 September 1932, 8; 15 September 1932, 23; 16 September 1932, 23; 17 September 1932, 17; 18 September 1932, 18; 26 September 1932, 3. See also *Real Estate News* 14 (January 1933): 12–13.

49 For more on the earlier activities of tenant organizations, see Spencer, "New York City Tenant Organizations and the Post–World War I Housing Crisis," 77–82.

50 Howe, *World Of Our Fathers*, 298.

51 *NYT*, 1 September 1932, 23; 2 September 1932, 17.

52 The *Forward* reported that twenty-five trucks filled with tenants arrived outside the courthouse; the *Times* estimated that the crowd numbered only seventy-five. *JDF*, 13 September 1932, 10; *NYT*, 13 September 1932, 8; for an example of Matthew Levy's disputes with Bronx municipal judges, see *JDF*, 16 September 1932, 1, 6; *NYT*, 16 September 1932, 23.

53 *NYT*, 26 September 1932, 3; *JDF*, 27 September 1932, 10.

54 *NYT*, 15 January 1933, sections 9 and 10: 2; 3 February 1933, 34.

55 *Real Estate News* 14 (January 1933): 8.

56 Ibid., 14 (February 1933): 50–51; ibid., 13 (June 1932): 196–97; ibid., 14 (September 1933): 308–9.

57 *Bronx Real Estate and Building News* 7, no. 3 (March 1933): 17; ibid., 7, no. 4 (April 1933): 16, 18; *Real Estate News* 14 (August 1933): 263; Naison, "From Eviction Resistance to Rent Control," 109–10.

58 *Real Estate News*, 14 (January 1933): 8; Arthur Hilly to Edward Mulrooney, 21 March 1933, reprinted ibid., (March 1933): 83.

59 *NYT*, 31 March 1933, 36; 2 August 1933, 16; Naison, "From Eviction Resistance to Rent Control," 110–11. The tenant movement, however, regained its momentum by 1934, sparked largely by activism in Harlem and in the Knickerbocker Village housing project. Differing in style from earlier agitation, the new wave of tenant activism emphasized creating alliances with liberal leaders and focused on hous-

ing reform. The City-Wide Tenants League, which emerged from this new wave of tenant protest, became a highly visible and effective advocate of housing reform in New York City. See ibid., 112–30.

60 For a few examples of relief bureau protests, see *JDF*, 29 October 1931, 1; 24 January 1933, 1; *Jewish Morning Journal*, 29 October 1931, 7; *NYT*, 20 April 1932, 24; 6 January 1933, 13; 18 March 1933, 15; 6 May 1933, 6; 9 August 1933, 7; interview with Irving Seid, 4 July 1976; interview with Anna Taffler, Oral History of the American Left.

    Mark Naison argues that after rent strikes were declared illegal, unemployed councils "changed their target from the landlord to the home relief system." Naison, "From Eviction Resistance to Rent Control," 111.

61 *NYT*, 16 April 1932, 18; 17 March 1933, 22. The names, ages, and often addresses of those arrested were regularly reported in the press.

62 Brendan Sexton, "Unemployed Organizations of the 1930s," Panel discussion at the 1983 New York State Labor History Association.

63 Saul Parker, ibid.; interview with Anna Taffler, Oral History of the American Left; Rosenzweig, "Organizing the Unemployed," 44.

64 Interview with Mollie Goldstein, 17 November 1981, Oral History of the American Left; Naison, "From Eviction Resistance to Rent Control," 110–12.

65 Unemployed councils remained active within Jewish neighborhoods, policing relief bureaus and agitating for greater government intervention. In 1936, Communists and socialists merged their efforts on behalf of the unemployed under the banner of the Workers' Alliance. The Workers' Alliance was the Socialist Party's advocate for the unemployed and its tactics were generally less confrontational than those of the Communist-led unemployed councils. The 1936 merger saw Communists take a minority role in the new organization, which retained the Socialist title. Klehr, *The Heyday of American Communism*, 295–96. By 1936, Roosevelt and the Democrats had won the allegiance of most Jewish Socialists. See, for example, *JDF*, 16 November 1936, 3; Moore, *At Home in America*, 220–30; Rosenzweig, "Organizing the Unemployed," 52–53; Naison, "From Eviction Resistance to Rent Control," 111–12.

66 For a few of the many accounts of the meat boycott, see *JDF*, 15 May 1935, 4; 26 May 1935, section 1: 12; 27 May 1935, 1, 9; 28 May 1935, 1, 3, 6, 14; 29 May 1935, 1, 13; 1 June 1935, 16; *The Day*, 25 May 1935, 2; 29 May 1935, 1, 5; 31 May 1935, 1; 1 June 1935, 1, 6; *NYT*, 28 May 1935, 27; 31 May 1935, 17; 1 June 1935, 8; *Bronx Home News*, 23 May 1935, 1; 24 May 1935, 3; 25 May 1935, 3; 28 May 1935, 3; 29 May 1935, 3; 31 May 1935, 3.

67 For examples of previous kosher meat boycotts, see Hyman, "Immigrant Women and Consumer Protest"; Frank, "Housewives, Socialists, and the Politics of Food"; Joselit, "The Landlord as Czar," 41–42.

68 For a few examples of arrests, see *The Day*, 31 May 1935, 1; *JDF*, 6 June 1935, 14; *Bronx Home News*, 31 May 1935, 3; *NYT*, 31 May 1935, 17.

69 *JDF*, 28 May 1935, 14. Jewish women perceived the boycott as a distinctly female

political activity and even suggested that women were more capable and committed to the campaign than men were. In a letter to the *Forward,* one woman implored Jewish men to stand firm in boycotting meat, expressing absolute certainty that women would never waver in their resolve. See ibid.

70 *JDF* 28 May 1935, 1, 3, 6, 14; 27 May 1935, 1, 9; *The Day,* 29 May 1935, 1, 7; *NYT,* 27 May 1935, 3; 28 May 1935, 27; *Bronx Home News,* 25 May 1935, 3. For more on the activities, composition, and accomplishments of the City Action Committee Against the High Cost of Living and of women's activism in the 1930s, see Annelise Orleck, *Common Sense and a Little Fire: Women and Working-Class Politics in the United States, 1900–1965* (Chapel Hill: University of North Carolina Press, 1995), 234–40. Orleck suggests that women's activism in the 1930s reflected more sophisticated political strategy, in part, because the women involved had participated in the garment industry strikes and unionization movement during the first decades of the twentieth century as well as in earlier neighborhood protests. Ibid., 228–29.

71 *The Day,* 1 June 1935, 1; 5 October 1937, 6; 10 October 1937, 6; *JDF,* 29 September 1937, 1; 4 October 1937, 1, 8; *NYT,* 22 September 1937, 33; 29 September 1937, 18; 5 October 1937, 3; Orleck, *Common Sense and a Little Fire,* 234–40; for more on the history of the kosher meat industry and attempts to regulate its policies and production, see Harold P. Gastwirt, *Fraud, Corruption, and Holiness: The Controversy over the Supervision of the Jewish Dietary Practices in New York City, 1881–1940* (Port Washington: Kennikat Press, 1974); on the federal regulatory attempts of the 1930s, see ibid., 41.

72 Cohen, *Making a New Deal,* 289.

73 Moore, *At Home in America,* 201–30; Feingold, *A Time for Searching,* 189–224. This study does not seek to repeat the detailed discussion of the Jewish entrance into the Democratic Party which has already been carefully presented in other scholarly works.

74 Roy V. Peel, *The Political Clubs of New York City* (New York: G. P. Putnam's Sons, 1935), 179. Peel counted 31 explicitly Jewish political clubs in New York City: 25 Democratic, 3 Republican, 2 Communist, and 1 Socialist. Many other clubs not identified as "nationality" clubs also contained large ethnic blocs in their memberships. See ibid., table 6, 265; see also Moore, *At Home in America,* 208–12.

75 Resolution of American Jewish Committee, as cited in Moore, *At Home in America,* 213.

76 Lillian Gorenstein, unpublished memoirs.

77 See letter reprinted in the *YMHA Bulletin,* 20 June 1930, 2; Peel, *The Political Clubs of New York City,* 286–87; Moore, *At Home in America,* 205–11.

78 Peel, *The Political Clubs of New York City,* 210, 216; *NYT,* 8 April 1933, 16.

79 *The Day,* 18 January 1930, 8.

80 As cited by Dinnerstein, *Anti-Semitism in America,* 125.

81 *The Day,* 16 October 1932, 10.

82  For a more detailed discussion of Jewish support for both Al Smith and Herbert Lehman, see Howe, *World of Our Fathers*, 385–91; Moore, *At Home in America*, 211–22; Bayor, *Neighbors in Conflict*, 46–56; Feingold, *A Time for Searching*, 198–204.

83  Bayor, *Neighbors in Conflict*, table 14, 147.

84  Fuchs, *The Political Behavior of American Jews*, 177–91.

85  Howe, *World of Our Fathers*, 392. See also Moore, *At Home in America*, 220–23.

86  *JDF*, 16 November 1936, 3.

87  Berrol, "The Jewish West Side of New York City," 34.

88  Sorin, *The Nurturing Neighborhood*, 75.

CHAPTER 6: PRIVATE JEWISH PHILANTHROPY IN THE WELFARE STATE

Notes to epigraphs: Lee K. Frankel, "Philanthropy—New York," in Charles Bernheimer, ed., *The Russian Jew in the United States* (Philadelphia: John C. Winston Co., 1905), 62; "A Proverb in the Discard," *Inside Information from the Jewish Social Service Association* (hereafter cited as *Inside Information*) 1, no. 1 (May 1934): 2.

1  Samuel Osgood, *New York in the 19th Century: A Discourse Delivered Before the New York Historical Society, November 20, 1866*, as cited in Rischin, *The Promised City*, 4.

2  Frankel, "Philanthropy—New York," 63.

3  Cohen, *Making a New Deal*, 218–38.

4  Abba Hillel Silver, "The Relation of the Depression to the Cultural and Spiritual Values of American Jewry," *JSSQ* 9, no. 1 (December 1932): 45; *JDB*, 6 January 1930, 4; 12 March 1930, 3–4; Minutes of the Board of Trustees Meeting of the New York Federation for the Support of Jewish Philanthropies (hereafter cited as FJP Minutes), 8 December 1930, Box 1086, FJP; B. M. Selekman, "The Federation in the Changing American Scene," *AJYB* 36 (1935): 68–69.
    Government welfare in New York became law with the passage of the Wicks Bill in the Fall of 1931. Emergency Work and Relief Administration of the City of New York, *Public Need and Public Welfare: New York City's Fight Against Hunger and Unemployment* (December 1933), 11–17; William W. Bremer, *Depression Winters: New York Social Workers and the New Deal* (Philadelphia: Temple University Press, 1984), 38–62.

5  Unemployment and numbers of welfare recipients were never accurately calculated. During the worst years of the Depression, an estimated 25 percent of workers were unemployed. Surveys indicated that unskilled workers suffered the greatest losses, comprising a higher percentage of unemployed and relief recipients than any other group. In contrast, white-collar workers fared better during the Depression, accounting for less than 20 percent of the unemployed. John A. Garraty, *The Great Depression* (New York: Harcourt Brace Jovanovich, 1987), 100–102; Kessner, "Jobs, Ghettoes, and the Urban Economy," 233–37.
    In 1934, the Bureau of Jewish Social Research found that in seven large

American cities. Jews comprised between 2.3 to 10.8 percent of white families receiving public assistance. Bureau of Jewish Social Research and National Council of Jewish Federations and Welfare Funds, *Notes and News*, 20 December 1934, 14.

6 Talmud Shevu'ot 39a; for an overview of Jewish communal organization in Europe, see Jacob Katz, *Tradition and Crisis: Jewish Society at the End of the Middle Ages* (New York: Free Press of Glencoe, 1961), 157–67; see also Goren, *New York Jews and the Quest for Community*, 1–12.

7 Reply of the Amsterdam Chamber of the West India Company to Peter Stuyvesant, reprinted in Paul R. Mendes-Flohr and Jehuda Reinharz, eds., *The Jew in the Modern World: A Documentary History* (New York: Oxford University Press, 1980), 358.

8 On earlier Jewish opposition to public welfare efforts, see Naomi W. Cohen, *Encounter with Emancipation: The German Jews in the United States 1830–1914* (Philadelphia: Jewish Publication Society of America, 1984), 117–19.

9 Maurice J. Karpf, *Jewish Community Organization in the United States*, 103.

10 For an overview of the history of the New York Jewish Federation, see *The Golden Heritage: A History of the Federation of Jewish Philanthropies of New York from 1917 to 1967* (New York: Federation of Jewish Philanthropies of New York, 1969); on the development of the Federation movement in New York during the 1920s, see Moore, *At Home in America*, 149–74.

11 Robert H. Bremner, *American Philanthropy* (Chicago: University of Chicago Press, 1960); Andrew Carnegie, *The Gospel of Wealth* (New York: Century, 1900); Paul Block cited in Moore, *At Home in America*, 159; Jacob Schiff cited in Naomi W. Cohen, "Responsibilities of Jewish Kinship: Jewish Defense and Philanthropy," in Gladys Rosen, ed., *Jewish Life in America: Historical Perspectives* (New York: Institute of Human Relations Press of the American Jewish Committee, 1978), 126.

12 Bureau of Jewish Social Research, "Supplementary Data on the Effect of Current Economic Conditions upon Jewish Social Work, Covering the Period January 1, 1930 to May 20, 1931," Prepared for the Continuing Committee of Jewish Federation Executives, June 1931, 1; *AJYB* 34 (1933): 35; FJP Minutes, 15 October 1930, Box 1086.

For an overview of national Federation budgets in the Depression years, see "Memorandum Prepared by the Bureau of Jewish Social Research, Federation Resources and Budgets, 1930–1933," December 1934, Box 166; Bureau of Jewish Social Research, Federation Financing of Jewish Social Work in 1932; Federation Financing of Jewish Social Work in 1934, Box 190, CJFWF.

13 Paul Block cited in, "New York Federation Attains Half of Goal," *American Hebrew*, 20 November 1931, 28.

14 Solomon Lowenstein, "Jewish Social Work in the Economic Depression," *JSSQ* 8, no. 2 (December 1931): 90; FJP Minutes, 25 June 1931, 12 October 1931, Box 1086; 12 December 1932; 13 November 1933, Box 1087.

15 "A Proverb in the Discard," *Inside Information* 1, no. 1 (May 1934): 2.

16 "Social Welfare Agencies" (first draft), 13 February 1941, WPA, Jews of New York, Box 3630, Folder "Social Workers—Training and Organizations."

17 I. M. Rubinow, "'What Do We Owe to Peter Stuyvesant?'—Relation Between Public and Group Responsibility," *PNCJSS* (1930): 93–94.

18 Ibid., 103.

19 John Slawson, Response to Rubinow, "'What Do We Owe to Peter Stuyvesant?'" ibid., 107; Maurice Taylor, ibid., 104.

20 Edward L. Israel, "Report of Committee on Social Policy of the National Conference of Jewish Social Service: Discussion," *JSSQ* 10, no. 1 (September 1933): 112.

21 Maurice Taylor, "The Functional Agency and the Federation in Community Planning: Discussion," *JSSQ* 9, no. 1 (December 1932): 62.

22 Maurice J. Karpf, "Wanted—A Return to Basic Values," *JSSQ* 8, no. 2 (December 1931): 59, 60, 63.

23 Bremer, *Depression Winters*, 25–27; for Rubinow's own reflections on the article and its rejection, see I. M. Rubinow, "Public Welfare and Jewish Social Work," *PNCJSS* (1935): 94; Garraty, *The Great Depression*, 34; for an overview of social work during the Depression, see F. Stuart Chapin and Stuart A. Queen, *Research Memorandum on Social Work in the Depression*, Social Science Research Council Bulletin no. 39 (New York: Social Science Research Council, 1937).

24 Report of the Welfare Council Committee on Unemployment, cited in Bremer, *Depression Winters*, 35; for more on the Welfare Council and the implementation of public welfare, see ibid., 25–62; Emergency Work and Relief Administration of the City of New York, *Public Need and Public Welfare*. See also Harry Lurie, The Financing of the Social Work Program During the Depression, 11 March 1932, Box 166, CJFWF.

25 For examples of the "*Forward* Fund" campaign, see *JDF*, 15 November 1930, 12; 20 November 1930, 1; 21 November 1930, 1; an example of *The Day*'s employment advertisements can be found in *The Day*, 6 April 1930, 1.

26 *JDB*, 2 February 1931, 2.

27 Many breadlines, not advertised as specifically Jewish, were also organized by Jews. The women's committee of the Socialist Party (which included many Jewish women) operated a kosher kitchen in lower Manhattan. *NYT*, 3 May 1930, 11; Bremer, *Depression Winters*, 32–33.

28 Karl Hesley to Lillian Wald, 28 February 1931, Welfare Council Correspondence, 1931–32, Box 33, Lillian D. Wald Collection, Rare Book and Manuscript Library, Columbia University, New York.

29 *NYT*, 18 February 1931, 10.

30 Karl Hesley of the Henry Street Settlement explained to Lillian Wald that closing the kosher kitchen was a sensitive matter and was best handled by Jewish social workers themselves. In reference to one Lower East Side kosher breadline, he explained, "There is no need for it but all the people concerned feel that since it is a koscher [*sic*] kitchen, it is a problem for the Jewish community to handle and

steps are under way now, I understand . . . with Frances Taussig [executive director of the Jewish Social Service Association] to try to close it." Hesley to Wald, 28 February 1931. Two weeks later, Welfare Council minutes report that the kosher kitchen had been closed and another in the city was being persuaded to do the same. Summary of the minutes of the Executive Committee of the Welfare Council's Coordinating Committee on Unemployment, 10 March 1931, Welfare Council Minutes, 1931, Box 34, Wald Collection.

31 John Slawson, Response to Rubinow, "' What Do We Owe to Peter Stuyvesant?'" 107.

32 Karpf, "Wanted—A Return to Basic Values," 60.

33 *JDF*, 6 April 1933, 8; *Jewish Morning Journal*, 1 September 1931, 4.

34 For a few examples of the many reports about Jewish federations and Jewish agencies carried in the Yiddish press, see *JDF*, 14 December 1931, 5; 18 May 1935, 14; 20 July 1935, 14; 9 November 1936, 1, 8; 8 February 1937, 2, 8; 30 October 1937, 4–5; 17 December 1937, 10; *Jewish Morning Journal*, 5 October 1931, 1, 2, 6; *The Day*, 8 February 1937, 2, 4. Bureau of Jewish Social Research, *Jewish Social Work* (1933), 20; for more on negative attitudes toward social workers, see Daniel J. Walkowitz, "The Making of a Feminine Professional Identity: Social Workers in the 1920s," *American Historical Review* 95, no. 4 (October 1990): 1065–69.

35 Shelly Tenenbaum, *A Credit to Their Community: Jewish Loan Societies in the United States, 1880–1945* (Detroit: Wayne State University Press, 1993), 59–64.

36 In 1938, the WPA sponsored a study of New York's Jewish landsmanshaftn prepared by the Yiddish Writers' Group of the Federal Writers Project. The findings are published in a collection of essays, *Di Yidishe Landsmanshaftn fun Nyu York*. See Isaac E. Rontch, "The Present Status of the *Landsmanshaftn*," in *The Jewish Landsmanshaftn of New York* [Yiddish] (New York: I. L. Peretz Yiddish Writers' Union, 1938), 16. See also Hannah Kliger, ed., *Jewish Hometown Associations and Family Circles in New York: The WPA Yiddish Writers' Group Study* (Bloomington: Indiana University Press, 1992).

37 Michael R. Weisser, *A Brotherhood of Memory: Jewish Landsmanshaftn in the New World* (Ithaca, N.Y.: Cornell University Press, 1985), 222–25.

38 Rontch, "The Present Status of the *Landsmanshaftn*," 17.

39 *The Jewish Landsmanshaftn of New York*, tables 1–10, 26–32. These tables summarize the findings of the landsmanshaftn study.

40 Weisser, *A Brotherhood of Memory*, 224.

41 "The Relation of the Jewish Social Worker to the Jewish Community: Report of the New York Committee of the Case-Worker Section of the National Conference of Jewish Social Service," *JSSQ* 11, no. 1 (September 1934): 82.

42 Karpf, "Wanted—A Return to Basic Values," 61.

43 Moore, *At Home in America*, 160–62. For an interesting discussion outlining the need to coordinate Jewish philanthropic efforts and create a broadly based Jewish coalition, see Letter and enclosure from Joseph Willen to Harry Lurie, 21 October 1933, Box 166, CJFWF.

One interesting attempt to make the Jewish community aware of the Federation's contributions and activities was the creation of a magazine filled with photographs documenting the Federation's work. First published in 1935, *Federation Illustrated* was billed as a "Graphic Report from Federation for the Support of Jewish Philanthropies of New York City." As its first issue explained, the magazine offered "an account, nearer flesh and blood than dry figures, of what [the Federation's] generosity means in tens of thousands of human lives." *Federation Illustrated* 1, no. 1 (May 1935).

44 Despite the lack of grassroots support, the Federation considered itself the representative institution of New York Jewry. "Every man, woman, and child belongs to our Federation whether he contributes or not," declared former Federation president Sol Strook. "Membership in Federation is automatic for all Jews in the community." *JDB*, 11 December 1929, 2. Moore, *At Home in America*, 173; For a breakdown of the amounts contributed to the Federation, see *Federation for the Support of Jewish Philanthropies of New York City: List of Subscribers* (1929), 134, Box 1126, and *Brooklyn Federation of Jewish Charities* (1929), 13, Box 1371, FJP.

45 Council of Fraternal and Benevolent Organizations, *Closing the Ranks in Jewish Life: A New Instrument for Community Understanding* (New York: Council of Fraternal and Benevolent Organizations, 1936), located in Box 1126, FJP. The pamphlet was circulated in both Yiddish and English; Moore, *At Home in America*, 160–62.

46 *Closing the Ranks in Jewish Life*, 4; Moore, *At Home in America*, 160–61.

47 The Federation did not require societies to pay membership dues, hoping instead that voluntary contributions would follow once Jews became more closely associated with the Federation. "From the beginning the voluntary character of Council association was stressed. Membership in the Council would entail no dues, nor any financial obligation on the part of any affiliated society." A year after the council was founded, Federation leaders reported, "Through the first year, little stress was placed on fund-raising in the Council. This would come in due course, it was felt, once understanding has been achieved. Happily, the beginnings of such support had already come and much more speedily than was hoped. In 1935 more than 400 societies contributed financially to the support of Federation. More than 5,000 members of societies were enrolled as Federation members from the Council." *Closing the Ranks in Jewish Life*, 8, 12.

48 FJP Minutes, 3 December 1934, Box 1087.

49 Goldwasser cited in, *Closing the Ranks in Jewish Life*, 4, 7.

50 National Council of Jewish Federations and Welfare Funds, "The Federation as the Vital Community Agency: A Report of the Committee on Finances and Governmental Welfare Policies of the National Council of Jewish Federations and Welfare Funds," 23 (1934) NYPL.

51 Samuel A. Goldsmith, "The Functional Agency and the Federation in Community Planning," *JSSQ* 9, no. 1 (December 1932): 53.

52  H. L. Lurie, "The Place of the Jewish Family Agency in an Economic Rehabilitation Program: Discussion," *JSSQ* 11, no. 1 (September 1934): 98.

53  Samuel C. Kohs, "Jewish Content in Jewish Social Work," *PNCJSS* (1936): 100.

54  George W. Rabinoff, "Where Is Jewish Social Work Going?," *JSSQ* 9, no. 2 (March 1933): 253.

55  William Hodson, executive director of the Welfare Council, to members of the executive committee of the Welfare Council Coordinating Committee on Unemployment, 13 November 1930, Welfare Council Correspondence, 1930, Box 33, Wald Collection; Bremer, *Depression Winters*, 35–37.

56  FJP Minutes, 12 December 1932; 13 November 1933, Box 1087; *JDB*, 1 March 1931, 2; 29 March 1931, 2; FJP Minutes, 13 February 1933, Box 1087.

57  FJP Minutes, 11 February 1935; 11 March 1935, Box 1087.

58  Ben Zion Bokser, "The Social Philosophy of Judaism," *PNCJSW* (1938): 30–31.

59  Israel Levinthal, "The Real Significance of the N.R.A.," *Brooklyn Jewish Center Review* 17, no. 34 (May 1933): 10.

60  Stephen Isaacs cited in Moore, *At Home in America*, 227.

61  Louis E. Levinthal, "Jewish Social Work and Jewish Living," *PNCJSS* (1936): 17.

62  Jennie Rovner, "Changes and Trends in Private Family Agencies," *JSSQ* 10, no. 1 (September 1933): 46.

63  Bureau of Jewish Social Research, *Jewish Social Work* (1933), 1–4; Jewish Statistical Bureau, *Digest of Events of Jewish Interest*, 9 April 1934, 49; National Council of Jewish Federations and Welfare Funds and Bureau of Jewish Social Research, "The Jewish Family Society in Its Relation to the Public Agency: A Study of the Current Relationship in Forty-Three Cities" (1935), 5; Welfare Council of New York City, Research Bureau, Statistics of Family Case Work in New York City—Review of Year October 1932–September 1933, 1–7, Rockefeller Family Archives, Record Group 2, Series "Economic Interests", Box 22, Folder 204, Rockefeller Archive Center, Tarrytown, New York.

64  Bureau of Jewish Social Research, *Notes and News*, 20 December 1934, 14. This statistic reflects a study conducted in seven major American cities, not including New York.

65  Report of Mayor LaGuardia's Committee on Unemployment Relief (1935), 31, NYPL.

66  Ibid., 29; Bremer, *Depression Winters*, 117–25; Solomon Lowenstein cited ibid., 119–20.

67  National Council of Jewish Federations and Welfare Funds and Bureau of Jewish Social Research, "The Jewish Family Society in Its Relation to the Public Agency," 3.

68  Bremer, *Depression Winters*, 123; *Inside Information* 1, no. 2 (June 1934): 1; 1, no. 7 (March–April 1935): 3.

69  Bureau of Jewish Social Research, *Jewish Social Work* (1933), 21, 18; Jewish Social Service Association, Annual Report, 1935, 9, 11, 22–24; Emergency Work and Relief Administration of the City of New York, *Public Need and Public Welfare*, 27; *JDF*, 14 December 1931, 5.

70  John F. Bauman and Thomas H. Coode, *In the Eye of the Great Depression: New Deal Reporters and the Agony of the American People* (DeKalb: Northern Illinois University Press, 1988), 92.

71  *E.R.B. [Emergency Relief Bureau] News*, 16 December 1935, 2; 2 December 1935, 3; see also Bureau of Jewish Social Research, *Jewish Social Work* (1933), 20.

72  *NYT*, 16 April 1932, 18. Interview with Mollie Goldstein, 17 November 1981, Oral History of the American Left Collection. Demonstrations outside New York's Home Relief Bureaus were a regular occurrence in the early 1930s. A few of the many examples are: *JDF*, 29 October 1931, 1; 24 January 1933, 1; *Jewish Morning Journal*, 29 October 1931, 7; *NYT*, 20 April 1932, 24; 17 March 1933, 22; Bremer, *Depression Winters*, 56–62.

73  Harry Lurie cited in, Bremer, *Depression Winters*, 57, 10.

74  Brandes, "From Sweatshop to Stability," 76–77; Jewish socialist support for Roosevelt grew steadily during the 1930s. By his second term, Roosevelt had won the approval of most Jewish socialists. See, for example, *JDF*, 16 November 1936, 3; Moore, *At Home in America*, 220–30.

75  "A Call to the President and Congress of the United States from the National Conference of Jewish Social Service," *JSSQ* 8, no. 1 (September 1931): 2.

76  Nathan Glazer, *The Social Basis of American Communism* (New York: Harcourt, Brace, and World, 1961), 130–68; Roy Lubove, *The Professional Altruist: The Emergence of Social Work as a Career, 1880–1930* (Cambridge, Mass.: Harvard University Press, 1965).

Jewish social workers became labor activists during the Depression, protesting against their Federation employers. In February 1934, Federation workers held a work stoppage to protest wage cuts, a Depression-era policy they had been criticizing for years. *JDF*, 7 February 1934, 12; *NYT*, 6 February 1934, 2; 8 February 1934, 8; for more on the activism of Jewish social workers, see Walkowitz, "The Making of a Feminine Professional Identity," 1051–75.

77  The Communist movement had an impact, particularly on the younger generation of Jewish social workers. A group of students published a pamphlet called "The Radical Therapist." Depression-era Jewish communal workers regularly discussed the need to reconcile "social work with the radical trends in present day society." Mordecai Kaplan reported that Jewish leaders responded to student movements by "giving a more intensively and affirmatively Jewish direction to the work at the school." Mordecai M. Kaplan Diaries, 2 April 1935, 1; 21 April 1935, 9.

78  Bureau of Jewish Social Research, *Notes and News*, 24 May 1934, 17.

79  Harriet Mowner, "The Future of the Family Agency," *JSSQ* 10, no. 1 (September 1933): 52; *Inside Information* 1, no. 1 (May 1934): 2; Rubinow, "Public Welfare and Jewish Social Work," 95; Bureau of Jewish Social Research, *Notes and News*, 24 May 1934, 17.

80  National Council of Jewish Federations and Welfare Funds, "The Federation as the Vital Community Agency," 4.

81  Morris Lewis, "New Communal Problems That Must Be Faced," *American*

*Hebrew* 22 January 1932, 284; National Council of Jewish Federations and Welfare Funds, "The Federation as the Vital Community Agency," 4.

82 In the late thirties, the Federation and the Joint Distribution Committee debated which organization should take responsibility for providing relief for European refugees. While Federation board members were divided on the issue, Solomon Lowenstein, the executive director, stated that "he could not see how Federation could take the position of expending its funds to aid non-citizens when it had to admit in the same breath that it had not the means to aid the Jewish poor of New York who were citizens and have been here for a long time." See Lowenstein's remarks and the ensuing discussion in FJP Minutes, 11 October 1936, Box 1088.

Lowenstein underlined his unwavering commitment to helping Jewish refugees, but believed that the Federation was not the organization to assume that responsibility. See also Solomon Lowenstein, "Trends in Jewish Social Work," *PNCJSS* (1936): 19. By 1938, however, the Jewish Social Service Association had begun serving the relief needs of refugees. Jewish Social Service Association, Annual Report, 1938, 4.

83 Jewish Social Service Association, Annual Report, 1935, 9, 11.

84 National Council of Jewish Federations and Welfare Funds, "The Federation as the Vital Community Agency," 23.

85 Bureau of Jewish Social Research, *Jewish Social Work* (1933), 20.

86 S. C. Kohs, "The Relation of Jewish Social Work to the Jewish Community," *JSSQ* 10, no. 4 (June 1934): 240.

87 Jewish Social Service Association, Annual Report, 1935, 10; see also Robert Morris and Michael Freund, eds., *Trends and Issues in Jewish Social Welfare in the United States, 1899–1952* (Philadelphia: Jewish Publication Society of America, 1966), 282; Walter A. Miller, Oral history, 19, Oral History Project, FJP.

88 Bureau of Jewish Social Research, *Jewish Social Work* (1933), 29.

89 Harry Greenstein, "The Relation of Public and Private Social Work," *JSSQ* 14, no. 3 (March 1938): 320–25; *The United Jewish Aid Societies of Brooklyn: Its Story of Service to the Largest Jewish Community in the World*, n.d., 2–6, United Jewish Aid Society of Brooklyn, Uncatalogued Collection, AJHS; *Inside Information* 1, no. 5 (January 1935): 2–3; Jewish Social Service Association, Annual Report, 1935, 22–24.

90 S. C. Kohs, "Current Fallacies Regarding Jewish Social Work: Is It Drifting Toward Extinction?" *JSSQ* 9, no. 3 (June 1933): 302–3.

91 Bureau of Jewish Social Research, *Jewish Social Work* (1933), 29. The establishment and activities of the Federation Employment Service are discussed at greater length in chapter 1.

92 Rubinow, "The Economic and Industrial Status of American Jewry," 36.

93 Rabbi Eugene Kohn, "A Cultural Program for the Jewish Community," *JSSQ* 12, no. 1 (September 1935): 75.

94 Federation Employment Service, "Towards Occupational Adjustment—Summary of Activities," Federation Employment Service, 1939, 12, FEGS.

95  Kohn, "A Cultural Program for the Jewish Community," 75.

96  Rubinow, "Public Welfare and Jewish Social Work," 104.

97  George W. Rabinoff, "Where Is Jewish Social Work Going," *jssq* 9, no. 2 (March 1933): 254, 255.

98  Kohs, "Jewish Content in Jewish Social Work," 108.

99  Kohs, "The Relation of Jewish Social Work to the Jewish Community," 240.

100  Mordecai M. Kaplan Diaries, 22 January 1939, 241.

101  fjp Minutes, 26 December 1932, Box 1087.

102  Ludwig Vogelstein to Solomon Lowenstein, 25 May 1932, 1, Box 166, cjfwf.

103  Memorandum on Problems of the 1933 Budget, 2, Box 166, cjfwf.

104  Morris D. Waldman, "The International Scene in Jewish Life," *jssq* 9, no. 1 (December 1932): 24.

105  Albert P. Schoolman, "Jewish Education and the American Jewish Community," *jssq* 9, no. 1 (December 1932): 40.

106  Vogelstein to Lowenstein, 25 May 1932, 1.

107  Only the Downtown Machzikei Talmud Torah was completely eliminated from the Federation's budget because board members believed that its students could be accommodated in other neighborhood schools. S. J. Cutler to Dr. Friedman, 8 June 1932, Re: 1933 Budgetary Program, 2, Box 166, cjfwf.

108  Memorandum Prepared by the Bureau of Jewish Social Research, Federation Resources and Budgets, 1930–1933, December 1934, 3, Box 166, cjfwf.

109  Mordecai M. Kaplan Diaries, 22 February 1933, 61.

110  Mordecai M. Kaplan, *Judaism as a Civilization: Toward a Reconstruction of American-Jewish Life* (Philadelphia: Jewish Publication Society of America and Reconstructionist Press, 1981; reprint, New York: Macmillian, 1934), 298.

111  Mordecai M. Kaplan Diaries, 14 August 1932, 300. Kaplan often expressed great concern that "Jewish life is at the mercy of the rich Jews." He noted that with the exception of Paul Warburg, Ludwig Vogelstein, Solomon Lowenstein, and a few other Federation board members, "no one in the Federation . . . was friendly disposed to Jewish educational work as a communal responsibility." See ibid., 8 October 1932, 28; 22 February 1933, 61; 7 February 1933, 57; 7 March 1933, 65.

112  For one example of a Jewish leader insisting that a distinct Jewish culture was incompatible with American democracy, see nyt, 31 January 1937, 34.

113  Mordecai Kaplan recorded these remarks made to him by Willen. Mordecai M. Kaplan Diaries, 12 November 1934, 253.

114  For Federation financing of Jewish community centers, see Jewish Welfare Board, Preliminary Report of Recommendations for Economies in Community Centers Affiliated with the Federation, 17 August 1932, Jewish Welfare Board Papers, ajhs.

115  Fifteen Jewish centers in Manhattan, Brooklyn, and the Bronx reported an increase in monthly attendance from 260,000 in 1929 to 492,953 in 1937. nyt, 28 November 1937, 15. On the ability of centers to withstand the economic

crisis, see *American Hebrew,* 28 April 1933, 426; for an example of membership and fund-raising appeals initiated by Jewish centers see: Jewish Welfare Board, Direct Mail Appeals for Membership Payments and Contributions, 1935, esp. 43–45, NYPL.

116 YMHA *Bulletin,* 9 January 1931, 2.

117 NYT, 3 January 1937, section 6: 7; on the number of unemployed and relief recipients attending Jewish centers, see ibid., 28 November 1937, 15; YMHA Bulletin, 24 April 1931, 4.

118 Bureau of Jewish Social Research, *Notes and News,* 11 November 1932, 15.

119 Harry Glucksman, cited in NYT, 24 April 1933, 4.

120 Jacob Billikopf, "Response to Rubinow, 'What Do We Owe to Peter Stuyvesant?'" 116–17. Providing perhaps the era's most crucial text advocating an increased emphasis on Jewish culture in America was Mordecai Kaplan, *Judaism as a Civilization.*

121 National Council of Jewish Federations and Welfare Funds, "The Federation as the Vital Community Agency," 29.

122 Viola Paradise, "Not by Bread Alone," a radio dramalogue presented by the Jewish Social Service Association of New York City on 6 November 1934 to mark its sixtieth anniversary and performed by the "March of Time" cast over the facilities of the Columbia Broadcasting Company (New York: Social Work Publicity Council, 1934), NYPL.

123 Kohs, "Jewish Content in Jewish Social Work," 101.

124 Joseph Proskauer, cited in YMHA *Bulletin,* 22 November 1929, 6.


CHAPTER 7: THE SPIRITUAL DEPRESSION

Notes to epigraphs: President's message, CCAR *Yearbook* 41 (1931): 193; Jacob Nathan, "An Ambulance or an Undertaker," *American Hebrew and Jewish Tribune,* 19 February 1932, 368.

1 Both Jewish and Christian leaders used the term *religious depression* during the 1930s. For example, in 1931, rabbis at the Rabbi Isaac Elchanan Theological Seminary and Yeshiva College resolved to fight the "'spiritual depression' in American religious life." NYT, 11 August 1931, 44. At the height of the Depression, a Dartmouth professor warned that "today we are passing through a period of religious depression not less severe than the concomitant moral and economic depression." William Kelley Wright, cited in Robert T. Handy, "The American Religious Depression, 1925–1935," *Church History* 29, no. 1 (March 1960): 3; see also Handy's complete discussion of the Depression's effects on American religious life, ibid., 3–16.

2 Significant differences existed among Reform, Conservative, and Orthodox synagogues during the Depression years. This chapter does not offer a comparative analysis of the three movements, but instead focuses on general trends in American synagogues.

250 Notes to Pages 168-70

3 The number of Jewish congregations in America grew from 1,619 in 1916 to 3,118 in 1926 to 3,728 in 1936. *Census of Religious Bodies, 1936-Jewish Congregations: Statistics, History, Doctrine and Organization* (Washington: United States Government Printing Office, 1940), table 2, 2. In 1906, New York State reported having 378 established synagogues; by 1936, the number had increased to 1,560. Ibid., table 4, 4.

4 Moore, *At Home in America*, 135. Moore provides a detailed discussion of the emergence of the synagogue center, 123–47.

5 Isidor Fine, President's message, Annual meeting, 19 January 1933, *Annual Report*, Brooklyn Jewish Center, 7, NYPL.

6 Minutes of Congregation Kehilath Jeshurun, 10 February 1931, Congregation Kehilath Jeshurun, New York; *Census of Religious Bodies, 1936-Jewish Congregations: Statistics, History, Doctrine and Organization*, 5.

Churches, which had also participated in a building boom during the 1920s, experienced similar indebtedness in the Depression years. For a discussion of the decline in contributions and an increase in congregational debts in Christian churches of various denominations, see Samuel C. Kincheloe, *Research Memorandum on Religion in the Depression*, Social Science Research Council Bulletin no. 33 (New York: Social Science Research Council, 1937), 17–30.

7 Silver, "The Relation of the Depression to the Cultural and Spiritual Values of American Jewry," 45.

8 Jack Wertheimer, "The Conservative Synagogue," in Jack Wertheimer, ed., *The American Synagogue: A Sanctuary Transformed* (New York: Cambridge University Press, 1987), 122–23.

9 Jacob D. Schwarz, *Financial Security for the Synagogue* (Cincinnati: Union of American Hebrew Congregations, 1935).

10 *The Guardian*, Bulletin of the United Synagogue of America, 1, no. 3 (February 1938), 3.

11 Mordecai M. Kaplan Diaries, 10 October 1930, 66; 5 December 1929, 219–20.

12 Silver, "The Relation of the Depression to the Cultural and Spiritual Values of American Jewry," 45.

13 Minutes of Baith Israel-Anshei Emeth-Kane Street Synagogue (hereafter, Kane Street Synagogue), 4 May 1932, Joseph and Miriam Ratner Center for the Study of Conservative Judaism, JTSA, (hereafter, Ratner Center).

14 Minutes of Congregation B'nai Jeshurun, 7 June 1933, Ratner Center; minutes of the Institutional Synagogue, 5 March 1931, Record Group 2, Yeshiva University Archives, New York.

15 Elias Cohen to Board of Directors, 15 November 1932, 5, Anshe Chesed collection, uncatalogued, Ratner Center.

16 Minutes of Congregation B'nai Jeshurun, 10 November 1931; A. H. Zinke to Members of the Board, 9 February 1931, Anshe Chesed collection; minutes of Congregation B'nai Jeshurun, 9 November 1932; minutes of the Kane Street Synagogue, 16 October 1933; all in Ratner Center.

17  Fine, President's message, Annual meeting, 1930, Box 3, BJC collection, Ratner Center; Fine, President's message, Annual meeting, 19 January 1933, *Annual Report,* 7–8.

18  Mordecai M. Kaplan Diaries, 22 April 1931, 89; 21 August 1931, 159.

19  Minutes of Congregation Kehilath Jeshurun, 1 June 1932.

20  Minutes of the Kane Street Synagogue, 4 May 1932, 3 April 1933.

21  A. H. Zinke to Members of the Board, 9 February 1931, Anshe Chesed collection.

22  For two of the many examples of the reduction of rabbinic salaries, see minutes of Congregation Kehilath Jeshurun, 9 November 1931, 17 April 1934; minutes of Congregation B'nai Jeshurun, 9 November 1932.

23  Mordecai M. Kaplan Diaries, 2 July 1931, 144; 23 April 1931, 91, 4 October 1932, 21.

24  A. H. Zinke to Members of the Board of Trustees, 9 February 1931, Anshe Chesed collection; CCAR *Yearbook* 41 (1931): 188–89; ibid., 42 (1932): 155; see also Michael A. Meyer, *Response to Modernity: A History of the Reform Movement in Judaism* (New York: Oxford University Press, 1988), 307–8.

25  Meyer, *Response to Modernity,* 307.

26  Joseph M. Schwartz, President's message, Annual meeting, 18 January 1934, 4, Box 2, BJC collection; on the sharp decline in synagogue memberships, see also Wertheimer, "The Conservative Synagogue," 122–23.

27  Meyer, *Response to Modernity,* 307; minutes of Congregation Kehilath Jeshurun, 9 November 1931, 23 March 1932; minutes of the Kane Street Synagogue, 27 February 1933, 10 July 1933.

28  Schwarz, *Financial Security for the Synagogue,* 12.

29  Fine, President's message, Annual meeting, 19 January 1933, *Annual Report,* 7; ibid., 21 January 1932.

30  Minutes of the Kane Street Synagogue, 4 May 1931.

31  Fine, President's message, Annual meeting, 19 January 1933, *Annual Report,* 7.

32  President's message, April 1931 (inserted within minute book); president's message, 17 April 1934, minutes of Congregation Kehilath Jeshurun.

33  Israel Goldstein to Isaac Landman, 1 September 1931, Congregation B'nai Jeshurun collection, Box 12, Folder "Correspondence-Miscellaneous, letters A-G, 1931–1946," Ratner Center.

34  Fine, President's message, Annual meeting, 19 January 1933, *Annual Report,* 7; Fine, President's message, Annual meeting, 1930, 2, Box 3, BJC collection.

35  Mordecai M. Kaplan Diaries, 12 September 1934, 236.

36  *Synagogue Service Bulletin* 1, no. 2 (October 1933), 9.

37  Personal interview, Sydney Evans, 18 August 1991, New Haven, Conn.

38  "Eliachar," (pseudonym of interview subject), quoted in Joseph A. D. Sutton, *Magic Carpet: Aleppo-in-Flatbush, The Story of a Unique Ethnic Jewish Community* (New York: Thayer-Jacoby, 1979), 124.

39  Edwin Shapiro, Oral history, 15, WWOHL.

40  Howe, *A Margin of Hope,* 3.

41  Kaplan, *Judaism as a Civilization*, 293.

42  Personal interview, Stanley Katz, 23 August 1991, New Haven, Conn.

43  Nathan, "An Ambulance or an Undertaker," 368.

44  *The Institutional* 21, no. 2 (3 September 1937), 1, located in the Institutional Synagogue collection, Yeshiva University Archives.

45  Kaplan, *Judaism as a Civilization*, 292.

46  W. A. C. to editor of *American Hebrew*, 26 August 1931, copy of the letter in Congregation B'nai Jeshurun collection, Box 12, Folder "Correspondence-Miscellaneous, letters A-G, 1931–1946," Ratner Center.

47  Israel Goldstein to Isaac Landman, 1 September 1931, Congregation B'nai Jeshurun collection, Box 12, Folder "Correspondence-Miscellaneous, letters A-G, 1931–1946," Ratner Center; Goldstein also suggested that the organizations of Reform, Conservative, and Orthodox synagogues should make adequate provisions for genuinely impoverished Jews who wanted to attend High Holiday services.

48  Hyman Reit, chairman of the United Synagogue's mushroom synagogue committee, cited in Moore, *At Home in America*, 140–41.

49  *Synagogue Service Bulletin* 2, no. 1 (August 1934): 18.

50  Minutes of the Kane Street Synagogue, 24 October 1932; 8 October 1934, 10 December 1934.

51  Fine, President's message, Annual meeting, 19 January 1933, *Annual Report*, 8.

52  Mrs. Phillip Brenner, Sisterhood report, 19 January 1933, BJC collection, Box 3.

53  Twenty-Fourth Annual Report, National Federation of Temple Sisterhoods, *Proceedings* 3 (1931–1939): 102.

54  Rabbi Jacob D. Schwarz, "The Temple Sisterhood and the Religious School," *Synagogue Service Bulletin* 1, no. 3 (November 1933): 2; Minutes of the Kane Street Synagogue, 10 December 1934.

55  Twenty-Second Annual Report, National Federation of Temple Sisterhoods, *Proceedings* 3 (1931–1939): 78.

56  Brenner, Sisterhood report, 19 January 1933.

57  Park Avenue Sisterhood skit cited in, Jenna Weissman Joselit, "The Special Sphere of the Middle-Class American Jewish Woman: The Synagogue Sisterhood, 1880–1940," in Wertheimer, ed., *The American Synagogue*, 219. In this article, Joselit discusses the evolution of synagogue sisterhoods.

58  *NYT*, 17 September 1931, 25.

59  *American Hebrew and Jewish Tribune*, 22 February 1934, 294; *The Orthodox Union* 1, no. 3 (October 1933): 1, 3.

60  *Synagogue Service Bulletin* 2, no. 8 (March 1935): 13–16.

61  For an example of one of Israel Levinthal's radio addresses, see "The Jew Looks at To-Morrow," broadcast on station WHN, 17 January 1937, Rabbi Israel Levinthal, Sermons and Addresses, Box 6, Ratner Center (hereafter, Levinthal collection); *NYT*, 26 October 1931, 3.

62  For an example of holiday broadcasts, see *JDB*, 20 April 1932; for an overview of Jewish programming on New York radio, see Beatrice Goldsmith, "Jewish Radio

Stations," n.d., WPA, Jews of New York, Box 3630, Folder "Jews of New York-Radio Management."

63 Herbert Goldstein, quoted in *The Orthodox Union* 1, no. 3 (October 1933): 1; ibid., 2, no. 11 (August 1935): 1.

64 Louis J. Moss to United Synagogue congregations, 3 October 1933, 1, in Congregation B'nai Jeshurun collection, Box 13, Folder "Correspondence-Miscellaneous, Letters T-Z, 1931–1946," Ratner Center

65 *The Institutional* 17, no. 4 (29 September 1933): 1.

66 *The Orthodox Union* 1, no. 2 (September 1933): 2.

67 NYT, 16 December 1933, 3.

68 Israel Levinthal, "A New Deal for Judaism," *Brooklyn Jewish Center Review* (September 1933): 1, 3; also cited in Deborah Dash Moore, "A Synagogue Center Grows in Brooklyn," in Wertheimer, ed., *The American Synagogue*, 310.

69 Louis J. Moss to United Synagogue congregations, 3 October 1933, 1; Report of the National Recovery Assembly of the United Synagogue of America, 12 November 1933, 1–3, in Congregation B'nai Jeshurun collection, Box 13, Folder "Correspondence-Miscellaneous, Letters T-Z, 1931–1946," Ratner Center.

70 Joseph L. Fink, "The Revolt Against the Synagogue," CCAR *Yearbook* 48 (1938): 205.

71 Report of the National Recovery Assembly of the United Synagogue of America, 2–3.

72 Louis Cohen, "Fostering Democracy in the Synagogue," *Synagogue Service Bulletin* 5, no. 1 (August 1937): 10.

73 Kaplan, *Judaism as a Civilization*, 427.

74 Report of the National Recovery Assembly of the United Synagogue of America, 3, 1.

75 CCAR *Yearbook* 41 (1931): 86–91; see also Meyer, *Response to Modernity*, 309–12.

76 Minutes of Congregation B'nai Jeshurun, 2 December 1930; *The Synagogue Light* (published by the Wall Street Synagogue) 1, no. 2 (October 1933): 17, NYPL; Meyer, *Response to Modernity*, 312.

77 Israel Levinthal, "The Heart of America on Trial," 5 November 1931, Levinthal collection, Box 5; Moore, "A Synagogue Center Grows in Brooklyn," 321.

78 *The Orthodox Union* 3, no. 6 (February 1936): 3.

79 Report of Social Committee, Annual meeting, 18 January 1934, Box 2, BJC collection; see also Joseph M. Schwarz, President's message, Annual meeting, 17 January 1935, 7, Box 2, BJC collection.

80 Rabbi Israel Levinthal, "Israel and the Red Sea—An Old Story and A Modern Application," 6 February 1931, Levinthal collection, Box 5.

81 *The Institutional* 21, no. 7 (8 October 1937): 1.

82 Kincheloe, *Research Memorandum on Religion in the Depression*, 1, 94–95.

83 President's message, CCAR *Yearbook* 42 (1932): 155.

84 Mordecai M. Kaplan Diaries, 4 October 1932, 21.

85 Martin E. Marty, *Modern American Religion*, vol. 2: *The Noise of Conflict, 1919–1941* (Chicago: University of Chicago Press, 1991), 258–302.

86 *The Christian Century* 52 (18 September 1935): 1168–70; Kincheloe, *Research Memorandum on Religion in the Depression*, 95.

87 NYT, 11 August 1931, 44.

88 Joseph L. Fink, "The Revolt Against the Synagogue," CCAR *Yearbook* 48 (1938): 204.

89 Uriah Zevi Engelman, "The Jewish Synagogue in the United States," *American Journal of Sociology* 41 (1935/36): 44.

90 McGill, "Some Characteristics of Jewish Youth in New York City," 253. Precise figures for synagogue affiliation and attendance during this period were never tabulated, but one 1928 national study indicated that fewer than 20 percent of Jews regularly attended Sabbath services. For a discussion of this study and other trends in synagogue attendance and affiliation, see Wertheimer, "The Conservative Synagogue," 120; Meyer, *Response to Modernity*, 322; Charles S. Liebman, *The Ambivalent American Jew: Politics, Religion, and Family in American Religious Life* (Philadelphia: Jewish Publication Society of America, 1976), 72–73; Nathan Glazer, *American Judaism*, 2d ed. (Chicago: University of Chicago Press, 1972), 85, 105.

91 Engelman, "The Jewish Synagogue in the United States," 50–51.

92 For a detailed evaluation of Kaplan and his work, see Mel Scult, *Judaism Faces the Twentieth Century: A Biography of Mordecai M. Kaplan* (Detroit: Wayne State University Press, 1993); for a discussion of the various sociological and philosophical influences on Mordecai Kaplan's thought, see also Ira Eisenstein, "Mordecai M. Kaplan and His Teachers," in Ira Eisenstein and Eugene Kohn, eds., *Mordecai M. Kaplan: An Evaluation* (New York: Jewish Reconstructionist Foundation, 1952), 15–25; Mel Scult, "The Sociologist as Theologian: The Fundamental Assumptions of Mordecai Kaplan's Thought," *Judaism* 25 (Summer 1976): 345–52.

93 Kaplan, *Judaism as a Civilization*, 426, 425; for more on Kaplan's critique of the American synagogue, see his "The Organization of American Jewry," PNCJSS (1935): 59–61.

94 As Charles Liebman observed, "Kaplan was not saying anything very new. He articulated in a provocative and intellectual manner the folk religion of American Jews." Liebman, *The Ambivalent American Jew*, 74.

95 Some Jewish leaders advocated other ways to expand the appeal of synagogues. For example, Judge Horace Stern, a prominent Jewish layman, proposed restoring the primacy of the synagogue by allocating all Jewish communal activities a place in synagogue programming. The 1931 "Stern Plan" recommended that each congregant join a synagogue committee devoted to Jewish philanthropy, Zionism, education, federations, or any other communal cause. According to Stern, national Jewish organizations would then rely on grassroots support emanating from the synagogue while, at the same time, Jews interested in extra-religious affairs would be drawn to congregational life. Horace Stern, "The Synagogue and Jewish Communal Activities," AJYB 35 (1934): 157–70; Meyer, *Response to Modernity*, 305; Kaplan, *Judaism as a Civilization*, 296–97.

96 Levinthal quoted in Marshall Sklare, *Conservative Judaism: An American Religious Movement* (Glencoe, Ill.: Free Press, 1955; reprint, Lanham, Md.: University Press of America, 1985), 136.

97 Silver, "The Relation of the Depression to the Cultural and Spiritual Values of American Jewry," 46–47.

98 Report of D. B. Kaminsky, chairman of the Physical Training Committee, Annual meeting, 16 January 1934, 17 January 1935, Box 2, BJC collection.

99 Herbert Goldstein, quoted in *The Institutional* 17, no. 32 (13 April 1934): 1–2.

100 *American Hebrew and Jewish Tribune*, 7 April 1933, 369; Joseph M. Schwarz, President's message, Annual meeting, 18 January 1934, 1–2, Box 2, BJC collection.

101 Louis J. Moss to United Synagogue congregations, 3 October 1933, 1.

102 Mordecai M. Kaplan Diaries, 2 February 1935, 272; 5 December 1929, 219. Kaplan had never regarded the synagogue center as the only solution to the problems of American Jewry. He had proposed "the reconstruction of the communal life of our people" through the creation of a comprehensive Jewish civilization. See, ibid., 2 February 1935, 272. For more on Kaplan, see Scult, *Judaism Faces the Twentieth Century*.

103 Mordecai M. Kaplan Diaries, 29 September 1930.

104 Ibid., 23 March 1935, 300.

105 Ibid., 11 August 1931, 147; Kaplan himself suffered significant financial losses in the Wall Street Crash. Some of his money was lost when the Jewish-owned Bank of the United States failed in 1930. See ibid., 29 December 1929, 244; 11 December 1930, 79.

106 Despite such bouts of despair, Kaplan continued his efforts to revitalize American Judaism, launching the *Reconstructionist* magazine in 1935 and moving tentatively toward establishing Reconstructionism as an independent religious movement. Yet Kaplan remained ambivalent about establishing an independent religious movement. Despite the creation of Reconstructionist clubs and a Reconstructionist press in the 1930s as well as the establishment of the Reconstructionist Foundation in 1940, a separate movement did not begin to take shape until the late 1950s and 1960s. Kaplan had hoped to "reconstruct" all of Jewish life and vacillated when it came to creating Reconstructionism as an independent movement. It was Kaplan's followers rather than Kaplan himself who pursued an active campaign to establish Reconstructionism as an institutionalized Jewish movement. For a detailed discussion of the Reconstructionist movement, see Charles Liebman, "Reconstructionism in American Jewish Life," AYJB 71 (1970): 3–99; Scult, *Judaism Faces the Twentieth Century*.

107 Samuel Wohl, "The Synagog in the Direction of Jewish Affairs," CCAR *Yearbook* 47 (1937): 244.

108 JDB, 30 December 1930, 2.

109 "Now or Never," *Convention Annual*, n.d., Council of Young Israel Organizations, Young Israel miscellaneous documents and publications, 1913–1973, Box I-240, Folder "Souvenir Journals," AJHS.

110 For example, after experiencing job discrimination in private employment agencies, Jean Margolies chose to register at a Sabbath-observant establishment. As she explained, in addition to the absence of anti-Semitism, there were other advantages to the Sabbath-observant employment agencies: "If you got a job, they had Jewish employers who were religious. You didn't get high pay in those places, but you had all your Jewish holidays and you never had to work Saturday or Jewish holidays." Personal interview, Jean Margolies, 27 August 1991, New Haven, Conn.

111 *Synagogue Service Bulletin* 1, no. 2 (October 1933): 12–13.

112 Dinnerstein, *Anti-Semitism in America*, 124–25.

113 Eugene Kohn, "A Cultural Program for the Jewish Community," *PNCJSS* (1935): 77.

114 Kaplan, *Judaism as a Civilization*, 76.

115 Bernard Revel quoted in *NYT*, 25 May 1931, 19.

116 Minutes of Congregation Kehilath Jeshurun, 26 April 1936, 5 January 1938; for more on the Ramaz Academy, see Jenna Weissman Joselit, *New York's Jewish Jews: The Orthodox Community in the Interwar Years* (Bloomington: Indiana University Press, 1990), 139–45. Report of the Hebrew Education Department, Annual meeting, 17 January 1935, Box 2, BJC collection; for more on the Brooklyn Jewish Center's educational programs, see Moore, "A Synagogue Center Grows in Brooklyn," 315–19.

117 *NYT*, 25 May 1931, 19; for more on Jewish education in the interwar years, see Nathan H. Winter, *Jewish Education in a Pluralistic Society: Samson Benderly and Jewish Education in the United States* (New York: New York University Press, 1966); Noah Nardi, "A Study of Afternoon Hebrew Schools in the United States," *Jewish Social Studies* (April 1946): 51–74; for a personal account of the development of Jewish education in the United States, see Alexander Dushkin, *Living Bridges: Memoirs of an Educator* (Jerusalem: Keter, 1975).

118 *The Day*, 14 December 1930, 8.

119 Minutes of the Institutional Synagogue, 5 March 1931; minutes of the Kane Street Synagogue, 11 December 1932.

120 "Open letter to Federations and Congregations from the Rabbinical Assembly of the Jewish Theological Seminary," *Jewish Education* 4, no. 3 (October–December 1932): 129–30; Alexander M. Dushkin, "Reaffirming Our Faith," *Jewish Education* 5, no. 1 (January–March 1933): 1–2; Ben Rosen, "The Effect of Economic Depression upon Jewish Educational Institutions," *Jewish Education* 3, no. 1 (January–March 1931): 4–9; Albert M. Schoolman, "Education and Philanthropy," *Jewish Education* 4, no. 3 (October–December 1932): 131–38; the pages of *Jewish Education* in the 1930s are filled with lively discussion about the effects of the Depression on Jewish education.

Mordecai Kaplan was terribly discouraged by the Depression's effects on Jewish education. See, for example, Mordecai M. Kaplan Diaries, 14 August 1932, 300.

121 Report of the Hebrew Education Department, Annual meeting, 17 January 1935, Box 2, BJC collection; Joseph M. Schwarz, President's message, Annual meeting, 16 January 1936, 4, Box 2, BJC collection; for examples of unpaid tuition see folders: "Hebrew School Correspondence, 1928–1931" and "Hebrew School, 1927–1935," Box 13, BJC collection.

122 Herbert Goldstein quoted in *The Institutional* 17, no. 32 (13 April 1934): 1–2.

123 After some debate, the New York Federation continued to support private Yeshivas and Talmud Torahs during the Depression. However, federations contributed only 10 to 15 percent of the schools' operating budgets. Without the support of a congregation, independent schools relied on tuition fees and voluntary contributions—both of which decreased dramatically during the Depression years. FJP Minutes, 26 December 1932, Box 1087; Dushkin, "Reaffirming Our Faith," 2; Schoolman, "Education and Philanthropy," 134. NYT, 7 July 1930, 40; JDB, 9 March 1932, 9.

124 Albert P. Schoolman, "Jewish Education and the American Jewish Community," JSSQ 9, no. 1 (December 1932): 40; for reports of strikes in New York Talmud Torahs, see JDF, 23 May 1935, 4, 10; *The Day,* 18 October 1930, 1; 7 March 1932, 1; 8 February 1934, 6; 24 May 1935, 4. NYT, 9 January 1933, 17; JDF, January 1933, 1; JDB, 10 January 1933, 2.

125 A. H. Friedland, "The Current Year in Jewish Education," JSSQ 11, no. 1 (September 1934): 39.

126 The Conservative and Orthodox movements were already overwhelmingly pro-Zionist (although the Agudas Israel represented a small but vocal anti-Zionist faction within the Orthodox movement). The Reconstructionist movement, which had barely begun to take shape in the mid-thirties under Mordecai Kaplan's leadership, was firmly pro-Zionist from the outset. For more on the Zionist positions within Jewish religious movements, see Samuel Halperin, *The Political World of American Zionism* (Detroit, Mich.: Wayne State University Press, 1961; reprint, Silver Spring, Md.: Information Dynamics, 1985), 61–111. The 1937 Columbus Platform supporting Zionism is reprinted in Meyer, *Response to Modernity,* 388–91; Meyer also provides a detailed discussion of the Reform movement's Zionist position in the interwar years, 326–34. For more on the development of Zionism in America, see Halperin, *The Political World of American Zionism*; Melvin I. Urofsky, *American Zionism from Herzl to the Holocaust* (Garden City, N.Y.: Anchor Press, 1975); Naomi W. Cohen, *American Jews and the Zionist Idea* (New York: KTAV Publishing, 1975); see also Yonathan Shapiro, *Leadership of the American Zionist Organization, 1897–1930* (Urbana: University of Illinois Press, 1971).

127 Halperin, *The Political World of American Zionism,* 262.

128 For a discussion of the Brooklyn Jewish Center's Zionist-oriented programming, see Moore, "A Synagogue Center Grows in Brooklyn," 317–18.

129 Morris Rothenberg, cited in NYT, 31 January 1937, 34.

130 Jacob S. Golub, "Trends Affecting American Jewish Life: Panel Discussion," JSSQ 10, no. 1 (September 1933): 21.

131 Jacob Marcus, cited in Halperin, *The Political World of American Zionism,* 25–26.

132 One study estimated that Jewish youth groups gained 14,000 new members between 1928 and 1933. Jewish Statistical Bureau, *Digest of Events of Jewish Interest,* 11 August 1933, 113. Similar findings are presented in Stanley A. Ginsburgh, "A Study of Nationally Organized Jewish Youth Groups in America as Educational Agencies for the Preservation of the Jewish Cultural Heritage" (Ph.D. diss., Massachusetts State College, 1940), Microfilm 74, American Jewish Archives, Cincinnati, Ohio; see also Janet Steinberg, "A Survey of Jewish Youth Movements," *JSSQ* 13, no. 1 (September 1936): 80–84; on the differing assessments of Zionist inroads among Jewish youth in the 1930s, see Halperin, *The Political World of American Zionism,* 263–64.

133 Many Zionist organizations were rooted in socialist ideology and emphasized creating a new Jewish economy as well as a shared Jewish culture. For a brief overview of the philosophies of various Jewish youth movements, see Steinberg, "A Survey of Jewish Youth Movements," 80–84; A. W. Rosenthal, "The Growing Role of the Jewish Center: Some Specific Proposals for More Effective Evaluation of Its Youth Programs," *JSSQ* 13, no. 3 (March 1937): 350.

134 H. L. Lurie, "Essentials of a Community Program for Jewish Children," *JSSQ* 11, no. 1 (September 1934): 113; I. M. Rubinow, "The Credo of a Jewish Social Worker—Presidential Address," *JSSQ* 10, no. 1 (September 1933): 16.

135 Judah J. Shapiro, "The Jewish Center and Jewish Youth," *PNCJSS* (1936): 86.

136 "Programs of Jewish Community Organization in the Light of Changing Trends: Panel Discussion," *JSSQ* 10, no. 1 (September 1933): 32.

137 Kaplan, *Judaism as a Civilization,* 328.

138 Abraham J. Karp, "Overview: The Synagogue in America—A Historical Typology," in Wertheimer, ed., *The American Synagogue,* 24.

139 Fine, President's message, Annual meeting, 19 January 1933.

140 On the growth of synagogues and the nature of the religious revival in the postwar era, see Karp, "Overview—The Synagogue in America," 24–28; Wertheimer, "The Conservative Synagogue," 123–32; Glazer, *American Judaism,* 106–28; Herbert Gans, "American Jewry: Present and Future," *Commentary* (May 1956): 422–30; a classic work on Judaism in the postwar era is Will Herberg, *Protestant-Catholic-Jew: An Essay in American Religious Sociology* (Garden City, N.Y.: Doubleday, 1960).

CHAPTER 8: AMERICAN JEWS AND THE AMERICAN DREAM

Notes to epigraphs: Sam Levenson, Oral history, 2, WWOHL; Peter I. Rose, "The Ghetto and Beyond," in Rose, ed., *The Ghetto and Beyond,* 12.

1 "Greetings," Jubilee Journal, Kolbuszower Young Men's Benevolent Society, 1931, Landsmanshaft Archive, RG 888, YIVO Institute for Jewish Research, New York.

2 David A. Bressler, "Looking Backward: A New Appraisal—A Quarter of a Century Behind Us," *American Hebrew and Jewish Tribune,* 29 April 1932, 616.

3 Phil Schatz, "Jewish Youth in the United States," *Jewish Life* (published by the New York State Jewish Buro of the Communist Party) 2, no. 8 (August 1938): 22.

4 Cited in Feingold, *A Time for Searching,* 150.

5 David Mogilensky, "Problems of Jewish Youth in America," *Betar Monthly* (December 1931): 4, 10.

6 *The Young Judaean* (September–October 1931): 14.

7 For a complete analysis of American anti-Semitism, see Dinnerstein, *Anti-Semitism in American History.* See also Strong, *Organized Anti-Semitism in America.*

8 President's Message, cCAR *Yearbook* 41 (1931): 195.

9 Selekman, "Planning for Jewish Economic Welfare," 31; Joseph Schwarz, president's message, Annual meeting, 1939, Box 3, BJC Collection, Ratner Center.

10 Sarah Rothman (pseudonym), as cited in Kramer and Masur, eds., *Jewish Grandmothers,* 28.

11 Howe, *A Margin of Hope,* 5.

12 Ronald S. Berman, "The American Experience: Some Notes from the Third Generation," in Rosen, ed., *Jewish Life in America,* 194.

13 For a discussion of Jewish family, occupational, educational, marriage, and fertility patterns, see Sidney Goldstein, "Jews in the United States: Perspectives from Demography," in Sklare, ed., *American Jews,* 49–119; Cohen, *American Modernity and Jewish Identity,* esp. 39–97, 113–33.

14 Cohen, *American Modernity and Jewish Identity,* 136; for a full discussion of these issues, see Moore, *At Home in America,* 201–30.

15 Karp, "Overview: The Synagogue in America," 24–25.

16 Will Herberg, *Protestant-Catholic-Jew: An Essay in American Religious Sociology,* 56–57.

17 Eugene Borowitz, cited in Karp, "Overview: The Synagogue in America," 26.

# Index

Abraham Lincoln High School, 56–57

Acculturation, 5–6, 8, 138–39, 163–65, 168, 202

Ahad Ha-am, 185

Allerton Avenue, rent strike on, 113–14, 116–18

Amalgamated Clothing Workers, 104

American Dream, 55, 127, 197–201

*American Hebrew*, 174–75, 198

American Labor Party (ALP), 134

Anshe Chesed, 170–71

Antin, Benjamin, 117

Anti-Semitism, 1–3, 31–32, 136, 158, 189–90, 197–201; and Bank of the United States, 14; employment discrimination, 21–24, 61, 188–90; and politics, 130–34; and rent strikes, 117; university quotas, 23–24. *See*

*also* Employment discrimination; *Fortune Magazine*

Apartments, 80; in Brownsville, 86; Co-operative Housing Projects, 93; in East Bronx, 91–92; on Eastern Parkway, 90; in Flatbush, 89; on Grand Concourse, 91–92; on Lower East Side, 84; on Upper West Side, 94–95

Assimilationists, 160–62, 204

Augenstein, Rebecca, 36–37, 40, 98, 100–101

Bank of the United States, 10–14

Barnett, Ida, 39, 45, 47

Baruch, Bernard, 133

Baxt, Roland, 70, 75

Belth, Nathan, 43